First World War
and Army of Occupation
War Diary
France, Belgium and Germany

14 DIVISION
Divisional Troops
89 Field Company Royal Engineers
22 May 1915 - 17 June 1919

WO95/1889/3

The Naval & Military Press Ltd
www.nmarchive.com
Published in association with The National Archives

Published by

The Naval & Military Press Ltd

Unit 10 Ridgewood Industrial Park,
Uckfield, East Sussex,
TN22 5QE England
Tel: +44 (0) 1825 749494

www.naval-military-press.com

www.nmarchive.com

This diary has been reprinted in facsimile from the original. Any imperfections are inevitably reproduced and the quality may fall short of modern type and cartographic standards.

© Crown Copyright
Images reproduced by permission of The National Archives, London, England, 2015.

Contents

Document type	Place/Title	Date From	Date To
Heading	WO95/1889/3		
Heading	14th Division 89th Field Coy. R.E. May 1915-Jun 1919		
Heading	14th Division 89th F.C.R.E. Vol: I 22 May 15 To 31st August 15		
War Diary	Havre	22/05/1915	23/05/1915
War Diary	Train	24/05/1915	24/05/1915
War Diary	Broxeele	25/05/1915	26/05/1915
War Diary	Zuytpeene	27/05/1915	27/05/1915
War Diary	Caestre	28/05/1915	28/05/1915
War Diary	Vlamertinghe	29/05/1915	05/06/1915
War Diary	Kersebroom	06/06/1915	16/06/1915
War Diary	Poperinghe	17/06/1915	18/06/1915
War Diary	Vlamertinghe	19/06/1915	24/06/1915
War Diary	Ecole At Ypres	25/06/1915	26/06/1915
War Diary	Ecole	27/06/1915	27/06/1915
War Diary	Ypres	28/06/1915	05/07/1915
Map	Appendix A		
Miscellaneous	O.C. 89th Fusiliers Appendix I	26/06/1915	26/06/1915
Miscellaneous Diagram etc	O.C.	27/06/1915	27/06/1915
Miscellaneous	O.C. 89th Coy RE Appendix 3	01/07/1917	01/07/1917
Miscellaneous	Appendix 4 No. 4 Section	06/07/1915	06/07/1915
Diagram etc	Appendix 4		
Miscellaneous	Appendix 4 O.C. no 2 Section	06/07/1915	06/07/1915
Miscellaneous	Appendix 5 Major Military	06/07/1915	06/07/1915
Diagram etc	Appendix 5		
Miscellaneous	Appendix 6 41st Infantry Brigade	06/07/1915	06/07/1915
Miscellaneous	2nd ? Crampton		
Miscellaneous	O.C. 89th Ouldco	26/06/1915	26/06/1915
Miscellaneous	43rd Infantry Brigade	26/05/1915	26/05/1915
Miscellaneous	2nd Brigade	27/06/1915	27/06/1915
Miscellaneous	Shovely & Picks.	27/06/1915	27/06/1915
Miscellaneous	O.C. 89	27/06/1915	27/06/1915
Miscellaneous	O.C. 1 Section	27/06/1915	27/06/1915
Miscellaneous Diagram etc	3rd 2 Llewellyn	28/06/1915	28/06/1915
Miscellaneous	2nd Lt. Calbert	28/06/1915	28/06/1915
Miscellaneous Diagram etc	O.C. 89th Grs	01/02/1915	01/02/1915
War Diary	Vlamertinghe	06/07/1915	04/08/1915
War Diary			
War Diary		10/08/1915	12/08/1915
War Diary	Ypres Cellars In Ramparts	13/08/1915	15/08/1915
War Diary	Ypres Cellars	16/08/1915	19/08/1915
War Diary	Vlamertinghe	20/08/1915	31/08/1915
Heading	14th Division 89th F.C.R.E. Vol 2 Sept & Oct 15		
Heading	War Diary Of 89th Field Coy R.E. From Sept 3rd 1915 To Oct 31 1915 (Volume)		
War Diary	Vlamertinghe	03/09/1915	14/09/1915
War Diary	Ypres	15/09/1915	04/10/1915

War Diary	Vlamertinghe	05/10/1915	31/10/1915
Heading	14th Division Nov 15 89th F.C.R.E. Vol. 3		
War Diary	Vlamertinghe	01/11/1915	19/11/1915
War Diary	Yperlei	20/11/1915	30/11/1915
Heading	14th Div 89th F.C.R.E. Vol: 4 Dec 1915		
War Diary		01/12/1915	02/12/1915
War Diary	Vlamertinghe	03/12/1915	17/12/1915
War Diary	Vlamertinghe Sheet 28 H.7.6.3-3	18/12/1915	23/12/1915
War Diary	Vlamertinghe	24/12/1915	31/12/1915
Heading	89th F C R E Vol 5		
War Diary	Vlamertinghe	01/01/1916	02/02/1916
Heading	89th F. C.R.E. 14th Div Vol 6		
War Diary		03/02/1916	08/02/1916
War Diary	Vlamertinghe	09/02/1916	13/02/1916
War Diary	Watou	14/02/1916	16/02/1916
War Diary	Herzeele	17/02/1916	20/02/1916
War Diary	On The March	21/02/1916	21/02/1916
War Diary	Near Amiens.	22/02/1916	22/02/1916
War Diary	Vignacourt	23/02/1916	23/02/1916
War Diary	Freschvillers	24/02/1916	24/02/1916
War Diary	On March To	25/02/1916	25/02/1916
War Diary	Humbercourt	26/02/1916	28/02/1916
War Diary	Fosseux	29/02/1916	29/02/1916
Heading	89th Coy RE Vol Vol 7		
War Diary	Fosseux	01/03/1916	01/03/1916
War Diary	Dainville	02/03/1916	07/04/1916
War Diary	Dainville And Agny.	08/04/1916	09/05/1916
War Diary	Dainville Hauteville And Agny	10/05/1916	27/05/1916
War Diary	Dainville Agny Arras	23/05/1916	06/06/1916
War Diary	Dainville	07/06/1916	07/06/1916
War Diary	Wanquetin	08/06/1916	20/06/1916
War Diary	Arras	20/06/1916	21/06/1916
War Diary	Warlus	21/06/1916	21/06/1916
War Diary	Arras	22/03/1916	31/07/1916
Heading	14th Division. 89th Field Company. Royal Engineers August 1916		
War Diary	Barly	01/08/1916	01/08/1916
War Diary	Le Bretel	02/08/1916	06/08/1916
War Diary	Le Bretel	07/08/1916	07/08/1916
War Diary	Dernancourt	08/08/1916	12/08/1916
War Diary	Fricourt	13/08/1916	14/08/1916
War Diary	Fricourt Mametz	14/08/1916	16/08/1916
War Diary	Fricourt Dugouts	16/08/1916	19/08/1916
War Diary	Near Fricourt	20/08/1916	21/08/1916
War Diary	Fricourt	22/08/1916	24/08/1916
War Diary	Fricourt On Mametz	24/08/1916	26/08/1916
War Diary	Sheet 62 D. F 4. C. 8.4 Near Mametz	27/08/1916	29/08/1916
War Diary	Dernancourt	30/08/1916	30/08/1916
War Diary	Move	31/08/1916	31/08/1916
War Diary	Frette Cuisse	01/09/1916	01/09/1916
Miscellaneous	Appendix Jan 24.8.16	24/08/1916	24/08/1916
Miscellaneous	Table Of Working Parties Night Of 22/23rd August	22/08/1916	22/08/1916
War Diary	Frette Cuisse	01/09/1916	08/09/1916
War Diary	And Ailly Sur Somme	09/09/1916	09/09/1916
War Diary	Dernancourt	10/09/1916	10/09/1916
War Diary	Fricourt Camp	11/09/1916	12/09/1916

War Diary	Fricourt Wood	13/09/1916	16/09/1916
War Diary	Fricourt Wood To Ribemont	17/09/1916	17/09/1916
War Diary	Ribemont	18/09/1916	22/09/1916
War Diary	Sus St. Leger	23/09/1916	26/09/1916
War Diary	And Hautville	27/09/1916	27/09/1916
War Diary	Hautville And Arras	28/09/1916	28/09/1916
War Diary	Arras	29/09/1916	31/10/1916
Heading	War Diary of 89th Fd Coy R.E. from 1st November 1916 to 30th November 1916 (Volume I)		
War Diary	Arras	01/11/1916	05/11/1916
War Diary	Gouy	06/11/1916	06/11/1916
War Diary	Gouy En Artois	07/11/1916	08/11/1916
War Diary	Monts En Ternois	08/11/1916	27/11/1916
War Diary	Monts En Ternois And Sericourt	28/11/1916	30/11/1916
War Diary	Sericourt	01/12/1916	14/12/1916
War Diary	Sombrin	15/12/1916	15/12/1916
War Diary	Duisans	16/12/1916	16/12/1916
War Diary	Arras	17/12/1916	28/03/1917
War Diary	Arras And Dainville	29/03/1917	29/03/1917
War Diary	Dainville	30/03/1917	08/04/1917
War Diary	Groupe Des Maisons	09/04/1917	12/04/1917
War Diary	Dainville	13/04/1917	13/04/1917
War Diary	Givenchy Le Noble	14/04/1917	14/04/1917
War Diary	Sus St Leger	15/04/1917	23/04/1917
War Diary	Bavincourt	24/04/1917	24/04/1917
War Diary	Basseux	25/04/1917	25/04/1917
War Diary	Telegraph Hill	26/04/1917	31/05/1917
Heading	14th Division "A".	03/07/1917	03/07/1917
War Diary	Telegraph Hill	01/06/1917	03/06/1917
War Diary	Neuville Vitasse	04/06/1917	11/06/1917
War Diary	Agny	12/06/1917	13/06/1917
War Diary	Beaumetz	14/06/1917	14/06/1917
War Diary	Saulty	15/06/1917	15/06/1917
War Diary	Authie	16/06/1917	28/06/1917
War Diary	Bailleul	29/06/1917	29/06/1917
War Diary	Shamus Dugouts To Wulverghem Wytschaete Road	30/06/1917	08/07/1917
War Diary	Shamus Dugouts	09/07/1917	29/07/1917
War Diary	Shamus Dugouts Wulverghem	30/07/1917	06/08/1917
War Diary	Le Brearde (27.V.5.C.7.3)	06/08/1917	06/08/1917
War Diary	Le Brearde	07/08/1917	15/08/1917
War Diary	Reninghelst	16/08/1917	19/08/1917
War Diary	Chateau Segard	20/08/1917	26/08/1917
War Diary	Wippenhoek Area	27/08/1917	29/08/1917
War Diary	Berthen Area	30/08/1917	02/09/1917
War Diary	Neuve Eglise	03/09/1917	06/10/1917
War Diary	Dickebusch	07/10/1917	31/10/1917
Miscellaneous	Report On The Crossing Of The River Lys On The 14th & 15th. Oct. 1918 By 89th Field Coy. R.E.	28/10/1918	28/10/1918
War Diary	Dickebusch	01/11/1917	10/11/1917
War Diary	Vlammertinghe Area	11/11/1917	12/11/1917
War Diary	Potijze	13/11/1917	22/11/1917
War Diary	Quelmes	23/11/1917	03/12/1917
War Diary	Canal Bank Kaai Ypres	03/12/1917	09/12/1917
War Diary	Canal Bank	10/12/1917	31/12/1917
War Diary	Canal Bank Ypres	01/12/1918	01/12/1918
War Diary	St. Martin Au Laert	02/01/1918	03/01/1918

War Diary	Bray Sur Somme	04/01/1918	22/01/1918
War Diary	Harbonnieres	23/01/1918	23/01/1918
War Diary	Gruny	24/01/1918	24/01/1918
War Diary	Quesmy	25/01/1918	25/01/1918
War Diary	Flavy-Le Martel	26/01/1918	26/01/1918
War Diary	Remigny	27/01/1918	26/02/1918
War Diary	Benay	27/02/1918	28/02/1918
Heading	14th Divisional Engineers 89th Field Company R.E. March 1918		
War Diary	Benay	01/03/1918	21/03/1918
War Diary	Jussy	22/03/1918	22/03/1918
War Diary	La Neuville En Beine	23/03/1918	23/03/1918
War Diary	Beaumont	24/03/1918	24/03/1918
War Diary	Rousson	25/03/1918	26/03/1918
War Diary	Moyvilliers	27/03/1918	27/03/1918
War Diary	Beaurepeape	29/03/1918	31/03/1918
Heading	14th Div. 89th Field Company, R.E. April 1918		
War Diary	Vellennes	01/04/1918	12/04/1918
War Diary	Bazinval	12/04/1918	21/04/1918
War Diary	Belloy Sur Somme	22/04/1918	30/04/1918
War Diary	Vaux-En-Amienois	01/05/1918	08/05/1918
War Diary	Le Cornet Brassart	08/05/1918	09/07/1918
War Diary	Lederzeele	09/07/1918	15/07/1918
War Diary	Terdeghem	14/07/1918	31/07/1918
War Diary	Lederzeele	01/08/1918	01/08/1918
War Diary	Eperlecques	02/08/1918	21/08/1918
War Diary	St. Jans-Ter Biezen	22/08/1918	31/08/1918
Miscellaneous	Training Programme. 89th. Field Coy. R.E.		
War Diary	Dirty Bucket Camp	01/09/1918	15/09/1918
War Diary	Ross Camp	16/09/1918	16/09/1918
War Diary	Orwell Camp	17/09/1918	19/09/1918
War Diary	Leger Fm	20/09/1918	30/09/1918
War Diary	Wulverghem	01/10/1918	17/10/1918
War Diary	Wervicq	17/10/1918	21/10/1918
War Diary	Tourcoing	22/10/1918	24/10/1918
War Diary	Mouscron	25/10/1918	31/10/1918
Diagram etc	To Carry 17 English Tons		
Diagram etc	Heavy Road Bridge. Wattrelos-Tourcoing Road. Reconstructed By 89th Field Coy R.E. Oct 1918 Map Ref (37a14b15:40) To Carry 17 Tons.		
War Diary	Coyeghem	01/11/1918	18/11/1918
War Diary	Tourcoing	19/11/1918	19/11/1918
War Diary	Helchin	20/11/1918	24/11/1918
War Diary	Tourcoing	25/11/1918	30/11/1918
Diagram etc	Inglis Bridge. Erected At 37/C/56 30:50 On 13-11-18 By 89th Field Coy. R.E.		
Diagram etc	Plan Of Ground Adjoining Destroyed Bridge. (37 N.W. C 5b3:5)		
War Diary	Tourcoing	01/12/1918	31/03/1919
War Diary	Petit Audenarde (Belgium)	01/04/1919	31/05/1919
Heading	War Diary 89th Field Co. R.E Final		
War Diary	Petit Audenarde	01/06/1919	17/06/1919

WO 1889/3

14TH DIVISION

89TH FIELD COY. R.E.
MAY 1915 - JUN 1919

14th Division

69th F.C.R.E.
Vol: I
22 May 15 to 31st August. 15.

June '19

121/6874

WAR DIARY
or
INTELLIGENCE SUMMARY.

(Erase heading not required.)

Army Form C. 2118.

Place	Date	Hour	Summary of Events and Information	Remarks and references to Appendices
HAVRE.	22.5.15.		The 89th Field Coy left ALDERSHOT at 10.55 am & 11.55 am (in 2 trains) & arrived at SOUTHAMPTON the same morning. All horses & vehicles were embarked on board, with 41 drivers under 2nd Lt. CALVERT. The remainder of the Coy embarked on the ST PETERSBURG. The dismounted portion of the Coy reached HAVRE at daybreak on Sat. 22nd & proceeded to REST CAMP. no 5. Spent the night there. Lt. Sgt Parks - W/S section & 18 NCO's & men? Lift at Aldershot as Isolation cases of Spotted fever. had	
"	23.5.15		At 7 am moved to R. Quay. dismebarked the transport, which had arrived that morning. Entrained at No 1. Point at 4.30 pm. Left HAVRE at 9 pm. While coy in 1 train — accompanied by 38 men & 2 officers of 14th Div Amn. Column. Sgt Mitchell, Pay Sgt ? Left at no 1. Isolation Camp Havre ? Spotted fever. Sgt Pickles, Sapr Fabian ?	
TRAIN.	24.5		Arrived ST OMER at 6.30 pm. detrained & moved to billets at BROXEELE. Capt Rein sent on ahead and to find position of billets. Coy v. bad driving. Company not settled down till 1.30 midnight.	Company unsteady thin smashings, King,
BROXEELE	25.5		1st parade 9 am. Routine orders read out. of opinion that they have come to France in a picnic late & general discipline bad. Then pushed in some sidings. Carriage bad. Horse lines moved to more concealed spot. Section lines adopted. D. Yearsley made A.L.Cpl (m.Cl)	

68 (FIELD COMPANY) ROYAL ENGINEERS

Army Form C. 2118.

WAR DIARY
or
INTELLIGENCE SUMMARY.
(Erase heading not required.)

Place	Date	Hour	Summary of Events and Information	Remarks and references to Appendices
BROXEELE	26.5		Rest Day. Men bathed at WATTEN. received orders to move at 11. p.m. Paraded 5.15 a.m. Marched with 43rd Inf. Bgde towards ZUYTPEENE. Arrived 9 a.m.	
ZUYTPEENE	27.5		Billets at L'HEY — 2½ miles W. of ZUYTPEENE. Casualties men & horses nil. Except one written manual to the Bgde. due to think to half walked, change of food & animals being soft after journey in boats & train. Paraded at 9.40 a.m. & marched with 43rd Bgde to CAESTRE. Arrived 9.30 a.m. Billets in farm close to the village. Casualties nil.	
CAESTRE	28.5		Corps Park Paraded 5.30 a.m. to march independently and to there receive orders from — . Went into billets in empty houses — all	
VLAMERTINGHE	29.5		to VLAMERTINGHE — R.E. advanced about 15 miles. C.R.E. 14th Division met S.O. to C.E. (capturing) at 2.30 to see what work was very dirty. A new line of support points, based on farms, to hold a platoon & 4 machine guns each (about). 8 points in all. 20,000 map. Sheet 28 N.W. All in H Square. 10. d. 5. 9.; #10. d. 7.3.; 17. a. 1.9; 17 c d; 23 b; 30 a 7.8; 30 b.d.; 30 d 6.4; Subalterns reconnoitred each; Section paraded 6 a.m. to commence work on the 1st 4 points. Sketched no 5 pst myself. Progress of work slow.	
	30.5		Coy. paraded 7 a.m. to continue work on the 1st 4 points. Dinner 12.30 – 1.30. Knock off at 4.30 in billets 5.30 p.m.	
	31.5		Ditto. Ditto.	
	1.6		Ditto. Ditto.	
	2.6		Ditto. Ditto.	
	3.6		Ditto. Work inspected by C.E. II Corps. 6 points laid out. Dug-outs completed. M.G. emplacements finished. A line of wire placed all round. A long day. Rec'd orders 9 a.m. to send Willth's party to DRANOUTRE and to return Abbey ville.	
	4.6. Friday		Commenced work 8 a.m. bring in men at work. Men came in by 12.30.	

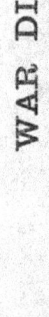

(FIELD) COMPANY
88
ENGINEERS

1577 Wt. W10791/1773 500,000 1/15 D. D. & L. A.D.S.S./Forms/C. 2118.

WAR DIARY or INTELLIGENCE SUMMARY

Army Form C. 2118.

Place	Date	Hour	Summary of Events and Information	Remarks and references to Appendices
	5.6.		Punched 6.30 a.m. trench at Willet near DRANOUTRE. 11 mile. Billetted in farm at KERSEBROOM. (L.S.11.C. 1/40,000 map). Lunched with got. 43rd Rifles. Under orders to report to S.O. 16 CE 2nd Corps for work on J.H.Q. Line.	
KERSEBROOM.	6.6.		Rear Party 8 men. 10 a.m. went round J.H.Q.3 Line with Capt. Walcot, Dunham & 6th KOYLI at work. Line running N & S. from S. of MT KEMMEL (DRANOUTRE – WELVERGHEM road) to BAILLEUL–ARMENTIERES road. Subalterns inspected 4 Section of the line in the aft. Saw CE IInd Corps in the aft. agreed to employ a Coy of Travailleurs Belges from middy. and about 500 civilians on Tuesday.	
	7.6.		Sappers worked at the lines, with the Inf., who knocked off middy. Travailleurs Belges arrived 2½ hours late, from LOCRE. They were only shown their work for the next day. Took over stores of R.E. tools from Inf.	
	8.6		Exceptionally hot weather. No IV Section to H & G Sections – with Belgian Travailleurs about 300 men. No I – " – E & F " with Ridge Travailleurs 250 men. No III & IV " – C & D " with 30 Belg. civilian. Sappers employed at strengthening the Inf. work with revetments & sandbags and fresh cover. Travailleurs Belge at work in trench in F. Sector. – They worked v. well.	Appendix I. Sums to C.E. 2nd Corps.
	9.6.		Joined the 4 R.E. Section to bivouac close to their work. CSM detailed in charge of provision of materials, who come from STRAZEELE & BAILLEUL. 2 lorries borrowed from ? Signal Coy, 1 from camp team dept BAILLEUL. Civilians employed. 2nd Lt. CALVERT (No 2. Section) on ask trenches & communication trench in H Sector. Good work. Capt. REIS Ye of payment & record of Civilians. L. Cpl. LONG. Spr. KING & MOSES detailed to work in BAILLEUL timber shops (by ORE baden).	
	10.6		Continuation of work. Men & workers have allowed to commence from 4 a.m. in order to avoid the heat. Progress fair. Civilian work v. well. Travailleurs slackening	

WAR DIARY
INTELLIGENCE SUMMARY

Army Form C. 2118.

Place	Date	Hour	Summary of Events and Information	Remarks and references to Appendices
	11.6.		Continuation of same. Completed map of works.	
	12.6.		Billets.	
	13.6. Sun.		Rest Day. Men bathed at BAILLEUL. Rec'd orders 3 a.m. on 14th to move at 8.45 with 41st Inf. Bgde. from HERZEELE to billets in L.8 (Sheet 27) near POPERINGHE. Collected Section at 5 a.m. Sergt. GRIGSON to report to C.R.E.	
	14.6		Moved off 7 a.m. Capt. REIS remained behind to pay civilians & to hand over to a representative of the C.E. 2nd Corps, Sent to BAILLEUL at 6.30 a.m. In billets at farm in L.9.c. at midday. Rec'd orders to build 4 huts for 16. Div'l Hqrs at once. Lt. Pippon in charge with the work.	
	15.6.		Employed 42 men on the huts - in 2 shifts. 2 road completed by 5 p.m. Sent 2nd Lt. CALVERT with 20 men to build a Dug-out for Div'l Hqrs. at VLAMERTINGHE. Rec'd orders 4.45 to be ready to move at short notice 15 Sept.18 & cease stop work on huts.	
	16.6.		No further orders. Continued work on huts. 10 a.m. rec'd orders to continue work as usual. 12 noon rec'd orders to dis continue & to billet near VLAMERTINGHE. 5.30 R.E. Coy. under 2nd Lt. Thompson.	
	17.		Left to go build my hut - Rode to R'nd Coy. found them without any instructions. Told O.C. 2 Section to entrain Hqrs. Dugouts. Not certain to make decision until. Am told that the hut has will not be required. Div'l Hqrs at Vlamertinghe. On return to Hqrs. found that Div'l Hqrs. four more huts for mess etc. have stopped the first building at Poperinghe.	
POPERINGHE	17.6			

88 (FIELD) COMPANY ROYAL ENGINEERS

Army Form C. 2118.

WAR DIARY
or INTELLIGENCE SUMMARY

(Erase heading not required.)

Place	Date	Hour	Summary of Events and Information	Remarks and references to Appendices
POPERINGHE	18.6		Gave notice at ABEELE for the new huts, which are to be built by the R^t ½ Coy. Complete the other huts near Poperinghe with the left half Coy.	
VLAMERTINGHE	19.6		Marched N^o ½ Coy + Hq^{rs} (less pontoon wagons) into VLAMERTINGHE. N^o ½ Coy continued on new hut + dug out for S.O.E. Confusion over posⁿ of Coy billets. Billeted in farm H.7.C.6.1	
"	20.6 Sun.		Moved to farm H.8.d.8.2 Village shelled at 8am & 8pm, men v. close to billets. Coy carpenter + No 3 Section continue huts. Rem^{dr} made Coy dug outs. Rec^d orders from C.R.E. to take on water supply of Div^l Area. Detail No 3 Section + Coy Carpenter under 2nd Lt Grissom to do this work. Also asked to improve the 3 main communication trenches in the Sector of front between MENIN road + ROULERS Rlwy. Reconnoitred them with 2nd Lt Calvert + Llewellyn. Sent Captⁿ Rees + Crompton to do the same in the aftⁿ.) as a 1st introduction to trenches. Arranged for work to begin night of 21st.	See appendix A
"	21.6 Mon.		Hut building con^d. Lt Crompton + No 2 Section with 1½ Coy of Liverpool Rgt (Pioneers) dug yards of new Comm. trench by night - under normal fire - a few close shells. No 2 Section d^o. No 4 Section improve S. branch trench in a v. useful place. 142 Section carry out samples + bay.	A
"	22.6 Tues		Owing to enemy attack + bombardment our actual commⁿ digging could be attempted. 4 + 2 clear up Telephone cable by day + turn up trenches 2 coys of Liverpools dig ritual S^s comm. trench from close to L'Ecole. Bad work.	

68 (FIELD COMPANY) * ROYAL ENGINEERS

Instructions regarding War Diaries and Intelligence Summaries are contained in F.S. Regs., Part II. and the Staff Manual respectively. Title pages will be prepared in manuscript.

WAR DIARY / INTELLIGENCE SUMMARY

Army Form C. 2118.

68 (FIELD) COMPANY ROYAL ENGINEERS

Place	Date	Hour	Summary of Events and Information	Remarks and references to Appendices
VLAMERTINGHE YPRES	23.6		Arrange to employ 2 Coys of Liverpools on N. Entrance under cover. & 2 Coys of 7th K.R.R.B. on a new line parallel to the S. Commn. Trench. Satisfactory work. 1 & 3 Sections out all night improving trenches. No 1 makes covering-iron culvert for stream through a Trench.	
	24.6		Arrange to employ 2 Coys of Liverpools on completing N. Trench. 2 Coys of 8th K.R.R. on retired S. Trench. 2 Coys " " " " near S. Trench. Nos 2 & 4 Sections assisting & supervising. Result satisfactory. Skilled out of Farm with Green Shutters close to VLAMERTINGHE & one C Farm near Drict Hqrs in Sheet 5g. Hut building & digging of Coy dug outs had been continued by the resting section all the week. SAP. CHAPMAN. F.G. SICK. EVACUATED.	
ECOLE at YPRES	25.6		Coy placed 2/c RE work in front line 43rd Bgde in trenches. Went round all trenches from 2 p.m. - returned 10 a.m. 26. Lined up ECOLE with Bgde Hqn. Nos. 1 & 3 employed on night ½ front. 2 & 4 on left ½ front. SAPPER ANSTEY. A. WOUNDED.	
	26.6		Maj. Mackesy R.E. made C.R.E. East of YPRES. Sections assist infantry in strengthening front line, sapping & improving communication trenches.	See op orders 1 as to work ordered. 

WAR DIARY or INTELLIGENCE SUMMARY

Army Form C. 2118.

68 (FIELD) COMPANY ROYAL ENGINEERS

Place	Date	Hour	Summary of Events and Information	Remarks and references to Appendices
ECOLE	27.6	Sun.	See appendix 2 for orders drafted by 8am. I am O.C. 89 as to work to be done by 43rd Bgde. Shelled out of ECOLE at 10 pm. Sap. Charles killed. Seven wounded. Hqrs. moved to cellar under rampart, between MENIN GATE & SALLY PORT in YPRES. Capt. Rein & self inspect round trenches from 9.30 pm until 2 pm. Progress in Sapping good. Line improving. Capt. Rycroft of Yorks & Lancs a suspected spy. SAPPER PEARCE W. WOUNDED.	2
YPRES	28.6		Sap. Airdon killed. Jones, Slater & Woodcock wounded. Explained previous days Brigade Orders to O.C. Battns. R.E. section employed on strengthening front, & carrying out of Bgde Orders. Wire not put out in view of a probable offensive. Section working 1, 2, 3, 2+4 on alternate days. Leave YPRES about 8.30 pm returning about 10 next night.	
" "	29.6		Borrowed 14 G.S. mules & went to camp to clean up programme of work with Major Mackesy. 41st Bgde takes over from 43rd on night 29/30. Relief miller & 20 20 chance of doing more work. Gave Section a rest.	
" "	30.6		Went round whole front with O.C. 41st Bgde (Gen. NUGENT) & B.M. (Capt. BAILEY) Lt Crompton & Chipun reported on front. Obtained continuing of 43rd Bgde work. Attack postponed.	
" "	1.7		Ordered Divnl. Magazine for ammunition in YPRES. c/Lt Norman & working pairs of B. & B. West round N. ½ of front. Sazarrad continuation of trench 10	

WAR DIARY
or
INTELLIGENCE SUMMARY.

(Erase heading not required.)

Army Form C. 2118.

Place	Date	Hour	Summary of Events and Information	Remarks and references to Appendices
YPRES.	2.7.		2 old French Trench. REIS took up notice boards by night. Sapping continued on whole front with greatest possible speed. CPL. HENLEY. T.S. SLIGHTLY WOUNDED.	Sapping ordered to be continued. Appendix 3.
	3.7.		Attended to papers & maps all morning. Section continued with on their respective fronts. Got permission to do some of the Sapping construction at once, bolder fighting dug outs arranged. 1ft ½ front had all notice boards erected. Spr. JUDSON seriously wounded - Sapping rifle bullet. Jan shells largely used by Germans against H.Q. 2 line. Inspected near communication trench in evening with Lt. ALTHAM (staff cope. 41st Regt). V. narrow scope. SAPPER KIRKPATRICK. F. ACCIDENTALLY. WOUNDED. SAP. HILL. J.A. SLIGHTLY WOUNDED.	
	4.7. Sun.		Arranged for Inf. to do all the Sapping. Sets 1+2+3 in trenches. Went round S. Sector with B.M. in the evening. Progress satisfactory, but enough loopholes being erected. Progress unsatisfactory in Comm. + Support trenches. SAP ANDREWS. F. WOUNDED.	
			Went round line with J.O.C. at 3 am. Ordered to employ 400 men at once on front Support trenches. Order cancelled. Considerable confusion existing as to who has to do work. Typed out a brief list of points needing to be cleared up for J.O.C. 41. Sapper Judson died of wounds.	
	5.7.		Handed over front line to 61st Int. Bg. Crompton & Pigeon handed over actual work. Got wolf report to fort. 14. Bn 5th on distribution of work on all	

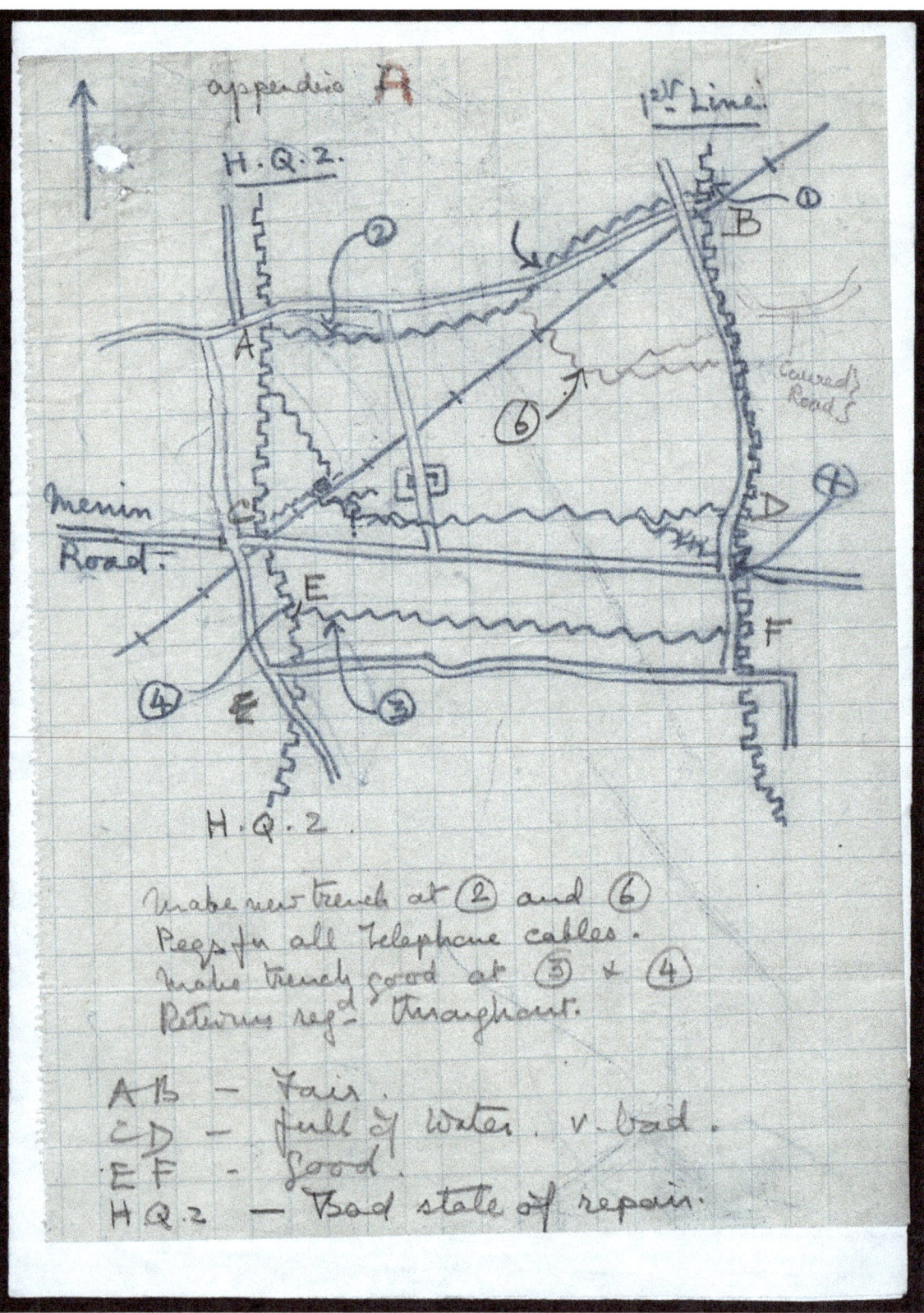

Make new trench at ② and ⑥
Pegs for all Telephone cables.
Make trench good at ③ & ④
Returns req'd throughout.

A B — Fair.
C D — full of water. v. bad.
E F — Good.
H Q 2 — Bad state of repair.

Appendix I

O.C. 89" Field Coy!

1/ With reference to my minute of 26/6/15 and interview yesterday.
The two Communication Trenches from F to G are not to be constructed but the Trench G is to be widened, or arranged, so as to admit of easy Communication.

2/ The date at which work has to be finished by is now brought to 6th July, and not as previously fixed. I presume your Cangel is all done by then. I am sending 141st Bde a copy of the work required too.

3/ You had better arrange a dumping place for your R.E. stores such as ladders for exit from trenches, materials for knife-rests etc. Somewhere towards left of Sector, as I am arranging that for right of sector at BIRR + roads. — Total!
Please let me know site you select & fix notice Board there ?

4/ There is also the question of improving the front line which you have in hand irrespective of the special preparations referred to above & in my minute of 26/6/15 —

5/ These improvements are
Connecting saphead from m.n.o and
running into trench 5.
Improvement of trench 5 at point x.
Connecting 12 to 10 by sap.
The saps facing enemy to be gradually
Converted to fire trenches.
To improve traverses in and build up parados
along trench 4.
To improve cover at Y in Trench 2. {minor point}.
Can you carry these out with assistance
of sawismo and your own Company.
If not please let me know how much you
think you can do.

17.40 p.m.
26/6/15

J P Mackeson
Major

O. C.

The following is a General scheme of work that is to be carried out under the supervision of Captain Benskin, R. E. and the 89th Field Coy. This work C.O's will please push on with at once.

It will be noticed that by pushing forward and getting closer to the Germans it will mean less shelling on the front line. It is a recognised fact that the closer you are the more comfortable you are.

(a) The whole section between the Menin Road and the Roulers Railway has been detailed by the Corps as Section D.

No 1 Trench.	I.18.a.6.7. to I.18.a.3.6. (Parallel to road).
No 2 Trench.	From Culvert on Menin Road to I.18.a.2.9.
No 3 Trench.	From the last named point I.12.c.3.2. to half way up South East face of triangle.
No 4 Trench.	From last named point to East point of triangle.
No 5 Trench.	From East point of Triangle to Junction of trenches at 12.c.1.5.
No 6 Trench.	From last named point to point 20 yards North of right hand listening post in Somersets lines.
No 7 Trench.	From last named point up to new communication trench about the left of Capt. Bellew's company.
No 8 Trench.	From last named point to bend in trenches next to northern listening post.
No 9 Trench	From last named to corner of trench at 11.b.9.1.
No 10 Trench.	From last named to Northernly corner of Railway Wood.
No 11 Trench.	From 11.b.6.4. to 11.b.6.6.
No 12 Trench.	From last named to junction of trench and Railway.

(b)   Work to be commenced forthwith.

(1)   To make new fire trench by sapping from Eastern point of Triangle, Square 12.c.45 to connect up with listening post in Trench 6, thence through the next two listening posts (the centre listening post to push out further East), from the latter point to sap North West to about the centre of Trench No 10, at the Eastern corner of Railway wood.

(c)   Other work to be constructed forthwith.

   To dig a communication trench from point 11.d.6.6. to present disused trench between North end of Y wood and Railway Wood. This latter trench will be cleared and cleaned as soon as possible.

(2)   The existing communication trench running from assembly trenches to the North end of Y wood, and lately commenced, is to be completed.

(3)   The construction of a new communication trench from the discarded trench mentioned in para C.(1).due East to Trench No 7.

(4)   To widen trenches No 3 and 4 by digging another trench four yards in rear and connecting up with passages.

All the above work will be sited by the R.E.

In some cases it will be possible to begin at once, but the work is to be completed as soon as possible.

R.E. Officers will meet the O.C. 6th Somersets at his Headquarters between 10.30.p.m. and 11.0.p.m. to-night, and the O.C. 10th Durham L.I. on the left of his line at the same time

27th June 1915.   Major,
                     Brigade Major, 43rd Light Infantry Brigade.

P.S.
      Troops must be warned about firing at night when this work is being carried out.

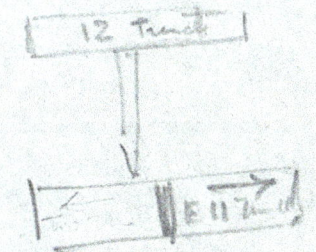
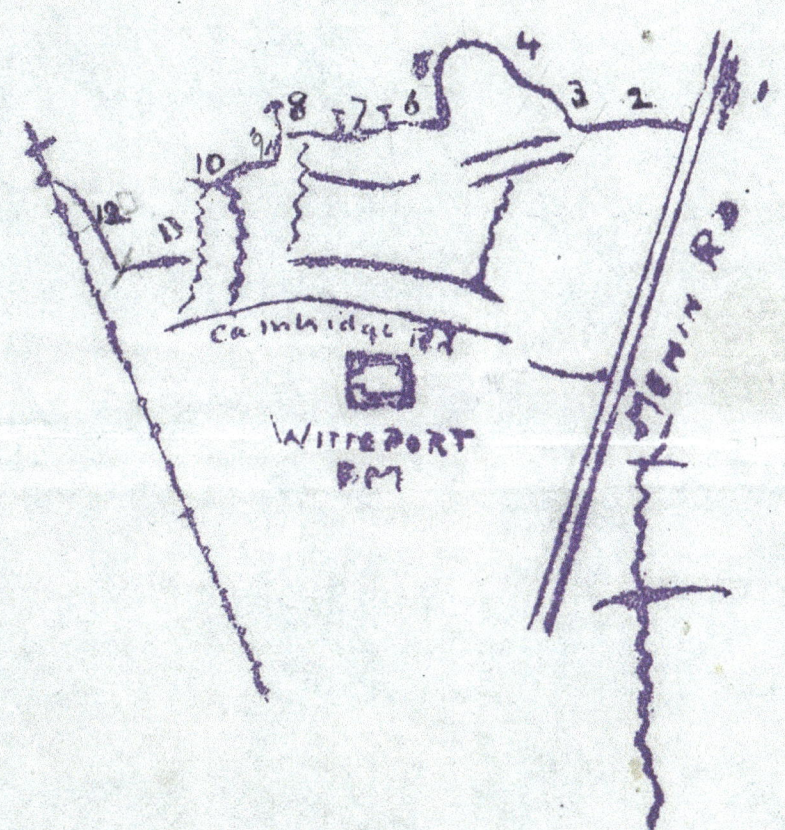

appendix 3.

O.C 89th Coy R.E.

The Corps Commander has ordered that the following work be done as soon as possible

(a) the reentrant 1, 2, 3, 4 to be eliminated by the construction of a sap from E of 1 towards 4

(b) the reentrant 10, 11, 12 to be eliminated by the construction of a sap from 12 towards 10.

2. It is considered that these objects can best be achieved as follows:—

(a) By starting a sap or saps from middle of 2 in an E.N.E. direction & forming T heads to join a sap to be run by 3rd Div. from near E. end of 1, thus:—

[sketch: Sap & T head; 3rd Div. Sap; points labelled 1, 2, 3, 4]

(b) By connecting up 10 & 12 by sapping out from both these trenches

If this is found to be impracticable, owing to proximity of enemy sap, our sap must run to the W. of, but as near as possible to the sap actually proposed.

3. It is understood that this work has already been commenced. If so please report progress.

3/. The General Staff have sent a minute to above effect to 41st Brigade, and request that the work should be completed as soon as possible.

Will you please assist them in having this done.

(b) appears to be the most important & this must be pushed on with.

4/7/15

Brackey Major RE

Appendix 4.

To No 4. Section.

You must be at H/qs 42nd Cycle the Brasserie W. of Ypres at 3 pm today — to explain tonight's work to representatives of Inf. Inf. are under orders to be at LILLE GATE at 6.30 pm tonight.

You will lead them to their work.

Your Section must
1. Lay trench boards at P^t E. These are stacked in F_2, & at BIRR x Roads.

2. Track down Notice Boards at BIRR x Roads & erect them. Consider the erection of more Notice Boards.

3. Assist & supervise the Inf.

The Communication Trench should be capable throughout of carrying a stretcher — unseen by day.

6.7.15   MW 89.

Appendix 4

F2 (old Trench 23)

Menin Road.

Note the names of the Commⁿ Trenches X, Y, Z

225 Infantry to be employed on improving the newly made commⁿ Trench (from A to B - (shown red) on night of 6.7.15. From C to D a deviation has been made to avoid water; a parapet built up from Borrow pits. Width of Trench must not be deepened.
Trench commences of at E   6.7.15

Appendix 4

O.C. No 2 Section

With the assistance of 25 Inf. you will make communications to & construct (complete) 3 Dug outs for Sig. 41st Inf Bgde.

The Inf. will be at the LILLE GATE at 8.30 pm tonight.

Details for work will be issued by me verbally to you.

6.7.15   WD sgd.

Appendix 5

Major Mackesy. R.E.

I attach a report on the progress of sapping.

Points a, b, c, have been mainly night digging, as the ground has been dead for a certain length.

h & k has been done by my own men.

The Infantry have been throughout rather averse to the sapping, having been too busy with their parapets, & there has been considerable misunderstanding as to who is to do the work.

L, as leading to the French trench has become popular.

The trench connecting ④ & ⑤ has been sapped, open digging having been impossible.

6.7.15

Kinahan
Capt RE
O.C. 59.

Appendix 5

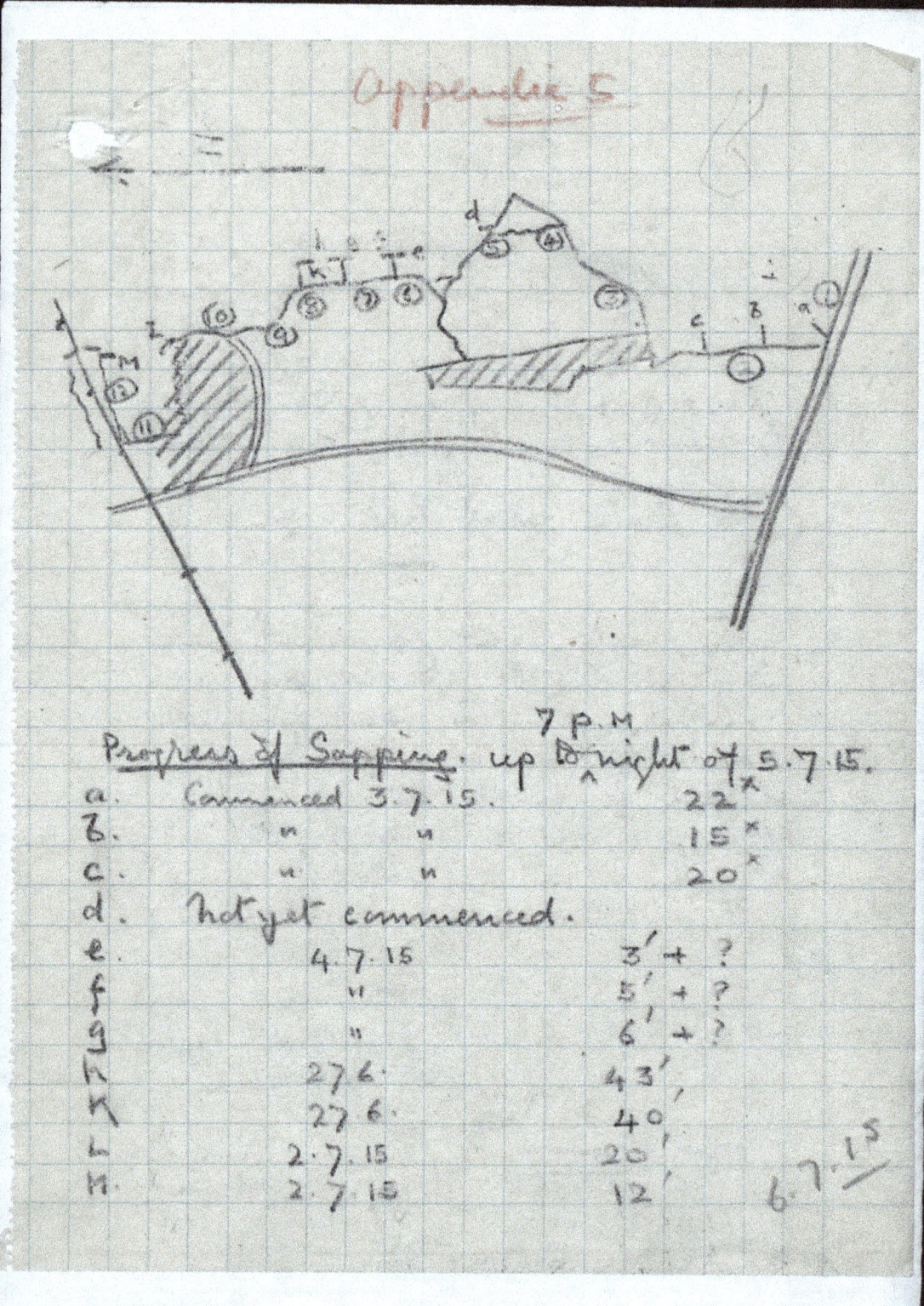

Progress of Sapping. up to night of 5.7.15. (7 P.M)

a. Commenced 3.7.15.   22 x
b.   "   "   15 x
c.   "   "   20 x
d. Not yet commenced.
e.   4.7.15   3' + ?
f.   "   5' + ?
g.   "   6' + ?
h.   27.6.   43'
k.   27.6.   40'
L.   2.7.15   20'
M.   2.7.15   12'

6.7.15

appendix 6

SECRET.   14th Divn
                                                           G. 2/5 S

41st Infantry Brigade.
42nd Infantry Brigade.
43rd Infantry Brigade.
11th Bn King's Liverpool Regt (Pioneers)
Major Mackesy.
C.R.A. (for information)

With reference to S/65/G dated June 10th, regarding division of responsibility in the construction and maintenance of defences, the distribution of work will be as laid down below.

At the present moment we are badly off for support trenches, and the only assembly trenches available for concentrating troops when the offensive is contemplated are in a shell swept area.

Our object is to avoid the latter area and to make our support trenches close to our fire trenches and certain assembly trenches indicated below in the area East of S 6 and S 8, in ground which is largely hidden from direct observation, except by aircraft.

We must be careful, however, to avoid constructing so many trenches in this area that we give the impression to hostile aircraft that they are likely to be used as assembly trenches.

I. <u>Work to be carried out under the orders of the Brigadier commanding 14th Division front.</u>

(a) Completion of fire trench from D 10 to D 12.

(b) Joining up and conversion into fire trench of T heads and saps from D 5, 6, 7 and 8.
    The exact line of this trench, and the point where it should join into D 5 ~~and the question of whether a further fire trench connecting D 4 and D 5 in rear of the point of the salient is desirable~~ requires to be definitely settled.

(c) Completion of saps A, B, and C from D 2, these saps to be joined by T heads with sap which 3rd Division is running out from the junction between 3rd and 14th Division fronts.

(d) Support trenches to be constructed in rear of D 6, 7, 8 and 9, and connected by frequent communication trenches with the fire trenches. A similar trench should be constructed E of S 3.

(e) Continuation of present scheme for "looping" the fire trenches and making dug-outs, so as to give alternative places for the garrison if subjected to heavy shell fire.

(f) Completion of new communication trench from BIRR cross roads to culvert at I.18.a.2.7.

II. <u>Work to be carried out under the orders of the C.R.E.</u>

(a) Construction of assembly trenches in rear of S 7, and S 9 ~~and S.10. An assembly trench might also be constructed in rear of S 5.~~

That part of S 4 which forms part of the communication trench from S 6 to D 2 should be maintained.
The remainder of S 4 and S 5, which are in an insanitary condition, should be abandoned. They should not be filled in, but left as dummy trenches for the enemy to practise on.

(b) Conversion of the first line of trenches in F 4, 7, 9, and 12 into good assembly trenches by deepening them and strengthening the traverses.

(c) Conversion of the first line of trenches in S 6 (N. of Y wood) and S 8, with the same object as in (b).

(d) Draining and improving existing communication trenches from the proposed assembly trenches (F 4, 7, 9, and 12) to proposed assembly trenches in S 6 and S 8; from proposed assembly trenches in S 6 and S 8 to proposed assembly trenches in rear of S 7 and S 9 ; and the communication trench from S 6 to that part of S 4 which is to be retained.

(e) Prolongation of communication trench W. through I.10.a to MENIN road about I.9.d.

(f) Construction of short assembly trenches leading out of communication trenches W.Y. and Z, each assembly trench to hold one platoon, and each of these communication trenches to have enough assembly trenches for half a battalion.

(g) The maintenance and improvement of existing communication trenches W.Y. and Z will be carried out by permanent parties detailed by C.R.E.

L. Isacke.

Lieut.Colonel
General Staff
6th July 1915.   14th (Light) Division.

2nd Lt. Crampton

Pl. come & see me at the ECOLE as soon as you can.

The whole Coy will be employed for present on Sapping in Att Spurs & on the extreme left of Durham's Front.

I wish to explain verbally instructions to Spilby & hand to you.

Nos 1 & 3 Sections will commence then work tonight.

2nd Lt Aryson must endeavour to obtain Sapping Tools of any sort from Corps Park. If unable, cut down

O.C.
89th Field Co.

Herewith copy of minute sent to 43rd Infantry Brigade for your information. On night 28th–29th the 43rd Infy. Brigade are being relieved by 3rd Division but your Company will still remain in charge of front trenches. The principal work is completion of the 2nd Communication trenches from C to D and doubling of line at D by construction of the new trench, there also to see that both old trenches along wood at F and F₁ and F₂ are made suitable for assembly trenches.

About 20 grapnels are being obtained to remove entanglements.

You should prepare means for men to get out of front trenches to assault and prepare & fix notice boards where required in your area.

26/6/15

J. Brunton
Lt/Ck. R.E. Major R.E.
YPRES.

Copy
43rd Infantry Brigade,

The following work has to be completed by night 30th inst - 1st July and I hope you will give every assistance in getting it complied. Captain Benskin RE, OC 89th F. Co. R.E. knows the details.

Completion of the two communication trenches from line along CAMBRIDGE Road at C to old front trenches at D.

Construction of second trench about 30" from and parallel to D.

Construction of 2 communication trenches from D to front line E.

Construction of 2 communication trenches from F to front line G.

(Copy has been given Capt Benskin)

(Signed) J. P. Mackesy
Major RE.
Acting CRE East of YPRES
for XIV Div.

26/5/15.
11.17 am.

49

P.S.— 10 (perhaps)

I am assuming that Jap will have arranged to demolish the blocked key behind their tank down in E.O. to be clear tonight. The E.S.M. should no-handing during its entr.

J 15
27-6-15

Winston
Churchill

44

Shovels, picks.
n.d Lt Griffin will march out Nos 1 & 3
Sections.
You will rejoin him as he passes.

I have arranged for Griffin to meet
O.C. Somersets at Kn Hege —
also for O.C. Inniskillings on his
return to Capt Grant at about 11 pm.

Woodward
Capt No.
5.15 pm.   Or. 9/9.
27.6.15.

O.C. 89 Coy.

I don't think the 43rd Inf Bde
will be relieved on 28 as previously
arranged, but they will probably continue on
in the trenches for a little time longer.
The work referred to in my minute of yesterday
at front need not now be finished on night
of 30th–1st but should be completed by that of
2nd–3rd prox at latest
The most important part is the support
trenches D for say 3 companies, but I
understand the Commn: trenches CD. must be
completed first for drainage purposes.

JB Mackesy
Major

27/6/15
8.35 a.m.

O.C. 1 Section
    2 ..
    3 ..
    4 ..

...in carrying out of the orders
... A copy is
attached.

...ing this report & copies to of
any matters of importance.

27.6.15

Hawkins
Capt. R.E.
O.C. Sig ... C/M

Pl. study the Bgde orders as regards
the numbering of trenches.
Sign Boards are now being made.
You will be responsible for the
correct placing of these Boards

2nd Lt. Llewellyn

Work to be done night 28/29
Sapping at C & D.
Locate the trenches in the
Somerset Area with a view
to placing up notice boards.

Report to me progress by the
Infantry & progress in the
Sapping.

28.6.15

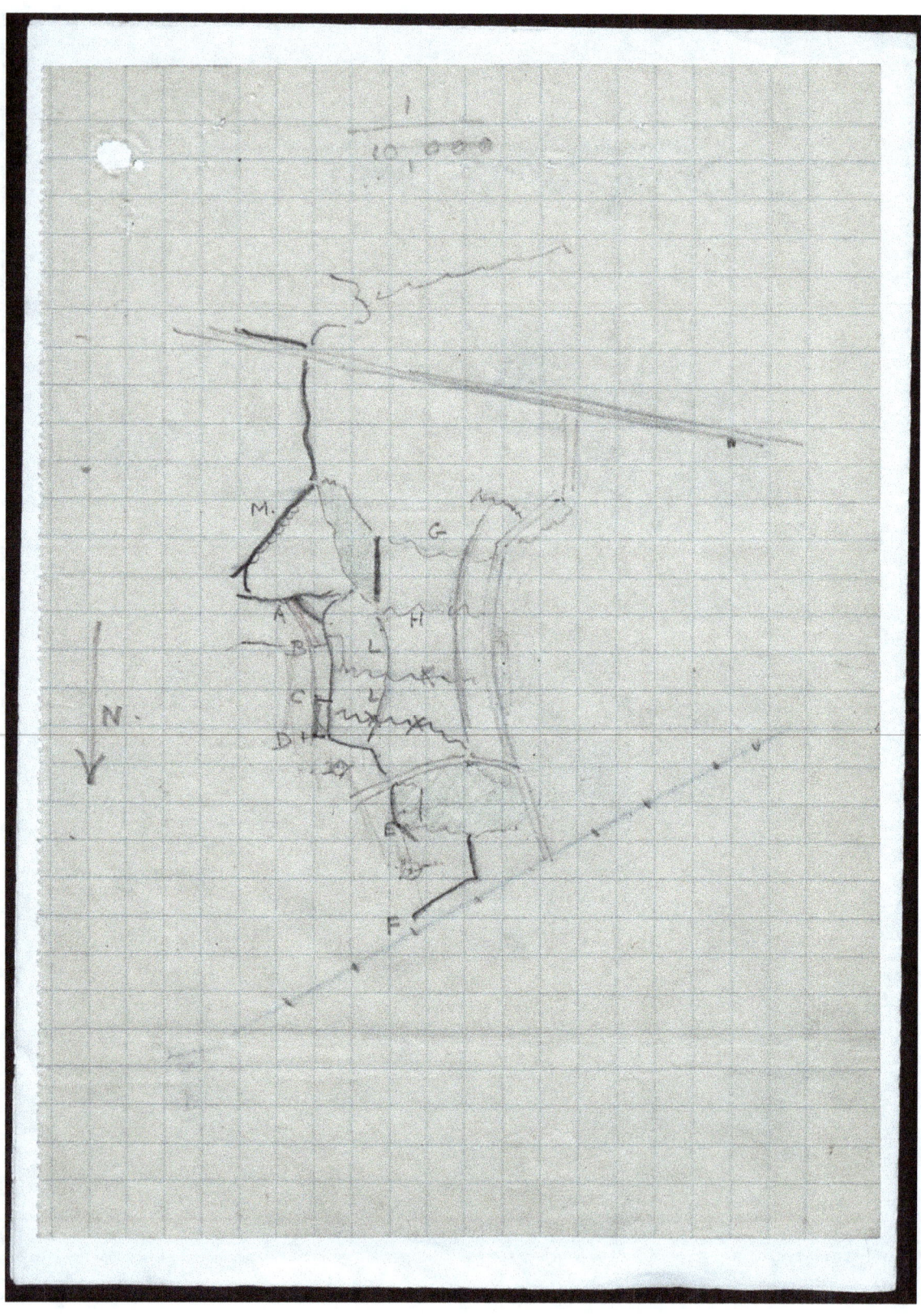

2nd Lt. Calvert

Work for 28/29
Report to Durhams about
10.30 pm, extreme right of
Somerset's front. 2 guides
will there direct you to work
to be done on salient — north
face —. This consists of
connecting up A & B by
utilising an existing ditch,
wh. was reconnoitred today

Take 500 Sandbags.
    Pickets.
    Trench wire.
all of wh. are at the
ECOLE.

Shovels not wanted.

Endeavour to mark down the
junction points of trenches.

      Benchidos
      Capt. RM
28.6.15   O.C. 89.

OC 89th Bde.

The date by which the special work, noted for completion by nights 4th 5th July, has now to be finished has been again postponed a few days, but every endeavour should be made to have it completed by night 4th-5th in case of any further alteration. This unless briefly:—

Construction & completion of 2 Communication Trenches from F9 to Old Trench S9 and thence to Front Trenches 6,7,&8.
Clearing & opening up of S9.
Clearing & opening up of S4 (62nd Coy during 5.5)
Construction of new trench about 30ft behind and parallel to S9.
Forming R.E. Depot upon Front Trenches & provision of notice boards.

2/ In addition to running Saps from 7, 10, & 12 as instructed to-day, the Extension of Those from Saps 6, 7, & 8 should be continued.

J P Macksey Major RE

1/7/15

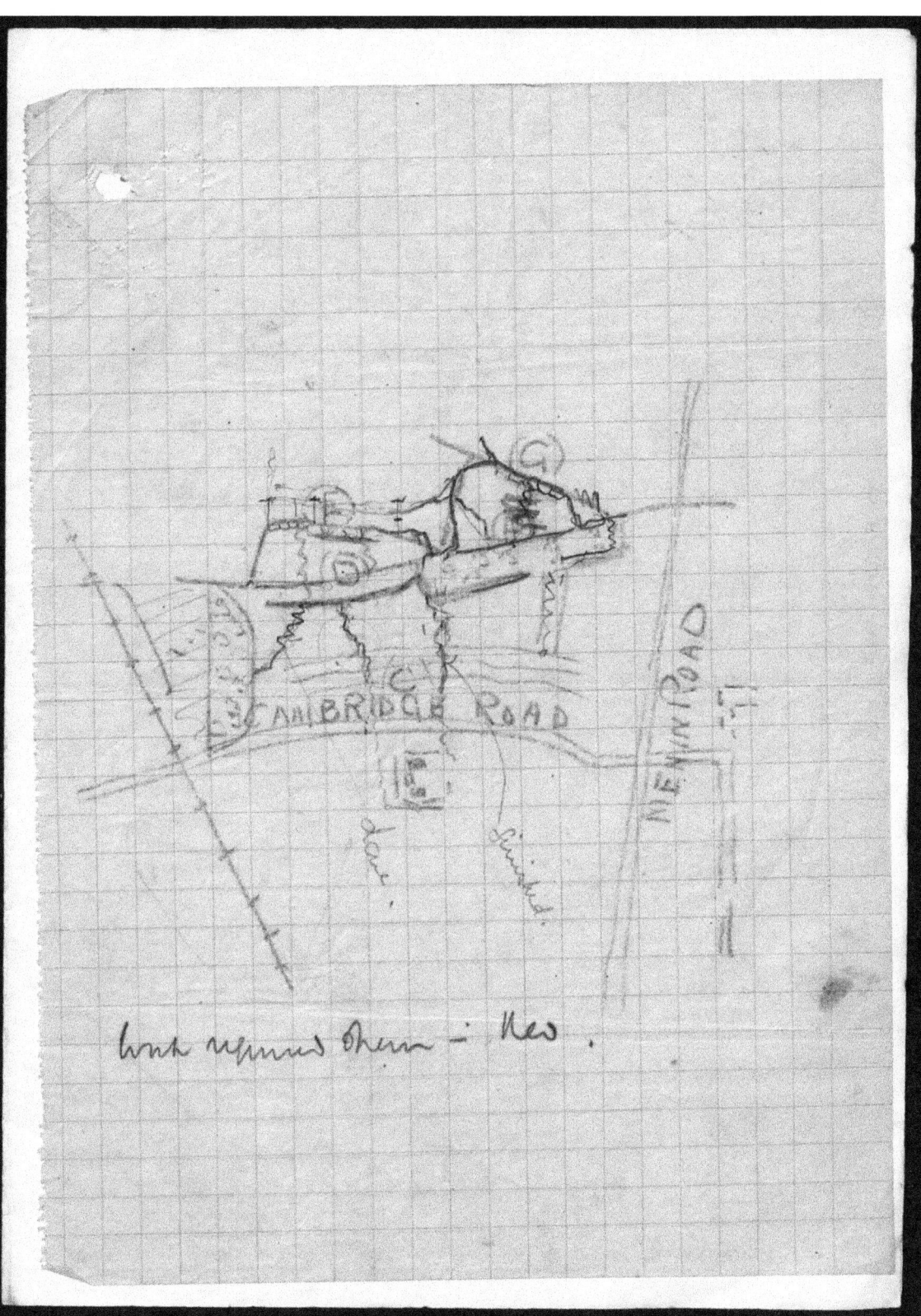

WAR DIARY or INTELLIGENCE SUMMARY

Army Form C. 2118.

Place	Date	Hour	Summary of Events and Information	Remarks and references to Appendices
VLAMERTINGHE	6/7		Men in trenches. Personally returned to VLAMERTINGHE with Capt. Rein. Took over communication trenches from O.C. 61. Gave section a rest. Coy. bathed at Poperinghe. Sap LANCASTER G. SLIGHTLY WOUNDED. Employed 250 O.R. & trench (42 Brigade) on improving trench Y. V. bad work. No 3 on Sec. 41. Coy. Cmd. No 4 supervising internally. Personally avoided supervision & selected site on T trench for Sec. 43. Returned 5 a.m. See appendices.	4 & 5
	7/7		Employed 500 R.O.F.! (43rd) on comm. trench Y. 5th Troops on & fifteen recc'd by day; see appendix. 5 distribution of work. Employed 1 platoon King's Liverpool on Comm. trench from 7.9. to S.8. Those at night not for night.	6
	8/7		No Inf. available for night work. Relief night. In accordance with orders from No for 14 Div. Capt. Rein made enquiries as to provision of Saw mill at Vlamertinghe. No 2. Select. - Ing adds for Sec. 41. No 4 improvements to Y trench. Congratulated by on good work in progress at Ypres was complete.	
"	9/7		350 1st Liverpool for night work - under Lt Trumpler. No 3 Section commenced 2nd rec. Dressing Station in G.H.Q.2 improved Y & 2. Worked at Vlamertinghe in morning. Bathed at Poperinghe in morning.	

WAR DIARY or INTELLIGENCE SUMMARY

Army Form C. 2118.

68 (FIELD) COMPANY ROYAL ENGINEERS

Place	Date	Hour	Summary of Events and Information	Remarks and references to Appendices
	10.7		2nd Lieut. W.T. Haughton killed instantaneously 7.30 pm between YPRES & G.H.Q. 2. T. Wash on Menin Road. G.H.Q.2. ("Rulli" and new junction of T with G.H.Q. 2. 5 new junction of Z. Dug out for Cpl 43rd Regt 43rd R.E. commenced. Wire Boards placed. Improvements to P₂. Y & Z. Dug out for Cpl. 41st Regt (commenced by 61st 7.9 Coy) continued by the 65th. SAP. READSHAW, F.S. SLIGHTLY WOUNDED.	
	11.7 Sun		Wash as above. Also day 3 new communication trenches on off shoots to Y & Z. See progress report dated 12.7.15. Ireland & step Dug out for Cpl 43rd Regt. SAP. SOUTHWELL, H. WOUNDED.	
	12.7		See progress report dated 13.7.15. Poor progress, partly due to a Relief night which had not been reported.	
	13.7		Being poor work indeed by the 11th Kings Liverpool. Reported this to O.C. Liverpool & to C.R.E. Programme of work as for the 10th finished. Dug out for Cpl 41st finished. SAP SOUTHWELL, H. DIED OF WOUNDS.	
	14.7		V. wet night. Progress under circumstances fair.	
	15.7		Reinforced Trenches with Capt Thurgood to find out how Drive & Comm. Trench	

WAR DIARY
INTELLIGENCE SUMMARY

Army Form C. 2118

89 (FIELD) COMPANY ROYAL ENGINEERS

Place	Date	Hour	Summary of Events and Information	Remarks and references to Appendices
	16-7		Round Common & Trenches with C.R.E. (Col SARGEAUNT). Capt Rein failed to deliver them to the trenches. Section work normal.	Orded out men. Previous day proposals approved.
	17-7		Laid out new trenches with C.S.M. Lockwood, & shared plans with Capt Langtown for work on 19.5. Capt Langtown for work on 19.5. Watches in the night by Capt Rein.	Shared plans to Capt Gray & 200 French troops brought to the
	18-7 Sun.		Commence new work, attacking good the cellars of the ECOLE made L. Talent & L. Llewellyn. L. Talent also by of trench troops & planter to Ser. o. Dry acts. Went round all night Standard of Livingroth N.A. Dressing Station completely to 3 Section. Progress V. satisfactory on S. Dressing Station. C.S.M. brought tables to ECOLE Stay work over trestles. Supply of Vlamertinghe & in district satisfactory under C/L Gain & C/L Long. SAP. WHITE. I.S. SLIGHTLY WOUNDED	
	19-7		C.S.M. started off turn & making re-inforced trench troughs at Gas Works Ypres. San. trains shelled on arrival. One horse — B.E.N. — hit — in by will piece of shell. G. Ward behaved very well.	
	20-7		Sent No. 2 & 4 Section to live at Ecole at 6pm. in easing from O.T. 61. Shelled when out there Ecole Gas shelled. Look over in supporting Point in the morning from O.T. 61.	Took over work on White Chatean Bridge. Blown house & burnt by shell fire at dawn. Erected Screen at Railway.

1577 Wt. W10791/1773 500,000 1/15 D.D.&L. A.D.S.S./Forms/C. 2118.

Army Form C. 2118.

WAR DIARY
or
INTELLIGENCE SUMMARY.
(Erase heading not required.)

Instructions regarding War Diaries and Intelligence Summaries are contained in F.S. Regs., Part II. and the Staff Manual respectively. Title pages will be prepared in manuscript.

69 (FIELD) COMPANY
A.S. / E. File

Place	Date	Hour	Summary of Events and Information	Remarks and references to Appendices
	21.		Nos 1 & 3 Section carrying on superintending the 4 Supporting Points. Progress satisfactory.	Norm 9-11; 12-4
	22.		400 Inf at White Chateau. Result disgraceful. Major Wylie arrived. Went with CRE to the White Chateau in car. Progress at 4 Supporting Points v.fair.	
	23.		90 Cav. & Cyclists employed at White Chateau. result v.good. Progress The 4 Section unsatisfactory. Progress of 4 Supporting Points very fair. visited them in the afternoon. Remodelled the Brickfields Water Supply. 62nd & 66 & no 2 sections also to live in the Ecole. encountered suitable bunk at ZILLEBEKE in nights - under Capt. Reid.	
	24.		Moved Sgt Sherman & Major Section C/P. Keith & no 1. Employed 30 Liverpools at various labour in making Handles. Went to Ecole by bike at 8.30 am. Our men began work at WHITE CHATEAU before 11 pm on night 23/24. Work very keen then satisfactory. visited 4 Supporting Points in the aftn. Bombed the shot. SAP. MAPSTONE, W. WOUNDED. PNR. WILLIAMS, T. SLIGHTLY WOUNDED	
	25 Sun.		Visited Ecole in morning. Work at chateau v.good indeed. 90 Cav & Cyclists & 40 D.A.C. employed that night. Good work. Progress Supporting Points satisfactory. 1½ Exemption sick. Improved in Aid Post Dug Outs. Ecole Dug Out satisfactory. 2ND (DFR): WRIGHT. D.G. ACCIDENTALLY WOUNDED	

1577 Wt.W10791/1773 500,000 1/15 D.D. & L. A.D.S.S./Forms/C. 2118.

Army Form C. 2118.

WAR DIARY
or
INTELLIGENCE SUMMARY.
(Erase heading not required.)

Instructions regarding War Diaries and Intelligence
Summaries are contained in F. S. Regs., Part II.
and the Staff Manual respectively. Title pages
will be prepared in manuscript.

68 (FIELD) COMPANY
ROYAL ENGINEERS

Place	Date	Hour	Summary of Events and Information	Remarks and references to Appendices
	26.7		No Inf available at night or by day - for Chateau or Supporting Points. Ordered to make a Field Water Short Round at 14th Divl Park. Ecole shelled 7.45 pm (27 shells) - no casualties. Billets at Poperinghe in afn.	
	27.7		Reconnoied chateau in morning with C.R.E. In need of discipline. New draft of 14 men (1 Driver) arrived. No Inf available for 4 Supporting Points. 40 Cdr. 50 Eyclist. 60 D.M.C. for Chateau. Wk with V.S. Gassing Station in Menin Road finished. Progress slow but satisfactory.	
	28.7		No Inf available for 4 Supporting Points. 400 Inf. 2/43rd Bgde for Chateau. Brought in two wagons from Menin Road. Sap'rs commenced making shot proof.	
	29.7 Thurs		Infantry failed to arrive 1st shift at Supporting Point. Reason to Aeroplane interference. Progress at Chateau good. Germans attacked Hooge at about 3 am. Rain with 50 men at mortar range v 30=.	
	30.7		No Inf available for any works. Work continued on the White Chateau satisfactorily by R.E. N. J Emplacement made at Supporting Point - also dug outs commenced.	
	31.7		No Inf available for any of the works. Sapper Brooker slightly wounded in Ypres when taking team for bricks. Sapper Stewart wounded.	

DRIVER KEIGH, D. WOUNDED SAPPER BROOKER, A. SLIGHTLY WOUNDED
1577 Wt. W10791/1773 500,000 1/15 D.D.&L. A.b.S.S./Forms/C. 2118.

WAR DIARY
or
INTELLIGENCE SUMMARY.
(Erase heading not required.)

Army Form C. 2118.

Place	Date	Hour	Summary of Events and Information	Remarks and references to Appendices
	1.8.15.	Sunday.	Nos 1 & 3 Sections rested all morning & relieved the 61st Fd Co the remainder S. of HOOGE & 3 Section living in SANCTUARY WOOD. Heavy shelling at Daybreak, & now with 1 & 3 Section) having been round the "part" practising with Crompton. Nos 2 & 4 caught work in Ecole. (I have about)	
	2.8.15.		2nd Section of Sent L' Knuckle with his 2 Section back to the 61st Fd Co. The 10th Durhams under 88 Superinion constructed a 2nd Line. The Situation was serious, as the front line was hardly tenable in ZOUAVE wood & there was nothing to stop the Germans pushing through. Dug out. Made a wire support to enlarge accommodation in the First Aid Post. Made a new RA.P. Hqrs. Dug out. No 1 Section under L' Crompton went to YEOMANRY POST between Cavalry Ln old wood's already there, & to help E. Coy 10 Durhams who were in Sanctuaryn. No 4 Section at ECOLE asked 1B made a strong Dug out at the MOATED GRANGE for Bgde Hqrs. No 2 Section continued at Ecole - no infantry working parties available.	
	3.8.15.		Continued as above. Progress all round v. satisfactory. At night Sections went to Yeomanry Post - Thence to Ecole for the night.	
	4.8.15.		Returned via 43rd Bgde Hqrs. L' Crompton wounded by a spent bullet in right 3/4. Progress all round v. satisfactory.	

WAR DIARY
or
INTELLIGENCE SUMMARY.

Place	Date	Hour	Summary of Events and Information	Remarks and references to Appendices
	10.8.15		No 2 Section moved to Ecole, & continued work commenced by No.1. Nos 1 & 3 resting. Remnants of 4 distributed among 1, 2 & 3. 43rd Inf. Bgde relieved the 42nd.	
	11.8.15		Nos 1 & 3 night work on Pts 8, 3, 7, 4 & 6. (Small Supporting Points Jn 30) No 2 cleaned up Ecole & rested. Liverpools worked on Q20 16 H.13. after I showed them the site. Lt. Macdonald (joined the Coy on the 10.) went to Ecole. SAPPER BERESFORD. W. WOUNDED.	
	12.8.15		Went round trenches from 2 a.m. to 8.30 a.m. Lt. BEASLEY joined the Coy. Lt. Talbot & Mr. Gerald disconnected for day work, which was to the continued. Nos 1 & 3 continued night work.	

WAR DIARY
or
INTELLIGENCE SUMMARY

Army Form C. 2118.

69 (FIELD) COMPANY

Place	Date	Hour	Summary of Events and Information	Remarks and references to Appendices
YPRES billets in ramparts.	13.8.		L^T Calvert found to be sick at the Ecole; he was sent back to camp. No 2 Section placed under L^T Macdonald + ordered to make Machine gun Cut in front line, + to assist by in front line. No 1 Section under Captⁿ Rein continue on R 4.5.6 No 3 " " L^T Grippen " R 8.3.7 L^T Beasley sent from camp to the Ecole to go round with Captⁿ Rein. Accompanied L^T Grippen in the evening + night. Found his work all wrong. R 8 in the wrong place. R 3 far too big. L^T Grippen apparently not his usual self. Work under Captⁿ Rein satisfactory. Liverpools conthⁿ on trench from H 13 to Q 20. 6th S^o Lancashires that 14 - have not done their share of their work - this is not understood. Slept in camp. PNR. DEACON. A. SLIGHTLY WOUNDED	
	14.8		L^T Grippen reports sick in the evening & removed by Ambulance to 14th Div. Rest Camp. in the morning.	
	15.8		No 3 Section sent back to camp in the afternoon. L^T Beasley left Y^e of L^T Grippen's work with Capt Fugle. Boyle + White to assist him. No 3 to make hurdles + dug out frames in camp - under L^T Calvert - remainder of men to work on Durham Redoubt near Vlamertinghe. Slept in camp. Work continued on shelters for the 13th.	

WAR DIARY
INTELLIGENCE SUMMARY

Place	Date	Hour	Summary of Events and Information	Remarks and references to Appendices
YPRES. Ellers.	16.8		Returned to Hyde Park in the morning and went round GHQ2 line with Capt De Houghton in the aft. to report on defences from Hell Corner to Shrapnel Corner. Work of the Coy. proceeded as before satisfactorily. The Brigade producing working parties generally as asked for. The standard of work done by the Durhams is not high on the main and V. trench. At 9 p.m. the ramparts were heavily shelled (about 6" guns). Several casualties in the Durhams & several shells v. close to HQrs. At 2 am. shelled with gas. (Sea Brooke) 4.3" & Capt De Houghton & Capt De Houghton to find out in eastern of the trench from H.13 to Q.20 has been satisfactory day. Q.20 found to be unreoccupied by the 6. G.H. returned 9 am. Ramparts shelled again in the early morning.	
	17.8	-	Section work continued normally. arranged for all but provided to act as carrying parties. The parties did v. badly. They were shelled by gas shells. Sept in camp. No 3 Section previous day & remd. an Durham Redoubt.	
	18.8		Returned to Hyde HQrs. Progress on Supports Road & Dug out stain. In the evening the Rampants & HQrs were shelled with 15" shells. V. close to HQrs. Progress of work normal. 2nd Lieut Perrott R.E. (regular) arrived in the evening.	
	19.8		89. relieved by 62nd Fd. Co, R.E. No 1. Section and Officers returned	

Army Form C. 2118.

WAR DIARY
or
INTELLIGENCE SUMMARY.
(Erase heading not required.)

Place	Date	Hour	Summary of Events and Information	Remarks and references to Appendices
			to camp. except Lt. Macdonald & No 2 Section who stayed on in order to take charge of work at White Chateau & to supervise Inf. working parties the same night. No 3 Section continued work as before. He returned to camp myself. Draft of 17 men arrived from ROUEN. C.S.M. sick. Lt. Calvert still sick. No 4 Section returned & placed Y/c of 2nd Lt PERROTT.	
FLAMERTINGHE.	20.8.		Work organised as below. No. 2 Section. Lt. Macdonald. Lining of ECOLE - WHITE CHATEAU. No. 1 Section. Capt. Rein. Laying Trolley line along Menin Road. Laying out defences for Ecole. Made good Menin Rd Dressing Stn. No 3 Section. Y/c of 3 Supporting Points (work on Somerset redoubt Y/c of 2nd Lt.) (no Inf. available) Lt Bewley. No 4 Section. Make forgoose at Menin Gate. Lt. Perrott. M.G. Emplacement in G.H.Q. Line Prepare Bridge. G for Demolition. No.3 Section shelled out of the Supporting Points. The German Artillery being directed against our 9.2 Howitzers. in the farm.	

WAR DIARY
or
INTELLIGENCE SUMMARY

Army Form C. 2118.

(Erase heading not required.)

Place	Date	Hour	Summary of Events and Information	Remarks and references to Appendices
	21.8		Progress considering the work only inch taken over - satisfactory. no Inf. Working parties available.	
	22.8	Sun.	Work as shown for the 20th continued with no Inf. available for Supporting Point. 150' of Trolley line laid. No casualties.	
	23.8		Work as shown for the 20th continued.	
	25.8		As for 22nd.	
	24.8		Spr. GRIERSON wounded at White Chateau. Slight. Small H.E. on parapet. Front round works by day. Progress generally satisfactory. Eagle Defences satisfactory continued. Capt. RE19 went on leave for 5 days. Spr. GRIERSON wounded at White Chateau. Slight. Small H.E. on parapet. Handed over 4 V. Countersch Support Points to 56th fd Coy. The work on these points had always been V. bad – due to Lack of continuity in the work. All worked proceeded as usual.	

WAR DIARY
or
INTELLIGENCE SUMMARY.

(Erase heading not required.)

Army Form C. 2118.

Place	Date	Hour	Summary of Events and Information	Remarks and references to Appendices
	26.6		Gen. programme of work continued. No. 2 Section moved from Ecole de Champs. Lt. Calvert still unfit for ordinary duties. City Inf. working party available was for White Chateau transferred all work at night. Scenic parapet erected on Rondere Rly. to take pl. of south parapet – invisible in order to 1st visible post. Trolley line reached Ecole John.	
	27.8		No special remarks. Gen. programme continued. A curved way marked out from Menin Gate to lead to West Lane.	
	28		As above. M.S. Emp: E not being provided with proper amount of head room. 2' ref. from above bottom of loophole.	
	29		Sunday. As above. Work at White Chateau unsatisfactory. Hurdles for revetment not secured fastened. & Traverses not being properly continued. Demolition of 9 Bridge ready. St Pierrene in Menin Gate ditto. " 10 " " being prepared. C.S.M. Lockwood proceeded on leave.	

89 (FIELD) COMPANY
ROYAL ENGINEERS

Army Form C. 2118.

WAR DIARY
or
INTELLIGENCE SUMMARY
(Erase heading not required)

22. 68 (FIELD) COMPANY

Place	Date	Hour	Summary of Events and Information	Remarks and references to Appendices
VLAMERTINGHE	30-8		No 1. Section. Lay Trolley line along Menin Rd. Defences of Ecole. No 2 " " White Chateau. No 3 " Ador. H.Q. Dugouts. Show progress on railway. No 4 " M.G. Emp^{ns} in G.H.Q. Comm^{ns} across Hell Fire Corner. Collected whole Coy in camp. Ecole too overcrowded when 62nd & 7th Coys in There; also heavy shelling in liable to recommence. Spr. M^cCLEOD slightly wounded on YPRES road. Shrapnel. Spr. BATTYE " " near Menin road. " " Capt. Reis returned from leave.	
	31-8		Show ground (examples of loopholes, dugouts etc etc) recommenced. Lt. 62 in charge. 10 men of 89th provided. Work carried normally as for the 30th. Wrote report on Drainage of H Sector. 425 Inf. being employed every night under direct Coy. supervision.	

12/7431

14th Division

89th F.C. R.E.
vol 2

Sep 1 & Oct 15

CONFIDENTIAL.

WAR DIARY.

of.

69th. FIELD COY R.E

from. Sept 3rd 1915 to Oct. 31. 1915.

(Volume 1) 2

Confidential

WAR DIARY. 2⁹ᵗ/ᵈ F. Cᵒ. RE.
or
INTELLIGENCE SUMMARY.

Army Form C. 2118

Place	Date	Hour	Summary of Events and Information	Remarks and references to Appendices
VLAMERTINGHE	3 Sept		CSM. retd. from leave. Work finished at the Shews Ground. Recreation room & horse shelter continued. Raining very hard & all work checked.	√
	4		Rained very hard. Trench drainage a prominent question. Lt. Macdonald ½ of drainage Stopped from employing men at the White Château by day – not considered safe. Work continued but little done	√

diary for Sept. 1. & 2:- not kept. √

[signature]

Army Form C. 2118.

WAR DIARY
or
INTELLIGENCE SUMMARY.
(Erase heading not required.)

Instructions regarding War Diaries and Intelligence Summaries are contained in F. S. Regs., Part II. and the Staff Manual respectively. Title pages will be prepared in manuscript.

Place	Date	Hour	Summary of Events and Information	Remarks and references to Appendices
VLAMERTINGHE	5th Sept		Capt Benakr went on leave, Capt Rees took over Section's work continued as before – rain ceased.	
	6th		No special occurrence – general work continued. No Infantry owing to wet day.	
	7th		L.u. work heavily shelled last night – parapets & parados damaged – no Infantry working parties owing to wet day. Sapping continued work of previous days.	
	8th		No raids available for hotley line. L.u. repaired where blown in by shell fire. Tunnel through Maxim R.P. at G.H.Q. completed. Read instructions to repair Signal loop dug-outs at J+3 – started work	
	9th		Ypres heavily shelled delayed working parties – repaired hotley line damaged by shell. Working party at L.u. increased to 2 reliefs of 200 Infantry each.	
	10th		Arranged with O/C 6.2 R.W.Ky. as taking over our work	

Army Form C. 2118.

WAR DIARY
or
INTELLIGENCE SUMMARY.
(Erase heading not required.)

Place	Date	Hour	Summary of Events and Information	Remarks and references to Appendices
Vlamertinghe	11. Sept.		Capt. Rankin ret.d from leave. 62nd relieved 62nd from front line work. 42nd Bgde in front trenches. Nos 1 & 4 Section living in YPRES & East of YPRES - moved in on 11th. No 3 still employed on L 4 work. No 2 in camp; employed on provision of stores, dugout frames etc. etc. 15 day pay & 10 day no 2 7.P. Spr. HACKETT brought up to drunk in camp. First case.	✓
	12.		Work as above. Spent morning taking over from Capt Reis & the aftr. in going round the trenches. State of Front line considerably improved during the last 14 days. Warned by ZRE that the 62nd will be relieved all work pending. plans for an attack by 41st & 5 Inf Bgde. Inf. employed at drainage of H Sector.	✓
	13.		Nos 1. Section & no 4 living in neat Rampart Tunnels & working on front line - vide detail of work with CRE. 14 Sept. No. 3. on L4y & No. 2 in Camp providing materials & assistance to Inf. for the same. Work mainly dugouts - aid posts.	✓
	14.		Capt Reis reported Lt. MACDONALD for misbehaviour as regards his manners to Officers & men. On investigation	✓

Army Form C. 2118

WAR DIARY
or
INTELLIGENCE SUMMARY.
(Erase heading not required.)

Instructions regarding War Diaries and Intelligence Summaries are contained in F. S. Regs., Part II. and the Staff Manual respectively. Title pages will be prepared in manuscript.

Place	Date	Hour	Summary of Events and Information	Remarks and references to Appendices
	Sept.			
Ypres.	15.		The matter was referred to the services. The Section was found upside down. Lt. Macdonald suspended work & recommended for renewal from the Coy. Work continued on the same lines.	W.
			43rd Bgde relieved 42nd Bgde in the evening. Our pub Ye of KAAIE Salient supervision of Sgt. (8th R.B. 1 Coy). Drainage continued nightly, work concentrated on the Beek.	W.
	16.		No special remarks.	
	17.		Went round KAAIE. which was overhanging the road. Capt Rain blew down part of the Cloth Hall road.	
	18.		Road Trench in the early morning. Heavy shelling on hill sides. 2 new trollops for trolley line down Menin Road arrived. No 3 Section also moved to Ypres Ramparts heavily shelled in the afternoon. Coy v. hard worked at strong dugout & many small works from 9 H.Q. early.	W.

27.

Army Form C. 21.

WAR DIARY
INTELLIGENCE SUMMARY.   89th - 3rd - Coy. R.E

(Erase heading not required.)

Place	Date	Hour	Summary of Events and Information	Remarks and references to Appendices
	19 Sept.		Nos. 1, 3, & 4 Sections living in the ramparts of YPRES continued making 4 Aid posts under the railway W. of Cambridge Rd -	Nil
	20		" " " " Menin Rd - at BIRR X Roads.	
	21		Many Rivet. Stores in front lines. Hqrs - Dug Out (4). Improvements to old dug outs. Shelters for Runners & many minor jobs.	
	22		These preparations continued every day & night in conjunction with the 43rd Inf. Bde. who provided covering parties & working parties as required. The 62nd Inf. Coy. was struck off all works (which fell on the 89.) whilst they prepared for the attack.	Nil
	23		Rail Bombardment of the Front Line E of Ypres. Coy. luckily escaped casualties except Spr. Smith - wounded by trench mortar.	
	24		3 Sections returned from YPRES at 5.30 a.m. having completed all the work allotted to it in connection with the attack arranged for the 25th - Baths allotted - but unable to make use of them. Men rested. Singsong in camp recreation room.	
	25		62nd Inf. Coy. partook in the attack. 89th in reserve. No 2 Section arrived at 9.30 to move to YPRES to assist 62nd if regd - 2/Lt. BEASLEY in charge. O.C. 62nd returned Lt. Beasley as not required. The section worked in squads under Lts. PRESCOTT & CLARKE of the 62nd.	Nil

WAR DIARY
INTELLIGENCE SUMMARY.

Army Form C. 2118

89 F.C. R/E

Place	Date	Hour	Summary of Events and Information	Remarks and references to Appendices
	25 Sept.		at erecting wire in front of front line. Spr UNDERWOOD killed. Several 62nd casualties. Work satisfactorily accomplished. Remainder of Company rested. Lt Cloake & 62 badly wounded helping Underwood. ↓ RE's Jordan	
	26		At request of O.C. 62 - rendered 3 Section were sent in the morning to relieve 62nd. On arrival at YPRES found O.C. 62 said that he had not wanted them. Address was 980, address we G Middle. So back they returned to camp. Made Trestle frames & tarred big trestles. Found that No 2 Section had not rec'd rations from the O.C. 62. Lt. Beasley to look after them. At night this section was employed in H.20 at revetments. Went round whole front with C.R.E. in the aft. Trenches very bad, & once more blown to bits. Only Johan head work made by the Infantry dug out made by the Coy still standing. Ordered to relieve the 62nd on the night of the 27th.	✓
	27		Light camp duties - & parkson drill in the morning. Found that O.C. 62 had sent my section back to camp in the night. Sent Nos. 2 & 4 back to YPRES in the evening.	

Army Form C. 2118

WAR DIARY
or
INTELLIGENCE SUMMARY.
(Erase heading not required.)

Place	Date	Hour	Summary of Events and Information	Remarks and references to Appendices
	27 Sept.		43rd July Hythe took over H. Sector. Remount Cellars that night & housed Nos. 2 & 4 Sections in the same place. 2.15. Perrot & Beasley i/c of the Sections worked at drainage that night. No. 3. Section placed at disposal of CRE for permanent work at making huts - under Lt. Tempeley of 61 Fd. Coy.	V2
	28.		At about 8.30 or 9 am a 17 inch shell landed on top of Hyde Alga. It pierced 20 ft. of soft earth, 4½' of brick - demolished a 10 ft. square area & caused a large amount of iron girders which strengthened the cellars & which had been placed as an additional splinter catcher - to collapse. Either 9 or 11 men with wickets etc were killed. Spr. Mogg of 89th peppered in face. Lt. Perrott badly shaken & slightly wounded. Beasley untouched. Remainder of men untouched. I was in the back part of cellars. Very narrow escape. I was also blown away & peppered. Men were hurriedly moved to the N. end of rampart. For afraid with me to send them back to do then work from dumps; as no safe spot	V2 · V2

WAR DIARY
or
INTELLIGENCE SUMMARY.

Army Form C. 2118

Place	Date	Hour	Summary of Events and Information	Remarks and references to Appendices
	29		our left in Ypres.) Had to go to bed, where goc. of D.I.S. ordered me to stay for the next day.	TK
	30		Stayed in bed. No. 1 Section provided materials to front line No. 3. Huts. 2 & 4 drainage.	TK
			41st Bgde taken over whole of H & A fronts. 87th Ordered to send 2 Section to work under 41st. No work given them that night other than making their own dugouts — of which No 2 helped them, returning to camp the same night.	TK
1 Oct.			C.R.E. represented that 2 Sections were too many for 41st Bgde. Arrangement made that each Coy was to furnish 1 Section to the front line, under the O.C. of the Coy normally officialed to the Bgde. O.C. 61.½. No 1 Section withdrawn. 2nd Lt. MOWBRAY, R.E. joined the Coy. S.M. DUDLEY ?? wounded in arm.	TK

31.   89th Fd. Co./N.E.

Army Form C. 2118

WAR DIARY
or
INTELLIGENCE SUMMARY
(Erase heading not required.)

Place	Date	Hour	Summary of Events and Information	Remarks and references to Appendices
	2		No 4 Section employed at enlarging R.4. & making a new group of dug outs in front. 150 Inf. employed by night on drainage – under No 2. Trolley line continued. Inf. clear under coy. at fd. Wales. No 3 – hutting. No 1. camp improvements.	W/e
	3		Went round by night. Ordered to send 2 Section to work with 43rd Bgde in DICKEBUSH front. Capt Rein went to make plans etc. Work as on the 2nd.	W/e
	4		Nos 1 & 2 Section to dug outs in VOORMEZEELE with 43rd Bgde. No 3 Section hutting. No 4 Section with 41st Bgde in Y Wood area. Went round front with ot.78 in field coy. from whom I took over works. Lt. Perrott returned from the Rest Camp.	W/e

Army Form C. 2118.

32/

WAR DIARY
or
INTELLIGENCE SUMMARY. of 89 Fd. Coy. R.E.

Instructions regarding War Diaries and Intelligence Summaries are contained in F. S. Regs., Part II. and the Staff Manual respectively. Title pages will be prepared in manuscript.

(Erase heading not required.)

Place	Date	Hour	Summary of Events and Information	Remarks and references to Appendices
VLAMERTINGHE	5		2nd Lt Roberts confined to bed vomiting. I went to Reninghelst to meet CRE 2nd & 3rd Div who were taking over from CRE 17th. (Leaving St. Eloi front) & arranged for 89th & 43rd Fd. Coys to hand over Dickebusch stores. Thence to 43rd Hqrs (Rode Huis.) Arranged for the 2 section at Voormezeele to continue the Voormezeele defences, with Suff. Labour in addition to the numerous other works handed over by 98, 79, 20.	nil
	6		Visited No 4 Section at No 10 Canal Bridge Dugouts in Ypres. Work satisfactory on all sides. No 1 × 2 – St. Eloi front. 3 – Hellfire. 4 – Ypres front – Y Wood area.	nil
	7		2nd Lt. COOPER. R.E.T.C. arrived in eve. Visited 2 sections at Voormezeele. Work all satisfactory. Took Lt. Cooper to join Capt Reid at Voormezeele. GOC. visited the 43rd & 2nd Suff. Bgde class which had been under instruction in my camp for 7 days, & which then terminated.	nil
	8		Ordered to make a M.G. Emplacement in camp above ground. Capt Renshaw's name forwarded & recommended by GOC. for Intelligence GSO3. Work continued as on the 6th.	nil
	9		Visited No 9, 1 & 2. Very Satisfactory Progress. No special remarks.	nil

33/

WAR DIARY
or
INTELLIGENCE SUMMARY

of 59th 3rd Coy. R.E.

Army Form C. 2118.

(Erase heading not required.)

Place	Date	Hour	Summary of Events and Information	Remarks and references to Appendices
	10.		No special remarks.	
	11.		Trolley line along Menin Road continued as far as practicable, to I.7.a.7.9. Visited No 4 Section. L/Cpl Sims made 2nd Cpl. C.R.E. ill. Work generally satisfactory.	W.
	12.		Work continued all round. No special remarks.	
	13.		Capt REIS wounded & evacuated in the evening. Rifle bullet in thigh. No special remarks.	W.
	14.		Nos 1 & 2 Sections returned to camp, handing over all work to the 24th Divn. No 3 Section Huts [ ] to 4. in front line (relieved have battled but not enough by Lt Beasley). Nos 3 & Ngn. battled.	W/2
	15.		Nos. 1 & 2 Bathed & then went to Cinema. Asked to congratulate the Coy. on its good work - by order of Gen. Distn. This is the 3rd time since the Coy has been in France. L/Cpl Shaw & C. Ward asked to receive Gd. Card for gallant and meritorious service from the G.O.C. This is a Divisional recognition of good work.	W.

Army Form C. 2118.

34.

WAR DIARY
or
INTELLIGENCE SUMMARY.
(Erase heading not required.)

Instructions regarding War Diaries and Intelligence Summaries are contained in F. S. Regs., Part II. and the Staff Manual respectively. Title pages will be prepared in manuscript.

Place	Date	Hour	Summary of Events and Information	Remarks and references to Appendices
	16.		No. 2 Section relieved No 4 in front line work. No. 1 Employed on Coote & Bolline, No. 3 Nutting No. 4. being relieved.	½
	17		Inf. Bde Field Works Class began. Work normal	½
	18.		No 1. Coote & Bolline. no. of Inf. working parties No 2. Front Line. under Ot. 62. No 3. Nutting No 4. Provision of Stores to old John. OT. visited the Bde field works course, under Sgt. Cornill. Satisfactory. Farmer's coat broken.	½
	19.		No special remarks. no Inf. working parties. Germans left the Coy. as interpreter.	Mons. DE LAVALETTE
	20.		Flooded Haymarket & Bond Str. in the night 19/20 from BELLEWARDE Lake. Inf. alarmed - not really serious 2/Lt. Parrott worked at The Bleak by night - after visiting it with me by day. Trouble in A Sector (not in H) & really due to The Bleak not having been sufficiently cleared in A Sector. Inf. working parties by night.	½

Army Form C. 2118

35

WAR DIARY of 89 Fd Coy
INTELLIGENCE SUMMARY.
(Erase heading not required.)

Instructions regarding War Diaries and Intelligence Summaries are contained in F. S. Regs., Part II. and the Staff Manual respectively. Title pages will be prepared in manuscript.

Place	Date	Hour	Summary of Events and Information	Remarks and references to Appendices
Vlamertinghe	21.		No special Remarks. Lt Rivett control drainage of Haymarket & the clearing of Beek.	X
	22.		No 2 Section returned from front. All Section in camp. No work on the front. The Division (including R.E. at rest). Time to be spent at training & cleaning up. Hour handed over to VI Div. Your CRE. (Col. STEPHENSON).	X
	23.		Coy. resting & only employed on camp improvement. Also cleaning kit, coats etc & 1 hour Coy. Drill. 43rd Div. Bde field water course conf. and No 3 Section com-at hutting.	
	24		V. heavy rain. 1 Section always at Hutting for Infantry.	} NZ.
	25		"	
	26			
	27		Coy Training. 1 Section daily employed at improvement to dugouts & paths and Section Stables. Training consisted of instruction in Bombing. Pontooning. Walden Trestle. and a little squad drill & saluting. OC presented II Cpl SHAW and L.Cpl WARD (no 2 Section) with Cards for Gallant & Distinguished Service.	
	28			
	29			
	30			
	31			

Sg. E.Z.C.R.E.
vol. 3

121/7673

14th Hussars

Nov 15

Army Form C. 2118

WAR DIARY
of 89th F^d. Coy. R.E.
INTELLIGENCE SUMMARY.

(Erase heading not required.)

Instructions regarding War Diaries and Intelligence Summaries are contained in F.S. Regs., Part II. and the Staff Manual respectively. Title pages will be prepared in manuscript.

Place	Date	Hour	Summary of Events and Information	Remarks and references to Appendices
VLAMERTINGHE	1st Nov.		14th Divⁿ still at rest. 89 F^d. Coy ditto. V. heavy rain. Camp converted to quagmire. No 1 - Route march. 2 & 4 - Camp duties - making paths - drains - improving dugouts. Huts. 3. Girl Hutting. Section further trained in Bombing. Capt. ALABASTER. R.E. joined the Coy.	
	2nd.		V. heavy rain. Coy battled in the aftⁿ. Nos 1 & 4 Coy Hut. 3. Girl Hutting. 2 Camp duties. Also further Bombing. L.C^{pl}. Bpr. LANCASTER killed by accident in Poperinghe street at about 5 pm. Concussion from a fall, when avoiding a wagon.	
	3rd.		V. heavy rain. Work as on the 2nd L.C^{pl}. Lancaster buried & court of Enquiry held. Cpl. GAIR died at Cambridge Hospital. Attended } when on leave.	
	4th.		Hut building continued. Work as on the 2nd	
	5.		No. 1 & 3 employed on Girl Hut. No 4 Coy. Hut & Potters etc No. 2. Trench sli[des] & a few Girl services.	1 Orderly cpl [?]

Stamp: 89 (FIELD) COMPANY · ROYAL ENGINEERS · 7 DEC. 1915

Army Form C. 2118

WAR DIARY of 89th FD. Coy.

INTELLIGENCE SUMMARY.

(Erase heading not required.)

Instructions regarding War Diaries and Intelligence Summaries are contained in F. S. Regs., Part II. and the Staff Manual respectively. Title pages will be prepared in manuscript.

Place	Date	Hour	Summary of Events and Information	Remarks and references to Appendices
VLAMERTINGHE	6.		No special remarks. A very quiet time for the Coy.	
"	7		for use in the I.L., which is employed as chalver. Trench railway materials nightly sent up to the Potijze Road for use when that work is to be resumed.	
"	8.		Weather again fine. Dug outs very damp & men being gradually moved into huts (5 nearly completed on 7th).	
"	9		Orders to layout trenches in rest area to Inf. to practice attack. An area of about 500' by 400' of German trench taken from aeroplane photos to be layed out. Site was selected with Sec. 4 & 3rd Bgde close to Bombing school.	
"	10		Section employed on following. Nos 1 & 2 Trench Stores. 3. Dist. Hutting. 4. Camp Mules. It is decided that breastworks are to be erected in front line. Hurdles & Gabions to be used for revetment. Nos. 1 & 2 Sections make Gabions, Hurdles, Trench boards.	
"	11		Went to HAZEBROUCK to 2nd Army Workshops to arrange construction of M.G. loopholes for Pivot mountings. Found they were being made. Laying out of German trench finished.	
"	12		It is decided that under the parapet dugouts be provided, for men lying down. Lt Mowbray employed on reconnaissance for building Decauville Rly. from Ypres to BRANDHOEK.	
"	13		Training of Inf. at breastworks commenced. V. wet & windy. Coy. employed on Trench stores & hutting.	
"	14		Sgt. Cowill to England on field works instructor. Training, under Capt. Alabaster's supervision. Work as before.	Cpl. Fogyle in charge of the Inf.

J. Oakeuta
Captain
89 (Field) Company
7 Dec. 1915
Royal Engineers

Army Form C. 2118

WAR DIARY
of 89 Field Coy. R.E.

INTELLIGENCE SUMMARY.
(Erase heading not required.)

Instructions regarding War Diaries and Intelligence Summaries are contained in F.S. Regs., Part II and the Staff Manual respectively. Title pages will be prepared in manuscript.

Place	Date	Hour	Summary of Events and Information	Remarks and references to Appendices
	15.		Visited the breastwork class. Satisfactory. Coy. employed at making breastwork materials & trench stores. No 3 Section hutting.	
	16		Capt Alabaster & I went round the new Sector to be occupied by 43rd Bde. Went to LA BRIQUE & ST. JEAN. Trenches all fallen in & up to ones thigh in mud & water. Shown round by a subs. of W. Riding Field Coy who was new to the ground. Wretched conditions. In the evening I sent Major JOSEPH RE of 1st London Field Coy to find out further information and the main drainage scheme. A fine day.	
	17.		Capt Alabaster showed Lts Cooper & Perrott round the Trenches S. of ST. JEAN. Worse than those visited on the 16th. Went to 43rd Bde Hqrs to discuss the erection of breastworks & recovery of trenches. 8 Coy hut completed for men's occupation. Shops being moved to close to main road. Wet & cold. Camp roads impassable.	
	18.		Aeroplane right over the camp at dawn. Bombs dropped in near fields. Trench stores continued to be made.	
	19		Nov. 1 Section (Lt. Cooper) & ½ No 4 Section (Lt. Perrott) and Coy. moved to dug outs vacated by the 12. P. Coy on the YPERLEI or C. 25. c. 7. 8. Section Officers & 2 C.O's reconnoitred the same night. Remainder of Coy remained in Camp under Capt. Alabaster. ½ of No. 3 Section permanently employed under Lt. Beasley at hutting. Remainder at provision of trench stores.	

Army Form C. 2

WAR DIARY
of 89th (A.) Fd. Coy.

INTELLIGENCE SUMMARY.
(Erase heading not required.)

Instructions regarding War Diaries and Intelligence Summaries are contained in F.S. Regs., Part II. and the Staff Manual respectively. Title pages will be prepared in manuscript.

Place	Date	Hour	Summary of Events and Information	Remarks and references to Appendices
YPERLEI.	20.11.15		Arranged to house 16 Inf. 4 from each Bn. Advised to sap French dug outs along the YPERLEI in continuation of the dugout lined in by 61st Fd. Coy. 20 Belgian permanently employed. Trolley line to be made back from St JEAN towards YPRES (point 12 d.2.7) also ban't on to WIELTJE. Drainage that considerable in trenches. All trenches in a deplorable state, & falling in. Hurdles collapsing from lack of anchors, & trenches 3' deep in places with water.	
	21.		Arranged to start an R.E. Dump at St JEAN. 10 D.L.I. attached for laying trolley line to WIELTJE. Men employed on drainage work - & recovery of trenches. Went to Potijze with C.R.E. about drainage of Bellewaarde Beek.	
	22.		Went round trenches with S.O.E. Generally employed on drains. recovery of trenches. Trolley line.	
	23.		Frost. 2nd Lt PERROTT suffering from strain; probably due to shock when nearly killed by 17" shell. Work on recovery of John St. & drainage in general. V. dark night. frost. Tried to shoot new line but failed for approval of S.O.C. Too dark. C.S.M. LOCKWOOD arrived to relieve 2nd Lt Perrott, who returned to camp.	

1577 Wt. W10791/1773. 500,000 1/15 D.D.&L. A.D.S.S./Forms/C. 2118.

1 DEC. 1915 — 88 (FIELD) COMPANY ROYAL ENGINEERS

Army Form C. 2118

WAR DIARY
of 89 Field Coy.
INTELLIGENCE SUMMARY.
(Erase heading not required.)

Place	Date	Hour	Summary of Events and Information	Remarks and references to Appendices
	24 Wed.		Spr. HOPKINSON wounded by Shrapnel. Spr. WIRE & TURNER about 3 pm. The coy. dugouts were shelled. 1. S.L.I. wounded. Ch. Long. 2nd Cpl. GRAY & Spr. WAKELEY very slightly touched. Glass in officers' mess shattered. Small shells luckily. 100 Inf. working party for raising of JOHN St. shored breastwork to 6.5 ft - ½ day. Shovel round St. Jean water. 20 ft drains to B.12 & B.13. Large quantities of stone received at St. Jean from camp. Capt. Alabaster R.E. reported on condition of works P1 & P2.	
	25 Thur.		Railway Trolley line proceeded satisfactorily. Further large quantities of materials for recently breastworks sent up. Sent round trench with S.O.C. + G.S.O.2. New line across high ground decided on - & ditto for line of wire.	
	26 Fri.		Working party of 70 - clearing JOHN St. & draining B.12 & 13. & laid out tapes for wire. Work commenced clearance of Hullenrade Beek finished. Progress in French dug-outs satisfactory.	
	27 Sat.		Big working party of 400 - employed on breastworks and on JOHN St. S.L.I. Work indifferent. Late in starting. But a certain amount of progress made. V. hard frost, which made it difficult to erect hurdles.	F. Oakley Capt.

88 (FIELD) COMPANY
1 DEC. 1915
ROYAL ENGINEERS

Army Form C. 2118

WAR DIARY of 69th Fd. Coy.
INTELLIGENCE SUMMARY.
(Erase heading not required.)

Instructions regarding War Diaries and Intelligence Summaries are contained in F.S. Regs., Part II. and the Staff Manual respectively. Title pages will be prepared in manuscript.

Place	Date	Hour	Summary of Events and Information	Remarks and references to Appendices
	28 Sun.		2.5 Inf. from each batt'n in Ryde attached to Coy for work. Night's work in general report – a v. dark night and absolute muddle on part of the Inf. working parties of 250. Rendezvous at 9.30. They arrived at 8.15. No. 1. Section had to knock off ¾ - ½ Inf. did the same. (determined) refilling a hand of smoke officers. No. 2. Section (2nd Lt. MOWBRAY) relieved No. 1 Section (2nd Lt. COOPER) at 12 mn. Breastworks handed over to the garrisons of trenches. Capt. Alabaster came round in the evening with one in order to see works in hand.	
	29 Mon		V. poor night's work, partly due to Inf. attached being strange. Difficulty in obtaining orders for Inf. attached. V. bad night. Wet & thawing. Work very difficult indeed. Sgt. BENSON hurt by falling down old trench. Removed on stretcher. Back hurt. No casualties.	
	30 Tues.		Coy. Dug Out. shelled about 9 am. About 40 shells within 15 yds of position. One dropped 300 slabs of guncotton buried 2 ft. Slabs scattered. Capt. Alabaster returned to camp. Arranged for 100 Inf. working party. Staff error to party never came. Work during the night was satisfactory, as the men knew what to do – but distributed by 2 "halts" at about 9 + 11 pm. Inf. attached worked well. 2.3 m Lockwood & I laid out the new trenches & wire for the same. About 200 yds. apron wire put up. Breastwork parados continued. Orders for Inf. attained. 2 Officers of S.I. shelled out spent night in my Dug.	

[Stamp: 89 (FIELD) COMPY ROYAL ENGINEERS 31 DEC. 1915]

Sgh R.C.R.E.
Vol: 4   Dec 19/15
121/7936

Army Form C.

WAR DIARY
of 89 Field Coy. R.E.
INTELLIGENCE SUMMARY.
(Erase heading not required.)

Place	Date	Hour	Summary of Events and Information	Remarks and references to Appendices
	1-12	Wed.	Heavy Artillery Bombardment N. No working parties - other than the attached men. Coy Dug Outs received a few shells. Rations going in not complete. Sent tool carts back to camp. They may have been attracting fire. Progress in French Dug Outs to date - 16 erected. 2 half erected. 10 being erected. General result of nights work good. LT. E.D. ALEXANDER joined the Company	
	2.12	Thurs	Capt. ALABASTER relieved Capt Rankin in front line work. Coy transport shelled when off loading rations at the Coy DugOuts at about 5.15 p.m. - in the dark. J? HILL slight wound in the foot. 1 mule killed at the site. 1 died in VLAMERTINGHE. 1 both hit (6 shrapnel) & brought back to camp. 1 Horse got away. Lost. Shortly after wards Capt Rankin & Lt Channing (adub) caught in a heavy shelling about 700 yds East of Brigade Hqrs. Crumps. Shrapnel & Gas. Lucky escape for both Offr. Working parties of 500 employed on making new Trench. and on repair of John St. also on trench water. But the work in general proceeding & under v. difficult conditions. 1 man of Notts & Derbys killed. 1 s.s.t. hit through lips.	

WAR DIARY
or
INTELLIGENCE SUMMARY.
(Erase heading not required.)

Army Form C. 2118.

Place	Date	Hour	Summary of Events and Information	Remarks and references to Appendices
VLAMERTINGHE.	3.12.15		No. 2 & 4 Section still on ST JEAN front. No. 7 employed on providing materials. ½ No 3 ditto. ½ No 3. on Hutting. No. 44107 L.Cpl. SMITH killed by shrapnel. Work on JOHN ST, GHQ breastworks and new trench in C.28.c.	
	4.12		Inf. working parts of 320 420 (additional to the 130 ordy attached to the Coy) Nos 2 & 4 Sections on ST JEAN front; No. 1 & ½ No. 3 making materials; ½ No 3 Hutting. 320. SHERWOOD FORESTERS & 100 D.C.L.I. on JOHN ST, new trench & C.28.c., GHQ. Breastworks and new drain behind S.9.a. B.G.C. 43rd Brigade and B.M. visited trenches with Capt. ALABASTER. 2/Lt. ALEXANDER arrived at advanced billets to see front line.	
	5.12		Capt. BENSKIN proceeded on leave. 100. CORNWALLS working parts on S.9.a. drain. No. 4 Section & ½ No. 2 returned from front line at 11 p.m. being relieved by No. 1. Works reorganised. ½ No. 3 Hermanently hutting, remainder of No. 3 divided among Sections 1, 2, & 4, which are divided into 1A. 2/C Cooper, 1B. S/Elton, 2A. 2/C Beasley, 2B. 2/Lt Mowbray, 4A. 2/Lt Alexander, 4B. CSM Lockwood. First three at front to effect reliefs with last three at alternate weeks. Front divided into three sectors	

WAR DIARY
or
INTELLIGENCE SUMMARY.
(Erase heading not required.)

Army Form C. 2

Place	Date	Hour	Summary of Events and Information	Remarks and references to Appendices
	6.12.15.		Relief effected without incident. Orders received from C.R.E. to have all in readiness to hand over to 6th Division. Details of drainage scheme sent to H.Q. 43rd Brigade. Working party of 100 D.C.L.I. opened up new drain in front of B.11. Work continuing normally on drainage and construction. Transport caught by shell fire between BRIELEN and VLAMERTINGHE on its return. Dr Gill wounded severely (several places) Dr Hill and Saper Foster also wounded, and three mules killed and one wounded.	
	7.12.15.		CANAL BANK shelled as usual. Artillery of both sides active. MAJOR HOWARD WEST RIDING R.E. at Canal Bank in afternoon, given copy of report on drainage with plans and a list of work in hand by 89th Coy, with notes as to requirements. Working party of 300 from 14th D.L.I. sent home with consent of B.M. 43rd Brigade owing to very bad weather which would make useful work almost out of the question. R.E. animals malleined. Preliminary instructions for a move too received. Work proceeding normally on construction and drainage. Report sent to C.R.E. 14th D. at H.Q. 43rd Brigade of all work done in WIELTJE sector.	No. 61185. Dr R. Gill at No. 53478 Dr W. Hill died of wounds received on 6.12.15.

1577 Wt. W10791/1773 500,000 1/15 D.D. & L. A.D.S.S./Forms/C. 2118.

WAR DIARY
or
INTELLIGENCE SUMMARY.

Army Form C. 2118

Place	Date	Hour	Summary of Events and Information	Remarks and references to Appendices
	8.12.15.		Nos 1A, 1B & 2A. Parties still in front line with attached Infantry. Three men of 105 D.L.I. attached to 89th Coy. tried by F.G.C.M. for absence, and handed over to 105 D.L.I. for custody. 2/Lt BARLOW and another officer of WEST RIDING R.E. taken round trenches. ST JEAN dump shelled 9 A.M., no harm done. Artillery near CANAL active all day. Work proceeding on trenches, drains and wiring. Report sent to C.R.E. on practical experience with breastworks and also a sketch showing positions of machine guns and occupied trenches. No. 17502. Pte W.WATTS, 6th S.L.I. wounded by shrapnel on CANAL BANK.	
	9.12.15.		Working parties cancelled owing to wet. 89th Coy R.E. and attached Infantry at work as usual.	
	10.12.15.		Lt Col BIGGE C.R.E. & Capt ALABASTER visited ST JEAN and new trenches; caught on return through ST JEAN at 12 noon by shrapnel; sprinkled but unhurt. Coy dugouts on YPERLEE shelled at 1.30 p.m. about 25 rounds 6" H.E. and shrapnel. L/Cpl D D MACDONALD wounded and several had lucky escapes.	89

Army Form C. 2118

WAR DIARY
or
INTELLIGENCE SUMMARY.

(Erase heading not required.)

Place	Date	Hour	Summary of Events and Information	Remarks and references to Appendices
	10.12.15.		Attached infantry sent to baths, not back in time for night's work. C.R.E. calls for names of those who have done consistent good work; number to be limited to 2 or 3; following submitted No. 52852. C.S.M. E. LOCKWOOD, No. 49000 S/t. P. ELTON No. 452181. 2c/pl C. SEARSTON, No. 63219. Lce C/pl J. WILLIAMS. Working party of 250 from 6th K.O.Y.L.I. Coy dug outs shelled at intervals during evening, and all trenches and YPRES - ST JEAN Road shelled heavily at 9 p.m. No. 45822. C/pl C.S. BURNS killed by shrapnel near CRUMP CROSS ROADS. Shelling of rain interfered with progress of work.	
	11.12.15.		Quiet day - fine night. No large working parties owing to infantry reliefs taking place. Warned by B.M. 43rd Brigade to be ready to hand over work on 17.12.15.	
ST JEAN	12.12.15.		Working parties S.O. S.E.I. on breastworks. No 1.A, 1.B, 2.A Sections relieved 12 midnight by 4A, 4B & 2B Sections respectively in front line. Orders received for handing over & return to camp on 15.12.15. ST JEAN & Canal bank shelled with normal ratio.	

WAR DIARY
or
INTELLIGENCE SUMMARY.

(Erase heading not required.)

Army Form C. 2118

Place	Date	Hour	Summary of Events and Information	Remarks and references to Appendices
	13.12.15.		Working party 250 s.a.l. on breastworks, new trenches and SHOREDITCH. Capt. BENSKIN returns off leave 12 noon. Five men of working party wounded.	
	14.12.15.		Working party 250 s.a.l. on breastworks & new trenches. Considerable artillery activity. New drain in front of B11 shelled by enemy. Work at night interfered with by shelling, rifle and machine gun fire.	
	15.12.		Capt. Alabaster & men in front dug out returned by small parties & without further trouble. The time spent on the ST. JEAN front had been very arduous, a very considerable strain, on the Coy. Dug outs were shelled every day and all work had been under fire of sort, which at times was very heavy. German activity in artillery has greatly increased on this front.	
	16.12.		Cleaning up camp. 50% of men given leave for the afternoon.	
	17.		Cleaning up camp. Return of surplus stores to AOD. Parking. 50% of men given leave for the afternoon.	

Army Form C. 2118

WAR DIARY
INTELLIGENCE SUMMARY.
(Erase heading not required.)

Place	Date	Hour	Summary of Events and Information	Remarks and references to Appendices
VLAMERTINGHE Sheet 28. H.7.B.3.3	18		Coy. employed at mobility at re-equipment. Surplus equipment returned to A.O.D. Camp cleared up and old dug-outs filled in. Xmas present given to men in the afternoon.	
	19		LT. MOWBRAY proceeded on leave. German gun attack at 5.40 am. V. heavy bombardment. Shells in huts field close to camp. 3 aeroplane bombs on camp. (1 dud) no casualties. Coy ordered to stand to. All wagons packed. 1 Section employed in aft. at making wire trestles.	
	20		2 N.C.O's & 6 Spr. went to report to O.1/c. Papering he for work at hutting C.T. Lorenca to VII Corps park 1/c stores. Coy employed in making trestles for wire. Col. CROSE arrived on C.M2.	
	21		LT. Mowfley & his 3 Section proceeded to O1/c. H. (LT. LONGSTAFF) for work at hutting in rest area.	
	22		Making trench boards. Wire trestles. Sending materials to Divl. Park.	
	23.		Employed as on 22nd. 2nd Lt TILLOTSON presented with card for gallant conduct.	

WAR DIARY of 89. Field Coy.

Army Form C. 2118

INTELLIGENCE SUMMARY.
(Erase heading not required.)

Place	Date	Hour	Summary of Events and Information	Remarks and references to Appendices
Vlamertinghe	24		Men bathed in the morning. Camp improvements & roads improved.	
	25		Xmas Day. Deana inspected 9 a.m. Check Parade 9 a.m. Driver & Section each row their own Xmas Dinner. Bad Turn out.	
	26		Nos 1, 2, & 4 Sections employed on more camp & trench boards. Drivers & horses out for exercise under Lt Alexander. Animals paraded again at 9 a.m. for inspection. Section v. good. Order for move cancelled. Great disappointment to all ranks. Lt Beazley returned to camp with his unit.	
	27		Visited camp of 2nd Fine War Riding Fd. Coy. & then round new front. The worst situation we have had to face. Camp & Adv. Dugouts both very poor — the latter being badly sited & constructed. Lt Beazley & ½ Section again sent off to build huts. Capt. Alabaster accompanied me round new front. V. badly shelled.	
	28		Lt. Cooper & Alexander went round keg in evening. Section employed on trench stores & camp improvements. Visited Sgt & 3 Sgt Byles in evening, with reference to new front & work.	
	29		Heavy shelling all day. 2nd Lt. Mowbray returned from leave.	

WAR DIARY of 89th Field Coy.
INTELLIGENCE SUMMARY.

Army Form C. 2118

Place	Date	Hour	Summary of Events and Information	Remarks and references to Appendices
VLAMERTINGHE.	29.	con-	43rd Inf. Bgde went into trenches. Lt. Cooper & 4 men went at 4 p.m. to take over dugouts, waders etc from Wool Ridge Field Coy. 16 men under Sgt. Elton went up at 9 p.m. Arranged for Lt. Alexander to commence work on a new trolley line from Bridge 7 to AGADIR Farm.	
	30		Men employed in moving on trench stores. Went out with Lt. Alexander at 4 a.m. to shew new trolley line — also to arrange with Maj. as to erection of French Dug outs along Ypres. Work commenced on new Bgde. Dump. New trolley line that night. Lines east of canal repaired & Coy. Dug outs improved. 20 D.L.I. arrived to erect French Dug outs in the night.	
	31		Capt. Alabaster & Lt. Mowbray inspected C Line Breastworks at dawn. 5 men sent to 2d. & 1st Wool Ridge Fld. Coy. billets to take over & to improve the accommodation. Visited them in the afr. & arranged for 2 huts — road material & trench boards to use in camp. No. 1. Section at Ypres bank worked on C. line with Inf. working party, also repaired trolley line E stand and supervised Inf at making French Dug outs. No. 2 Section on road loop Brass Brigade Dump.	

Denakin
O.C. 89. Fd. Coy. Coys R.E.

Sg 74 FORE.
fol: 5

14

Army Form C. 2118.

WAR DIARY

INTELLIGENCE SUMMARY.
(Erase heading not required.)

Instructions regarding War Diaries and Intelligence Summaries are contained in F. S. Regs., Part II. and the Staff Manual respectively. Title pages will be prepared in manuscript.

88 (FIELD) COMPANY
2 FEB. 1916
ROYAL ENGINEERS

Place	Date 1916	Hour	Summary of Events and Information	Remarks and references to Appendices
VLAMERTINGHE	1st Jan		Nos. 1 & 2 Sections continued as before. Lt. Cooper failed to cut down 1/2 a tree near the canal bank, which was (& he afterwards replaced by a steel model of the stump (as an R.A. observation post). Nos. 3 & 4 Section contd. on trench stores, & improvements to old & new Hqr. Camp. Went up & round in the morning.	
	2nd		Lt. Beasley returned from 8% Nutty — leaving him near Tree. Work on front continued much as before. e.sm. failed to fell the tree. 7 cases of rheny, colds & tumurin on horses legs from mud. Other units worse. Lt. Cooper walked	
	3rd		Lt. Beasley & I went round the Brigade front at early dawn. Lt. Cooper walker muddled about all his work. Proper poor! No 4 Section under Lt. Alexander progress good. Lt. Cooper again failed to fell the tree – hopeless. Condition of animals not really bad.	
	4th		Sent Capt. Alabaster up to go round & see if he could fell the tree. He did it. Took more settled in front. consisted of erection of French dry culv- Vicar's Lane (from progress) improvement of trolley lines & drainage. Improvement of new camp. Hqrs. continued.	
	5th		Relieved No 1 by No. 2. No. 4 by to No. 3 (remain on fail hutting). No transport available for bringing up French dugouts. No night working party.	

Army Form C. 2118.

WAR DIARY
or
INTELLIGENCE SUMMARY.
(Erase heading not required.)

Instructions regarding War Diaries and Intelligence
Summaries are contained in F. S. Regs., Part II.
and the Staff Manual respectively. Title pages
will be prepared in manuscript.

[Stamp: 88 (FIELD) COMPANY * ROYAL ENGINEERS * 2ⁿᵈ FEB. 1916]

Place	Date	Hour	Summary of Events and Information	Remarks and references to Appendices
	6ᵗʰ		Went round trenches as far as possible by day & at night. Found that portion of front which the 4.3.d.l. Bgde will be taking over from the 9.J.L. Murkney in charge of front work. 200 & being part by night. Better progress. French dug out work delayed by lack of materials. Warned C.R.E. that we should need 50 half culls on our front line dug out.	
	7ᵗʰ		Spr. MARLOW wounded & shortly on road at Brielen (?) buying letters from Capt. Alabaster round trenches by night. French Dug out work progressing fairly. Trade full up. French Dug out along Ypres-BOESINGHE railway & right.	
	8		No night working parties. Trolley made 4 trips in night with French Dug outs. Progress in French dug outs good. Released up all correspondence to date. No night working parties. Circulated further note on trench drainage to the Brigade. Raised question of honour for men of the Coy.	
	9		Capt. Alabaster laid up — sore leg. Went round in afft. Walk in front satisfactory. French dug outs coming in satisfactory numbers at last.	
	10.		Went round new portion of front with O.C. & 2ⁿᵈ in command. Section in front made to mix front & dug outs or 1½ hours notice — no accommodation. No Sgt. working party. Work in general satisfactory. New portion of line not too bad & much better than that taken over from 49 — Bgde.	

1577 Wt.W10791/1773 500,000 1/15 D. D. & L. A.D.S.S./Forms/C. 2118.

Army Form C. 2118.

WAR DIARY

of 89th Field Coy

INTELLIGENCE SUMMARY.

(Erase heading not required.)

Place	Date	Hour	Summary of Events and Information	Remarks and references to Appendices
VLAMERTINGHE	11.	10 a.m.	Capt. Alabaster sick in camp. Went round the new trolly line from Bridge 6 to Anstalit farm by m/car. Satisfactory. Lt. Alexander sent to reconnoitre front before relieving Lt. Moseling. Work all round generally satisfactory.	
	12.		Went down the area to be taken over by 43rd Inf. Bgde. transport from the 146th Bgde. (49th Divn). Camping area so individually failed that proceeded that the area be abandoned. No. 4 Section relieved No. 2 at front line work. No. 1 relieved No. 3. Men bathed in the afternoon.	
	13.		No. 3. continued on improving new quarters or new camp. Capt. Alabaster still sick in camp — Bad leg. Remainder as before.	
	14.		To the advanced dugouts to arrange Lt. Alexander's work — which appeared satisfactory. No. 1 Section still working on the trolley line from Bridge 6. Remainder of Coy on camp improvements & huts. D.O. John 1 N.C.O. & 3 men of No. 2 Section sent to Calif. 3. new area to build.	
	15.		2nd Lt. Roseley acted to proceed to England & report to R.S.O. Made extra report on 43 Inf. Bgd. Transport & Quartermaster's lines. 1 N.C.O. & 3 men of No. 3 Section sent to camp 4 new area to build. Capt. Alabaster still light duty. Neuve Yeper Line finished. Nottington 89th Yd etc.	

Army Form C. 2118.

WAR DIARY
of 89th Field Coy R.E.
INTELLIGENCE SUMMARY.

(Erase heading not required.)

Instructions regarding War Diaries and Intelligence Summaries are contained in F. S. Regs., Part II. and the Staff Manual respectively. Title pages will be prepared in manuscript.

Place	Date	Hour	Summary of Events and Information	Remarks and references to Appendices
Same	16		2nd Cpl GRAY (seriously) & Spr McKINLEY wounded by m.g. while making a new track for Infantry behind Willow Walk. Spr PRIOR showed considerable gallantry in attending to them. West round Vicar's Lane & CLIFFORD's Lane with 13.M and Lt Alexander. Work is satisfactory. Enemy machine gun fire far too active. Inf- got their wind up rather at Jr. Wiring of advanced field gun finished. New trolley line between progressing with a permanent roof. P & 8 Liverpool. Coy accommodation improving. No night working parties.	
	17		CSM Lockwood taking over from Lt Kearsley. Capt. Alabaster nearly fit. Trolley line from Bridge 6 to Australia Farm finished. Company becoming seriously depleted of nco.'s who have been scattered in small parties to various Infantry working parties. Estd hutting	
	18		No 1 Section took over hutting & water supply work. Improvement A hut. Water supply at Steenbje & Dragenbote. New camp finished.	
	19		Relieved No. 4 Section by No.s 2 & 3 (2nd Lt Mowbray & CSM) under Capt. Alabaster. Relief satisfactory. Sent up Aster engine for lighting dugouts. Very heavy machine gun fire by night on left half of sector - prohibitive to work. Luckily no working party that night.	

1577 Wt. W10791/1773 500,000 1/15 D. D. & L. A.D.S.S./Forms/C. 2118.

Army Form C. 2118.

WAR DIARY of 89 ... Field Coy R.E.
or
INTELLIGENCE SUMMARY.
(Erase heading not required.)

Place	Date	Hour	Summary of Events and Information	Remarks and references to Appendices
Same	20		No.1 Section on water supply w.of. Poperinghe. No.4 & 1 battled in the afternoon. Work satisfactory in front line. No special remarks.	
	21		Reconnoitred for 2 more Brigade Transport Camps. Vicar's Lane & Clifford's. Big water party. Vicar's Lane & Clifford's taken. is satisfactory. Lt. ALEXANDER went on leave. 10 Inf. from Cy. dugouts joined Coy. Hqs. for a rest from drainage.	
	22		Work of No. Section all very satisfactory. Sent in scheme for 2 Brigade Transport Camps to the next area. Obtained all timber for construction of 11 R.A. huts by bringing them from VII Corps Park in a railway truck - satisfactory.	
	23		Visited advd dugouts in morning. Satisfactory. Arranged to relieve Capt. Alabaster myself. The same night after helping to lay out new trench to connect WILLOW'S walk & GAWTHORPE road, as reconnoitred by Capt. Alabaster it. Infl plans in Cy. dugouts in working order, but unable to do more owing to lack of fittings. New trench laid out 11.30 p.m., Capt. LONG, ComᵈG D Coy 11ᵗʰ KING'S REGT., who will carry out the work, being present.	
	24		C.S.M. LOCKWOOD injured on duty 400 yds East of CANAL BANK at 1.45 a.m. Temp/May 2Lt. V.C.D.BOYD CARPENTER, R.E. reported for duty 7.A.M. Capt. Alabaster returned to camp.	

Army Form C. 2118.

WAR DIARY
of 89th Field
INTELLIGENCE SUMMARY.

(Erase heading not required.)

89 (FIELD) COMPANY
1 2 R FEB 1916
ROYAL ENGINEERS

Instructions regarding War Diaries and Intelligence Summaries are contained in F. S. Regs., Part II. and the Staff Manual respectively. Title pages will be prepared in manuscript.

Place	Date	Hour	Summary of Events and Information	Remarks and references to Appendices
Sand.	24	con.	Working party of 200 Inf. on Clifford's Tower & Vicar's lane. Good work - but parties very late - owing to breakdown of bus. Improved Coy Dugouts & pathway in front of same.	
	25		Continued on French Dugout by day. V. will working the party from D.L.I. as usual. Improved pathway along Canal. Wired hurdles put in by Carpenter, & put up faire steps. Very dark night.	
	26		Continued wiring hurdles & erection of this step of Vicar & Clifford's Tower. Improved Engine house. Most certain the "cheeks" for distruction of Bridges 4 & 4A.	
	27		Working party of 200 Inf. on Clifford's Tower & Vicar's lane. Work poor. Punctual. Relieved Nos. 1, 2 & 3 Sections by Nos. 1 and 4. on the site of work. Relieved the 10 Sup. kitchen.	
	28		No. 2 Section - odd jobs. Water Supply, wire hurdles. No. 3 " " Hutting under Lt. T.T.J. Boyd - Carpenter. Front line work satisfactory.	

WAR DIARY
of 89th U. Field Coy. R.E.

INTELLIGENCE SUMMARY.
(Erase heading not required.)

Army Form C. 2118.

89 (FIELD) COMPANY * ROYAL ENGINEERS * 2 FEB. 1916

Instructions regarding War Diaries and Intelligence Summaries are contained in F. S. Regs., Part II. and the Staff Manual respectively. Title pages will be prepared in manuscript.

Place	Date	Hour	Summary of Events and Information	Remarks and references to Appendices
29.	Same place.		Gas alert. No special remarks. Wake in front end of Coy. Hqrs. proceeding on normal lines.	
30.	Sunday.		Cloudy & windy. Went to see Alabaster at Adv. Bnge-outs. Everything satisfactory. Big working party that night. Good work. 200 Inf. on Vicar's Lane & Clifford's Tower.	
31.			Major Lawrelitte returned from leave. Spr. Prior no. 97515 awarded D.C.M. for gallant behaviour on the night of 16/17th inst. Lt. Alexander returned from leave. Sgt. Elton withdrawn to Coy. Hqrs. from Adv. Bnge Out - to act as A.C.S.M. Brigade police to make good existing works in view of coming wire.	
Same	Feb 1st		2nd Lt. Best of 96th Fd. Coy. no a. given joined the Coy. for 2 days in order to see condition of work in the sector. Took him to Alexander up working party on the Canal Defence - about 200 Inf. Satisfactory. Alabaster requested to be left at Adv. Bnge Cut.	
	2		No special remarks. 4 recruits joined the company. Big working party on improving Vicar's Lane & Clifford's Tower. Working in front of these trenches.	

J. Oakleton
Capt. R.E.
for OC. 89 FF Coy. R.E.

84 a J.C.R.E.
14 d Dw
Vol 6.

Army Form C. 2118.

WAR DIARY
or
INTELLIGENCE SUMMARY.
(Erase heading not required.)

Instructions regarding War Diaries and Intelligence Summaries are contained in F. S. Regs, Part II and the Staff Manual respectively. Title pages will be prepared in manuscript.

89 (FIELD) COMPANY
27 MAR. 1916
ROYAL ENGINEERS

Place	Date	Hour	Summary of Events and Information	Remarks and references to Appendices
	FEB	3rd	Nos 2, and 3. Sections relieved Nos 1 and 4. Sections respectively on CANAL BANK at 11 p.m.	
	Feb	4th	O.C. 89th Coy relieved Capt ALBASTER at the same hour. One shell killed 12 horses at Coy dump and caused some Belgians who were looting. Lt WILLIAMS, 96th Field Coy R.E. reported for instruction at Canal Bank. 2 Lt BEST, 96th Field Coy R.E. returned to this unit after course of instruction.	
	Feb	5th	Veterinary officer inspected all animals, satisfactory. Brig workshops on roadmaking and wiring of VICARS LANE, CLIFFORDS TOWER, POND COTTAGE, CANAL BANK, with good results on night of 5/6.2.16. 2 Cpl WHITE injured on duty on night of 4/5.2.16.	
	Feb	6th	Divisional Meritorious Service Card presented to Sap. PRIOR, D.C.M. No special remarks. A very quiet night.	
		7.	Jth relieved by Capt Alabaster. No special remarks. Work normal. Aeroplanes over camp.	
		8.	Large working party as in the 5th. Good work done.	

1577 Wt. W10791/1773 500,000 1/15 D. D. & L. A.D.S.S./Forms/C. 2118.

WAR DIARY of 89th Field Coy. R.E.
INTELLIGENCE SUMMARY.

Place	Date	Hour	Summary of Events and Information	Remarks and references to Appendices
VLAMERTINGHE	9.		Capt. STOREY of 96th Fd. Coy. visited HQrs. Camp for purpose of taking over front line information. Lt. MOWBRAY and No 2. Section returned to HQrs. the same night without event. Decided to steal 2 Sawyer's Stove & make a Coy. kitchen on a hand cart.	
	10.		Lt. TRAIN of 96 Fd Co arrived to take over unexpected while hut from 89th. collected men scattered on detachments. Sgt rid of Barrel always came.	
	11.		Capt. ALABASTER & Lt. BOYD-CARPENTER returned with No 3. Section Reported evacuation to CRE. Very cold & wet day. Sgt rid of Lt Marston's horse. Travelling kitchen made. Weak order. 10 Jay of road attached for a night. Also, Joy officer	
	12.		German attack on Gd & French front to the nopr. 11/12. Heavy shelling all day. Id Coy. not affected, having just handed over. Result not known. 62 Id Coy & CRE. marched away. Spent the day clearing up & leaving camp & packing. Q. asked me to finish off Sd Camp & Compensation claims.	

Army Form C. 2118.

WAR DIARY
of 89 Field Coy
INTELLIGENCE SUMMARY.
(Erase heading not required.)

Instructions regarding War Diaries and Intelligence Summaries are contained in F. S. Regs., Part II. and the Staff Manual respectively. Title pages will be prepared in manuscript.

Place	Date	Hour	Summary of Events and Information	Remarks and references to Appendices
	13		Company paraded at 9.45 am to leave VLAMERTINGHE (same farm for 6 months), having been shunted to the Prison (turn out) was excellent. Marched to new billets in the rear area about 11 miles. Strong head wind & raining. 3 parties marched about 11 miles. Strong head wind & raining. Packed with troops (20-gr, relieving the 4th). Men's feet very soft; after continued trench work & gun trots. Animals in fair condition. Roads bad. Cafe of small improved kitchen hutches available. Capt Aldriatt stayed behind & got it moved arriving at billets or about 5 pm. Billets at Sheet 27 N.E. K. 9 a. Fine evening. Men shake down well.	
WATOU	14		From LAVALETTE & Lt ALEXANDER investigated compensation claims. Lt MOWBRAY received leave. Men rest for 24 hours. Walk without packs to keep fit. One walk of 2 hours with a picked shovels.	
same	15		Company went for a 3 hour road march in full marching order - without transport. Lt dealt with several claims for damages for Division. Bad weather & wet. Asked to be ready to move billets on the 17th. Horse standings very bad.	
same	16		V. bad weather. Moved horse & mules to standings on a road.	

WAR DIARY of 89. Field Coy R.E.
INTELLIGENCE SUMMARY

Army Form C. 2118.

61.

88 (FIELD) COMPANY 2 MAR. 1916 ROYAL ENGINEERS

Place	Date	Hour	Summary of Events and Information	Remarks and references to Appendices
HERZEELE	17		Had Church the Company to fresh billets 1 mile N.E. of Herzeele. Left watou at 9.45 am. Weather - sent an empty pontoon back to bring these on. No motor lorry available for two billets in 4 farms. Men's standings on a farm road good. Lavalette & Lt. Alexander went in advance billets claim.	
"	18		Heavy rain in morning. Able to do a little squad drill in morning. Lavalette & I went to ESQUELBEC. Sgt. Major about claims.	
"	19		Rain. Squad Drill. Lecture on demolitions. Lt. LLEWELLYN rejoined the Coy. unexpectedly.	
"	20		Major LAVALETTE left the Coy. Squad Drill. Fine day. Rest.	
On the march	21		Lt. COOPER strained his back & was handed over to the Field Ambulance. Left HERZEELE at 2.45 pm & marched to CASSEL for entrainment. Very steep hill at Cassel. Arrived 7.30 - entrained by 10. — left 10.30	

1577 Wt.W10791/1773 500,000 1/15 D.D. & L. A.D.S.S./Forms/C. 2118.

62.

WAR DIARY
of 89th Field Coy RE
INTELLIGENCE SUMMARY.
(Erase heading not required.)

89 (FIELD) COMPANY
2 MAR 1916
ROYAL ENGINEERS

Place	Date	Hour	Summary of Events and Information	Remarks and references to Appendices
near AMIENS.	22	-	Arrived at DOBREAUX (?) at about 8.30 am. Train late 1 hour. Clear of the Station in 1 hour. Marched 15 miles through AMIENS to VIGNACOURT. Snow blizzard very cold. Satisfactory billets.	
VIGNACOURT	23	-	Led to understand that Division would be resting for 3 weeks or so, what Coy would remain in its present billets. C.R.E. visited me in the afternoon. Took over R.E. work from Capt. BRODIE of 221st A.T. Coy R.E. Also took over a small store near the Rly. Stn. of timber & iron. Reconnoitred the possibilities of the village as regards materials & saw mills. Snow & frost.	
FRESCHVILLERS	24	-	Received orders in the middle of the night that the Brigade (a W.) were to move. Coy to march at head of Brigade to FRESCHVILLERS leaving the billets at 9.30 am. Very hard frost in night. Horses endeavoured to get hines roughed in time. Mules were difficult. Unable to move the heavy carts in time. Been arrived at head of Inf. at about 3.30 pm. Cart, which had been continually delayed arrived at 8 pm. Billets in farms. Fair	89

63.

WAR DIARY
of 89th Field Coy, R.E.
INTELLIGENCE SUMMARY.
(Erase heading not required.)

Place	Date	Hour	Summary of Events and Information	Remarks and references to Appendices
On march	25		Ordered to march to HUMBERCOURT & to join in behind the Brigade at DOULLENS. Roads very slippery. Head not followed by snowstorm & frost. Distance to march about 9 miles but the worst in my experience. Roads blocked everywhere. Most of animals were not roughed & were falling down every yard. Brigades mixed up at LUCHEUX. Luckily road fairly flat. The greater portion of Brigade transport was stranded in the snow & on the road all night. 89th did very well. All the Sappers were distributed among carts to help the falling mules & horses. Got the whole Company into billets by about 9 pm except 1 pontoon & supply wagon. So everything in & about 1 am.	
HUMBERCOURT	26		Still freezing. Fine day. Brigade ordered to reassemble & collect its scattered kits. Ambulance carts & animals & roughed the latter again. Spr WILLIAMS broke his leg under a cart on the 25th.	
	27		Brigade still at HUMBERCOURT. Company went for a 10 mile route march. Roughing of animals continued.	

Army Form C. 2118.

64

Instructions regarding War Diaries and Intelligence Summaries are contained in F. S. Regs., Part II. and the Staff Manual respectively. Title pages will be prepared in manuscript.

WAR DIARY
or
INTELLIGENCE SUMMARY.

(Erase heading not required.)

Place	Date	Hour	Summary of Events and Information	Remarks and references to Appendices
HUMBERCOURT	28.		Capt BENSKIN, 2nd Lt. LLEWELLYN and 2 Sappers left at 7a.m. for DAINVILLE to act as advance party and for reconnaissance of front. Remainder of company marched to FOSSEUX at 10 a.m., arriving 1.30 p.m. One mule died of colic on night of 27/28. Roughing of animals resulted in easy march. Thaw.	
FOSSEUX	29.		Orders received at 10.15 p.m. for company to follow 51st Coy at 2.30 p.m. and march to DAINVILLE, taking over billets from 17/1 C.ie du Genie. Capt Benskin & 2. Lt Llewellyn went round night & left sections of French post at AGNY & ACHICOURT respectively. Condition of trenches very good. Thaw.	

29

14

89 Fd Coy R.E.
Vol

Vol 7

:65.

WAR DIARY 60th FIELD Co. R.E.
or
INTELLIGENCE SUMMARY.

(Erase heading not required.)

Instructions regarding War Diaries and Intelligence Summaries are contained in F.S. Regs., Part II and the Staff Manual respectively. Title pages will be prepared in manuscript.

*[Stamp: 68 (FIELD) COMPANY 2118. Army * ROYAL ENGINEERS * 1-APR. 1916]*

Place	Date	Hour	Summary of Events and Information	Remarks and references to Appendices
FOSSEUX	1.3.16		Coy. left FOSSEUX at 2.15 pm & marched to DAINVILLE (west of ARRAS). Road very crowded with troops. Arrived about 7 pm & entered billets without trouble, same having been taken over from French. R.E. Coy at 1/day by o.z. 89. Men. officer's billets & office still occupied by French. O.C. acted as Town Major for one day.	
DAINVILLE	2.3.16		French left by middle. Went round trenches in afternoon with Capt. Alabaster. Lt Llewellyn cleared up 15 Carpenters & Knocking round. Men cleaned up. men in billets. C.R.E. as Town Major.	
"	3.3.16		Spr Bowen given 28 days Field Punishment No 2 by O.C. for Drunk in quarters. (CRE). Here continued to clean up & improve billets. Sent Nos 1 & 3 Sections to Château D'AGNY dugouts by night - took own pack there. Meant to stay overnight	Went round AGNY with Capt A.
"	4.3.16		Went round rifle Range with Capt. Alabaster. Went to Capt. J. Duguid in Château D'AGNY, guaranteed to attend by fourteen wagons. Improved billets at DAINVILLE by day. Etc. continued	Arranged for stores etc.
c	5.3.16		Capt. Alabaster inspected Nos 1 & 3 Section in Adat Dugout. Nos 1 & 3. on improving Château & making near Dugouts. Nos 2 & 4 making Trench stores.	Lt Alexander reconnoitred French. V.G.

1577 Wt.W10791/1773 500,000 1/15 D. D. & L. A.D.S.S./Forms/C. 2118.

WAR DIARY
of 89th Field Coy. R.E.
INTELLIGENCE SUMMARY.
(Erase heading not required.)

Army Form C. 2118.

89 (FIELD) COMPANY
ROYAL ENGINEERS
1 APR. 1916

Place	Date	Hour	Summary of Events and Information	Remarks and references to Appendices
DAINVILLE	6.3		O.C. went round left sector of Brigade with B.M. & Lt. MOWBRAY R.E. Coy ordered to make dugouts in main 2nd line, as required. Work commenced at the Chateau & reconnaissances made in 2nd line. Snow & wet, frost at night.	
	7.3		Lt. ALEXANDER ordered to assist R.A. at construction of 4 Heavy gun Emplacements to be tunnelled into railway cutting - a big job, owing to big angle of fire - 90°. O.C. visited advanced dugouts & materials for the dugouts in front line. Sent up remainder of No.3 section to advanced dugout. First day snow & frost at night. 8 new men arrived as reinforcement.	at Chateau D'AGNY and where required
	8.3		Fine day. O.C. visited advanced dugouts & Battn Hqrs. Ch. D'AGNY Work normal & satisfactory. Dugouts commenced. Strengthened up. O.C. visited R.A. Batteries. Work normal. Coy paid.	
	9.3		O.C. visited Bgde Hqrs. & R.A. Hqrs. 47th Bgde (RFA) as to requirement. Lt. Thurburn sent to assist Capt. ALABASTER 8 subs in front line at making a report for CRE on the whole of the front defences, from all points of view.	
	10.3		Report on above received. (Conference with O.C. Battns held by Gen. at AGNY on all defence works to be carried out, and on various points of discipline.) x Work continued. Relief again for Inf.	

x This was an H.S. W.

Army Form C. 2118.

WAR DIARY of 69th Field Coy. R.E.
INTELLIGENCE SUMMARY.

(Erase heading not required.)

Place	Date	Hour	Summary of Events and Information	Remarks and references to Appendices
DANVILLE	11.3		(See no. 3.15) Work normal.	
	12.3		O.C. went round M.S. Impts. of G.B. line with Capt. DE HOUGHTON Bgde. M.G.O. & LT HAYES S.L.I. On return visited the haritzer Gun Emp'g in the Railway Cutting. O.C. was just expressing doubt as to strength of structure to Lt. Alexander, when the entire structure collapsed. Very serious accident. Sgt. LONG, Spr. DUNN and 1 Gunner killed. LT. HAYES, Capt. FABER & LT. ALEXANDER just escaped. Capt. BENSKIN buried, & had wonderful escape - not really hurt - only bruised, & was extricated in 2 hours. Men killed must have died nearly instantaneously & nothing could be done. Accident due to the whole side of the trench breaking down & carrying away the girders which had been put up. Work as usual. Fine day. AGNY shelled with shrapnel – (1 L.Cpl. & 2 Spr.) arrived 3 reinforcements – about 8 casualties – not R.E. Sgt. Long & Spr. Dunn buried at Dainville cemetery. Also Lt. Hayes & the Gunner. Work as usual. Certain amount of shelling near Adv'd Dug out. No casualties. Aeroplane activity.	
	13.3.			
	14.3		O.C. at duty. Fine day. Lt. Alexander to WARLUS to arrange for improvements to R.A. Mgn. Lt. Mowbray making a covered trench nr[?] of Bgde. Hq. Nos. 1 & 3 continued at Ch. D'AGNY, their work being 2-line mined dugouts, and several mine front line jobs. Nos. 2 & 4 at Dainville employed at improving the dams in the village, preparing materials for 1 & 3, signboards & various minor jobs. 6 reinforcements arrived.	

68.

WAR DIARY of 89th Field Co. R.E.
INTELLIGENCE SUMMARY.

Army Form C. 2118.

(Erase heading not required.)

89 (FIELD) COMPANY
1 APR. 1915
ROYAL ENGINEERS

Place	Date	Hour	Summary of Events and Information	Remarks and references to Appendices
DAINVILLE	15th	3.16	Lt. Mowbray cont.d to make his map of trenches. Lt. them employed as on 14th.	
	16th		O.C. wired that he would be relieved. Found shortage of timber. Saw Mill (water power) fixed up near Plateau at Agny Girls' School, as M.Z. Instructor. As before. O.C. to ARRAS to find siding for moving emplacement, now decided to be at AGNY in Chalk Pit shelling near the Advanced Dep Cuts in the Caves of the Chateau	
	17th		O.C. on reconnaissance in morning. Reports prepared by Officers for handing over. No 1 & 3 sections returned to Headquarters at Dainville, and No 2 & 4 took over — No 4 from No 1 & No 2 from No 3. Lts. Alexander + Mowbray went up in afternoon to take over & then sections followed on after dusk. O.C. to quite fit again Capt. Alabaster stayed on.	
	18th		O.C. handed over to Capt. Alabaster before proceeding to Hauteville, to duty with Div.l School. No 1 + 3 spent day in settling down, having baths, getting paid, etc. Capt. Alabaster returned from line about 1 p.m. No 2 + 4 sections spent day in settling down, taking over R.E. Park at Chateau Agny, etc. Ap.d 3 See proceed.	
	19th		No 3 Sec.t proceeded to Hauteville before dawn for construction of accommodation for Officers + men at 14th Div.l School. O.C. followed on about 11 p.m. Work normal — One emplacement B/49 + 2 M.G. Emplacements taken in hand. Parting notice (No 1) of leading, construction of cellar work, etc. Capt. Kr. Renwick R. Engine A.D.B & A form. S. 1.13.N E. a.a.B.S.A form... Lieut. W. Renwick, left as acting O.C.	422

G57 Hr W 10996/B574 500000 1/15 P.I.D & E.C C.a.a.B.S.S. Forms/C. 2118. N E.

WAR DIARY

89th (Field) Coy, R.E.

INTELLIGENCE SUMMARY.

(Erase heading not required.)

Place	Date	Hour	Summary of Events and Information	Remarks and references to Appendices
DAINVILLE	20th 3-16		Weather fairly fine. Work normal. Both front line & Div.l School at Hauteville supplied with timber. Shortage of square timber in particular. Adj.rs Dainville arrange for transport of timber – heavy work for transport. Girders purchased from Arras. Work satisfactory.	
	21st		Several orders for notice boards have come in, notably from A.P.M. Party from No. 1 Sec.d sent into Arras to cut girders. Pontoon waggon sent in for then removal to Chateau etc. try for front line work. Cpl Williams taken off in ambulance, later evacuated from Div.l area with suspected Spotted Fever.	
	22nd		Work normal. Large quantity of timber in demand. Sergt. Matthews sent into Arras to purchase to-ll-ld. Lt. Waters R.E. reported for duty to be attached to us for instruction. Construction of gas proof curtain frames in hand by No. 1 Sec.d at Headquarters. Work at Hauteville by No. 3 Section very satisfactory. Nothing further received about Lt. Williams. Work as usual. 2 reinforcements arrived (on special authority). ☒ Report of work done by the Company from arrival in this area up to 22nd forwarded to C.R.E.	
	23rd		Lt. Rawlings made to Hauteville to inspect improvements to R.A. Hodge.— party working on this sent back to Camp – and to draw cash from field Cashier. Lt. Waters R.E. who reported yesterday, transferred by C.R.E. for duty with 1st Div.l Signal Coy.	

WAR DIARY of 89th (Field) Coy. R.E.

(Erase heading not required.)

(FIELD) COMPANY
68 ROYAL ENGINEERS
1st APR. 1916

Place	Date	Hour	Summary of Events and Information	Remarks and references to Appendices
DAINVILLE	24th	3-16	Work normal. More girders were transported from Arras to Château Agny. Horse died of Internal haemorrhage at 5a.m. and was buried. Tracing of maps of Agny are in progress by draughtsman of No 1 Section. Printed fames are being made to take blue-paper prints, tracing from aeroplane photos commenced. Signal dug-out in 2nd line practically finished. Nos 2 & 4 Sections employed on construction of one new dug-out in B (2nd) line, & improvement of others, strengthening M.G. Emplacements, fixing gas-proof curtain frames to dug-outs & fixing up bunks in some crowded infantry dug-outs behind front line. Lt Kenelly went out on reconnaissance for materials for front line. Road-finger posts (13) sent to A.P.M. at Warlus.	
	26th		Work in line normal. 1 N.C.O. + 4 men sent to Toreux to construct an incinerator for 25th Sanitary Section, 4 men sent to Warlus to erect 2 Armstrong Huts for R.A. Coy. Hqrs. 1 N.C.O. + 8 men are sent up to Château Agny every night to work on improvement of accom of Coy's advanced billets.	
	27th		Work normal. Sergt Matthews sent into Arras to pay for girders used by Nº 4 Sect. in construction of Gun Emplacement B/Ag. Dr Taylor tried 5 days' pay for insolence to a N.C.O. Nº 1 Sect is kept fairly busy, as they have to provide loading parties for timber sent to front line + Hillerville, in addition to other work, which is very satisfactory, fine but cloudy day.	4/3?

1577 Wt. W10791/1773 500,000 1/15 D.D. & L. A.D.S.S./Forms/C. 2118.

WAR DIARY
of 89th (Field) Coy. R.E.
INTELLIGENCE SUMMARY

Place	Date	Hour	Summary of Events and Information	Remarks and references to Appendices
DAINVILLE	28 3-16		Work normal. Some shelling near Dainville station. Dump about 10.30 a.m. Spr. No 41273, D/fr Patterson awarded 28 days' F.P. No 1 for being Drunk on Duty. One of our horses had a serious accident that night + had to be shot — about 12.15 p.m. — after Vet. had seen it. Buried later. It was very difficult to tell if the animal had been hit by a shell, or had run into something, as the driver was thrown + stunned after hearing an explosion (one of our own guns) + the horse bolted. Lt. Llewellyn rode over to Warlus to inspect smashing Huts erected for R.A., + then to annexe to inspect incinerator. Very bad weather. 6 men employed on firing sign-posts for A.P.M.	
	29th		Work normal — same as before, on dug-outs, M.G. Emplacements, etc. Serious shortage of running dressing for mined dug-outs which rather holds up the work. Trg uns Blackening up. Several more moving up.	
	30th		Work normal. Fine day. Lt. Llewellyn went out in morning to correct a portion of the map. Alsu trying to get rid of a worthless mule, that has been dumped on us by the 62nd Coy.	
	31st		Work satisfactory. Lt. Llewellyn rode over to Foreseux to inspect work done on incinerator. 2 wire days reqd. to complete this Coy. accounts closed. Some shelling near Station dump — no casualties. Working parties there had to be withdrawn. Capt. Alabaster returned from leave about 6.30 p.m. Lt. Boyd — Carpenter + No 5 Sec. (Class 3 men) returned from Hauteville	V.P.?

1577 Wt. W.10791/1773 500,000 1/15 D.D. & L. A.D.S.S./Form/C.2118.

Army Form C. 2118.

WAR DIARY
or
INTELLIGENCE SUMMARY
(Erase heading not required.)

89 (FIELD) COMPANY
1 MAY 1916
ROYAL ENGINEERS

Place	Date	Hour	Summary of Events and Information	Remarks and references to Appendices
DAINVILLE	1.4.16.		2⁺ LLEWELLYN with N°1 Section and 2⁺ BOYD-CARPENTER with N°4 relieved 2⁺ ALEXANDER with N°4 at 2⁺ MOWBRAY with N°2 on front line work with advanced billets at AGNY CHATEAU at 7.30 p.m. Relief carried out without incident. CAPT ALABASTER inspected jobs.	
	2.4.16		Front line work consisting of M.G. emplacements and dugouts proceeding well. Incinerator at FOSSEUX finished.	
	3.4.16.		Advanced billets and dump treated with 5.9's and strip bombs. Capt ALABASTER inspected all M.G. emplacements with 2⁺ WOODS, 43ʳᵈ Bde M.G. Coy, and prepared table of jobs to be done.	
	4.4.16.		2⁺ BOYD CARPENTER reported on water supply of horse on BOCRUVY ROAD near A3 line) well 80 ft deep, water requires 2 scoops per water cart. Girders purchased in ARRAS and sent to AGNY. Bde Defence scheme received.	
	5.4.16		Work proceeding normally. Enemy machine guns near have their tails down. Capt ALABASTER inspected Left Sect⁰	
	6.4.16.		Work for Ambulance at FOSSEUX started. Advanced billets shelled. 2⁺ BOYD CARPENTER measured flow of R. CRINCHON as 2500 J per minute.	
	7.4.16		Additional dugout accomodation for advanced sections started. New communication trench from DAINVILLE Brickfields to railway taped out.	

73.

Army Form C. 2118.

Instructions regarding War Diaries and Intelligence Summaries are contained in F. S. Regs., Part II. and the Staff Manual respectively. Title Pages will be prepared in manuscript.

WAR DIARY
or
INTELLIGENCE SUMMARY

(Erase heading not required.)

Place	Date	Hour	Summary of Events and Information	Remarks and references to Appendices
DAINVILLE and AGNY.	8.4.16		Work on Brigade front proceeding well. 170 yds of communication trench from BRIQUETTERIE dug.	
	9.4.16		Very quiet day on our front, in spite of "Granny" registering. Positions of machine gun on right of section, and for dugouts in second line on Bryan I and FICHEUX Road reconnoitred.	
	10.4.16		B.G.C. wishes some of the houses in AGNY salient identified. C.R.E. directs reclamation of best wells in AGNY. 1 Section will have to hut hand at HAUTVILLE soon.	
	11.4.16		Work on dug outs and M.G. emplacements proceeding well. Recommendations for Military Medal submitted.	
	12.4.16		C.R.E. visits some of jobs on hand. CHAT MAIGRE staff postponed. Lewis gun emplacements started.	
	13.4.16		Leave suspended. All to report on 18th. Administration Comm at HAUTVILLE will accommodate No 1 Section on 15th. Searchlight section to be sent to base.	

74.

Army Form C. 2118.

WAR DIARY
or
INTELLIGENCE SUMMARY

(Erase heading not required.)

Instructions regarding War Diaries and Intelligence Summaries are contained in F. S. Regs., Part II. and the Staff Manual respectively. Title Pages will be prepared in manuscript.

Place	Date	Hour	Summary of Events and Information	Remarks and references to Appendices
DAINVILLE and AGNY	14.4.16		Relief of Nos 1 & 3 Sections by 4 and 2 carried out without incident. During relief all work suspended except that on Lewis gun battle positions. Men employed on these worked till 3 a.m. in the front line and then returned to DAINVILLE.	
	15.4.16		No.1 Section under Lt LLEWELLYN proceeded to HAUTEVILLE at 7.30 p.m. Captain Alabaster went to Advanced Billets to take Command of No 2. Section pending the return of 2/Lt MOWBRAY from leave. All Lewis gun emplacements in left sector completed.	
	16.4.16		All work as usual in front line. Lewis Gun emplacements in right sector completed. Reclamation of Agny Wells still in progress. Sub-sections being made in the erection of huts at Hautville. Company in Dainville had a half holiday to play football against 61st Field Co R.E. 88 (F) Field Co. lost by 4 goals to nil. Nothing special to record. Work in front line consisting mostly of Reclaiming Wells in Agny and reclaiming various dugouts in the support lines. Sappers returned to Camp (DAINVILLE) preparatory to departing for Base for searchlight work.	
	17.4.16		3 N.C.O.s and 6 Sappers left this morning for the Base for searchlight work.	
	18.4.16			
	19.4.16		2/Lt MOWBRAY returned from leave and took over command of his section. Artillery active at night strafing Boche transport.	
	20.4.16		Boche strafed AGNY about 7.30 p.m. No harm done. New G.S. line laid out from GIRL to GUN STREETS.	

WAR DIARY or INTELLIGENCE SUMMARY

Army Form C. 2118.

Place	Date	Hour	Summary of Events and Information	Remarks and references to Appendices
DAINVILLE and AGNY	21.4.16.		Nothing unusual happened. Capt ALABASTER returned from front line.	
	22.4.16.		Work on LIVERPOOL ST switch postponed owing to wet.	
	23.4.16.		Hollow log periscope for use in cup heads made and approved by B.G.C. 43rd Bde.	
	24.4.16.		Holiday for section in rear. Front line work proceeding normally. O.C. inspected L.G. emplacements with M.G.O.	
	25.4.16.		Rail cutting carried out in ARRAS. Dead mule cast. O.C. visited No 1 sect at HAUTEVILLE. Arrangements for reliefs made. Race course grand stand set on fire by Boche shelling.	
	26.4.16.		Work on front line progressing well. CSM's LOCKWOOD & ELTON inspected gun carts Lt/M.G.C. 14 5/D for suitability and wantonness ground in Ypres Salient from May 15 to Jun 16.	
	27.4.16.		No 3 Section relieved No 2 on front line.	
	28.4.16.		No 2 section relieved No 1 at HAUTEVILLE.	
	29.4.16.		No 1 Sect relieved No 4 in front line. O.C. inspected L.G. emplacements and chose sites for new ones with M.G.O. 175 yds of LIVERPOOL ST SWITCH cut.	
	30.4.16.		Lt ALEXANDER goes on leave.	

J. Vechang
Capt
O.C. 89 F.W.5 R.E.

WAR DIARY or INTELLIGENCE SUMMARY

89th Fld Coy R.E.

Place	Date	Hour	Summary of Events and Information	Remarks and references to Appendices
DAINVILLE and AGNY.	1.5.16		No 1 Section, O.C. 2/Lt B. LLEWELLYN } at CHATEAU D'AGNY for front No 3 Section, O.C. 2/Lt D. BOYD-CARPENTER } line work. Work, strengthening Lewis Gun emplacements, reclaiming dugouts, and reclaiming walls in AGNY. No 2 Section, O.C. 2/Lt M. MOWBRAY at HAUTEVILLE erecting tanks and doing general engineer services. No 4 Section, O.C. Lt E.D. ALEXANDER on leave, at DAINVILLE, erecting tanks and preparing materials for front line. Capt BENSKIN at 14th Divn School. Capt ALABASTER O.C. Coy. 2Lt LLEWELLYN admitted to hospital sick at 8 p.m.	
	2.5.16		O.C. visited front line and arranged for work for ensuing week, also inspected work on Vickers gun emplacements being erected by Capt LAIRD, 2/2 London Fld Coy RE, on R. CRINCHON and advised solution of difficulties. C.S.M. ELTON assumes temporary command of No 1 Section. 2/Lt LLEWELLYN to 44th Fld Amb: 2/Lt ALEXANDER from FOSSEUX Open Ground, a fortnight. 10 mn No 4 Section attached to 61st Fld Coy at WANQUETIN.	

Army Form C. 2118.

WAR DIARY
or
INTELLIGENCE SUMMARY

(Erase heading not required.)

[Stamp: 88 (FIELD) COMPANY ROYAL ENGINEERS 1 JUN. 1916]

Instructions regarding War Diaries and Intelligence Summaries are contained in F. S. Regs., Part II. and the Staff Manual respectively. Title Pages will be prepared in manuscript.

Place	Date	Hour	Summary of Events and Information	Remarks and references to Appendices
DAINVILLE and AGNY	3.5.16 &		Work on M.G. Emplacements on R. CRINCHON taken over from 2/2 LONDON Fld Coy R.E. Other work on front line altered accordingly.	
	4.5.16.		Bde notify that they will give us our own time to do L.G. Emp, so that alterations found necessary may be done thoroughly. Trench mortars distinctly unpopular, blowing up Boche and delaying work	
	5.5.16.		House in AGNY salient prepared for demolition	
	6.5.16.		Bde will issue orders protesting during coming week for setting off the charge in the house above mentioned. One recruit developed any worm. Isolated and treated alone.	
	7.5.16.		C.R.E. arranges for 43rd Bde to supply parties for CRINCHON machine guns, and extra details of reqirements. Lewis gunners continue their roughness in leaving loopholes open; new N° 11 on the BOCQUOY Road now necessary	
	8.5.16		Lt BOYD-CARPENTER came to DAINVILLE to talk over details of work.	
	9.5.16.		Work proceeding normally in front line.	

WAR DIARY
or
INTELLIGENCE SUMMARY

(Erase heading not required.)

Army Form C. 2118.

78.

89 (FIELD) COMPANY
1 JUN 1916
ROYAL ENGINEERS

Place	Date	Hour	Summary of Events and Information	Remarks and references to Appendices
DAINVILLE HAUTEVILLE and AGNY	10.5.16		No. 57367 S/Sgt T. WHEELER detailed for collection of stores in event of a move. Work on brigade recreation room started. Lt ALEXANDER returned from leave at midnight	
	11.5.16		No. 4 Sect relieved No. 3 in front line.	
	12.5.16		No. 3 Sect relieved No. 2 at HAUTEVILLE. Lt ALEXANDER relieved Lt BOYD CARPENTER in front line.	
	13.5.16		No. 2 Sect relieved No. 1 in front line. Lt MOWBRAY returned to DAINVILLE, Lt BOYD CARPENTER went to HAUTEVILLE. Lce C/pl HOPE wounded in AGNY by a bullet in the column.	
	14.5.16		Second blanket withdrawn.	
	15.5.16		C.R.E. directs cessation of work on rear villages as soon as material on hand is used up. X=D.L.I. finished cut of new communication trench from Brickfields G.R.S.	I.O.P.

Army Form C. 2118.

WAR DIARY
or
INTELLIGENCE SUMMARY

(Erase heading not required.)

Instructions regarding War Diaries and Intelligence Summaries are contained in F. S. Regs., Part II. and the Staff Manual respectively. Title Pages will be prepared in manuscript.

68 (FIELD) COMPANY ROYAL ENGINEERS — 1 JUN. 1916

Place	Date	Hour	Summary of Events and Information	Remarks and references to Appendices
Hambrith	16.5.16		V9. emplacement shelled. Six hits by whizz bangs. Damage nil. This is our weakest emplacement.	
	17.5.16		M.G.O. 43rd Bde and Capt ALABASTER selected sites for new V9. and V15. O.C. also inspected R.G.N.Y. dressing stations and CRINCHON strongpoint. Work proceeding well in front line and DAINVILLE. Boche retaliated with 68 - 5.9" on Stokes gun near G21. One fell right into half built new emplacement for L.G.11. Result no emplacement.	
	18.5.16		New L.G.11. sited; arrangements made for acting sentry station in G.B. line. O.C. visited HAUTEVILLE. Sapr McMILLAN wounded by stray bullet on CRINCHON.	
	19.5.16		2/L LLEWELLYN returned from hospital.	
	20.5.16		Quiet day. Work proceeding normally. Bullet which went through L/Cpl HOPE's arm extracted from BESSIE's croft.	
	21.5.16		2/L BOYD CARPENTER relieved by 2/L LLEWELLYN at HAUTEVILLE.	
	22.5.16		2/L B.C. on leave; No. 3 returned from HAUTEVILLE to DAINVILLE.	1/79

Army Form C. 2118.

WAR DIARY
or
INTELLIGENCE SUMMARY

(Erase heading not required.)

Instructions regarding War Diaries and Intelligence Summaries are contained in F.S. Regs., Part II. and the Staff Manual respectively. Title Pages will be prepared in manuscript.

Stamp: 68 (FIELD COMPANY) ROYAL ENGINEERS 1 JUN 1916

Place	Date	Hour	Summary of Events and Information	Remarks and references to Appendices
DAINVILLE, AGNY, ARRAS	23.5.16		N°1 Section goes to ARRAS to help 11th LIVERPOOLS on ARRAS defences.	
			N° 2 at AGNY.	
			N° 3 in DAINVILLE	
	24.5.16		O.C. Coy went round ARRAS defences with C.E. and G.S.O. VIth Corps and O.C. 11th LIVERPOOLS. O.C. Coy also visited 2/611 and V9 with M.G.O., very good work. 43rd & 63rd decide not to change up dug outs in G.1.6 but other overhead wire blocking track with praying below.	
			2/Lt G. R. M. MILLEN reports for duty.	
	25.5.16		Demonstration of trench block by C.S.M. ELTON meets with approval of Mr 43rd Bde. 2/Lt MOWBRAY, Spr DUNN, Spr WHITAKER volunteer for raid.	
	26.5.16		O.C. and 2/Lt MILLEN visit front line work and L/S ALEXANDER. Preliminary arrangements for raid discussed 8.30 p.m.	
	27.5.16		N° 3 relieves N° 2 in AGNY. 2/Lt MILLEN ordered to join 62nd at Sten ordered to remain temporarily with 89th. Lt. and 2/Lt MILLEN inspect ARRAS with 2/Lt LLEWELLYN. 2/Lt MOWBRAY with S.L.I. accommodation site of raid.	

Army Form C. 2118.

WAR DIARY
or
INTELLIGENCE SUMMARY

(Erase heading not required.)

Instructions regarding War Diaries and Intelligence Summaries are contained in F. S. Regs., Part II. and the Staff Manual respectively. Title Pages will be prepared in manuscript.

Place	Date	Hour	Summary of Events and Information	Remarks and references to Appendices
DAINVILLE AGNY ARRAS	28.5.16		O.C. and 2Lt MILLEN relieve Lt ALEXANDER at AGNY. 2Lt MILLEN ordered to join 62nd Field Coy & return to DAINVILLE. Lt ALEXANDER returns to DAINVILLE. Preliminary preparations for raid. Orders for action in event of mine exploded.	
	29.5.16		2nd Lt MILLEN reports to 62nd Field Coy for duty. No 2 section under temporary command of Lt ALEXANDER, Relieves No 1 in ARRAS. No 1 section relieves No 4 at AGNY. No 4 section returns to DAINVILLE. 2 Lt MOWBRAY left in charge at DAINVILLE. Cpl SEARSON volunteers for raid. Preliminary training for raid carried on. O.C. returns to camp.	
	30.5.16		O.C. goes to Third Army School demonstration. DAINVILLE shelled at night.	
	31.5.16		Work continuing well in AGNY, ARRAS and DAINVILLE.	

J Ouhlnets
Captain E
OC 89th Field Coy R.E.

2449 Wt. W14957/M90 750,000 1/16 J.B.C. & A. Forms/C.2118/12.

WAR DIARY
or
INTELLIGENCE SUMMARY
(Erase heading not required.)

Army Corps 89ᵗʰ Fᵈ Cᵒʸ R.E.

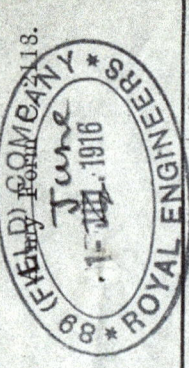

Vol 10

Place	Date	Hour	Summary of Events and Information	Remarks and references to Appendices
H.Q. DAINVILLE AGNY & ARRAS.	1.6.16.		2/Lt BOYD-CARPENTER returns from leave. No 1 & No 3 under 2/Lt LLEWELLYN in AGNY, 43ʳᵈ Bde front. No 2 under Lt ALEXANDER in ARRAS, Boulevard defences. No 4 in DAINVILLE resting and doing odd jobs.	
	2.6.16.		2/Lt MOWBRAY, Cpl SEARSTON, Spr DUNN, Spr WHITTAKER spent day Capt BENSKIN at 14ᵗʰ Divn School. Protected look-outs in G.S. line started.	
	3.6.16.		Raid abandoned owing to secrecy not being observed. Capt BENSKIN awarded D.S.O., 2/Lt LLEWELLYN Mil. Cross, 2/Lt (late CSM) LOCKWOOD D.C.M. 2/CSM EATON Mil: Medal. G.O.C. VIᵗʰ Corps inspected animals and expressed satisfaction.	
	4.6.16.		Rearrangement made for relief of 89ᵗʰ Fᵈ Cᵒʸ by 61ˢᵗ on 7.6.16.	
	5.6.16.		O.C. visits WANQUETIN & ARRAS. DAINVILLE shelled in morning and at night.	
	6.6.16.		O.C. with O.C. 61ˢᵗ visit works in progress on front line. Three sections of 61ˢᵗ Cᵒʸ arrive in DAINVILLE.	

WAR DIARY or INTELLIGENCE SUMMARY

Army Form C. 2118

Instructions regarding War Diaries and Intelligence Summaries are contained in F. S. Regs., Part II. and the Staff Manual respectively. Title Pages will be prepared in manuscript.

Place	Date	Hour	Summary of Events and Information	Remarks and references to Appendices
DAINVILLE	7.6.16.		Relief of section in PGNY of ARRAS by 615 Coy carried out by daylight. Sec moving off in pairs.	
			2/Lt MOWBRAY & advance party proceed to WANQUETIN by daylight. 89th Coy march out of DAINVILLE at 8.30 p.m. and arrive Coy H.Q. at WANQUETIN.	
WANQUETIN	8.6.16		Rest day for all ranks.	
	9.6.16		No 4 Section employed on sinking shaft on Terrain Militaire and on en bloc service in WANQUETIN. Remainder employed on training, drill and sports.	
	10.6.16.		Work of previous day continued.	
	11.6.16.		Rest day.	
	12.6.16.		No 3 Section T.A.B. inoculation. No 4 " on works. 1&2 " training. 2 Names submitted for Military Medal for good work.	

WAR DIARY or INTELLIGENCE SUMMARY

(Erase heading not required.)

Instructions regarding War Diaries and Intelligence Summaries are contained in F.S. Regs., Part II. and the Staff Manual respectively. Title Pages will be prepared in manuscript.

Place	Date	Hour	Summary of Events and Information	Remarks and references to Appendices
WANQUETIN	13.6.16		Nos 1 and 2 Sections Training	
			No 4 " On works	
			No 3 " Light duties after inoculation	
	14.6.16		Nos 1 and 2 " Rifle Range	
			3 " Training and in afternoon proceeded to DAINVILLE on special work for CRE.	
			4 " works	
	15.6.16		Capt ALABASTER proceeded to ENGLAND on leave	
			Nos 1 and 4 Sections TAB inoculation	
			No 2 " works	
	16.6.16		Nos 1 " 4 " Light duties after inoculation	
			No 2 " Works	
	17.6.16		as for 16.6.16	
			No 3 Section returned from DAINVILLE in afternoon	
	18.6.16		Rest day.	
	19.6.16		LT. ALEXANDER and 2LT BOYD-CARPENTER proceeded to ARRAS to reconnoitre K section prior to relief of 1/2 DURHAM FIELD COY R.E (T.F.)	
			Coy instructed in new method of carrying Sho tubes in GAS ALERT periods.	
	20.6.16		Coy gas helmet drill, company drill in morning.	
			2LT. MOWBRAY and 16 O.R. proceeded to ARRAS in advance party & to reconnoitre K. Section.	
			LT ALEXANDER arranged billets & horse lines for Coy transport in WARLUS and visited C.R.E.	
ARRAS		9 pm 1 marched to ARRAS and while Coy transport left WANQUETIN at 9 pm 1 marched to ARRAS arriving at midnight & billeted in BARRACKS, BOULEVARD CARNOT		£729
	21.6.16		all officers + NCOs made reconnaissance of trenches in K. section. Work on Mine craters taken over 12 midnight. Sgt Palus left WANQUETIN at 9 pm & marched to WARLUS
WARLUS			Coy Transport under Sgt Palus left WANQUETIN at 9 pm & marched to WARLUS	

WAR DIARY
or
INTELLIGENCE SUMMARY
(Erase heading not required.)

68 (FIELD) COMPANY
Army Form C.
1- JUL. 1916
ROYAL ENGINEERS

Instructions regarding War Diaries and Intelligence Summaries are contained in F. S. Regs., Part II. and the Staff Manual respectively. Title Pages will be prepared in manuscript.

Place	Date	Hour	Summary of Events and Information	Remarks and references to Appendices
ARRAS	22.6.16		Work continued on various works in K.Sec.N. C.R.E. & Lt. ALEXANDER visited 412 Bde Hqrs & arranged programme of work. 1/2 DURHAM FIELD COY. R.E.(T.F.) vacated billets vacated bed at 10 p.m. 2/Lt. LLEWELLYN reported for duty.	
	23.6.16			
	24.6.16		CAPT ALABASTER reported for duty 12.30 a.m. on return from leave. Trench 105 destroyed. Work on craters impossible, but no casualties thanks to steel helmets.	
	25.6.16		Work carried out by day in craters. Work at night interrupted by enemy to stop on 41st-63rd front.	
	26.6.16		C.R.E. and O.C. Coy visited craters. Field shelling of ARRAS in afternoon.	
	27.6.16		B.G.C. 41st Inf Bde and O.C. Coy visited craters and settled on details of work. Gas alert from 2.30 p.m. till 5.00 p.m.; gas discharged 3000 yds by ARRAS on narrow front against wind, the retaliation on ARRAS. 2/Lt. MOWBRAY located hostile machine gun 11.30 p.m.	
	28.6.16		Work proceeding normally. Our artillery active in afternoon, observing retaliation by our front. ARRAS shelled twice during the p.m.	

86.

WAR DIARY
or
INTELLIGENCE SUMMARY

Place	Date	Hour	Summary of Events and Information	Remarks and references to Appendices
ARRAS	29.6.16		Three reinforcements received from base. Work proceeding normally.	
	30.6.16		O.C. visited K1 sector with Bde M.G. Officer at selected site; decided not to erect of B.G.C., on open emplacements with dugouts for team. ARRAS shelled lightly at intervals throughout the night.	

J. Oakeladen
Captain.
O.C. 89th Fd. Cy. R.E.
1.7.16

WAR DIARY
or
INTELLIGENCE SUMMARY

Army Form C. 2118.

14 July
Vol II
89 — Field Company
87

Place	Date	Hour	Summary of Events and Information	Remarks and references to Appendices
ARRAS	1.7.16.		Company engaged on following work in K sector:— Consolidation of craters, T.M. Emplacements, M.G. Emplacements dugouts, Water supply in ROCLINCOURT and Redoubt line. Whole company in the line. Transport at WARLUS	
	2.7.16.		Big mine blown at about 2 a.m. at K.113. 2/Lt MOWBRAY helped repel enemy offensive in consolidation; Sapr SORNES & DICK did well. O.C. Coy visited site during morning, reported to C.R.E.	
	3.7.16.		C.R.E. visited 113 crater; O.C. inspected 110, 107, 105.	
	4.7.16.		O.C. Coy visited 113 with B.G.C. 41st Bde. Scheme settled on. 2/Lt MOWBRAY at 18 O.R. R.E. started consolidation in rear of it.	
	5.7.16.		Enemy very troublesome; trench mortared before-of 110; blew away log-top of 107 & shelled rear of 113 during wire. In spite of being twice cut & work being knocked in four times, 2/Lt MOWBRAY and his party showed great gallantry & worked till daylight, for men never got much thank.	Coy

Army Form C. 2118.

WAR DIARY
or
INTELLIGENCE SUMMARY

(Erase heading not required.)

Place	Date	Hour	Summary of Events and Information	Remarks and references to Appendices
PARAS	6.7.16		M.G.C. 14th Divn, B.G.C. 41st Bde, various staff officers & O.C. Coy visited craters.	
			Report on state of consolidation sent to C.R.E.	
			Application made for authority to get reinforcements to replace 21 men effective.	
	7.7.16		Sapper KANE recommended for an immediate award for gallantry.	
			2Lt MOORE at one section 612th by R.E. relieved for duty on consolidation of 113 crater.	
			2Lt WHEELER " " " " " " 106 & 111 craters	
			62nd Coy R.E.	
			2Lt MOWBRAY recommended for an immediate award for gallantry.	
	8.7.16		Work proceeding normally in K. Sector.	
	9.7.16		General scheme prepared for employed of large working parties of other division in K. Sector. Estimated that 440 will be needed in addition to the Cyclists and Battn in Bde Reserve.	
	10.7.16		C.R.E. visited QUATRE VENTS, site for Bde battle H.Q.	
	11.7.16		C.E. VIIth Corps and C.R.E. 14th D. visited craters in K. Sector.	

Army Form C. 2118.

WAR DIARY
or
INTELLIGENCE SUMMARY

(Erase heading not required.)

Place	Date	Hour	Summary of Events and Information	Remarks and references to Appendices
ARRAS	12.7.16		O.C. Coy visited ST VAAST and directed scheme for reclamation of dug out.	
	13.7.16		O.C. 184th Coy discussed situation of K Sector from moving point of view. ARRAS shelled during night.	
	14.7.16		O.C. Coy visited 113 Crater and FISH AVENUE. B.G.C. 41st Bde. considers that Medical authorities in ROCLINCOURT have enough accommodation.	
	15.7.16		O.C. Coy visited Redoubt line & work in progress.	
	16.7.16		O.C. Coy visited works on craters carried out by section 62nd Fd Coy R.E.	
	17.7.16		Sections 61st & 62nd Fd Coy negotiated assets. Permanent working parties arranged. 2nd Monkey reconnoitred OBSERVATORY at THELUS Redoubt.	
	18.7.16		Work at Quatre Vents at ST VAAST progressing well. 2° Boyd Carpenter reconnoitred ROCLINCOURT.	
	19.7.16		O.C. Coy visited all K Craters and prepared scheme for work thereon by garrison.	
	20.7.16		C.R.E. inspected work at QUATRE VENTS.	
	21.7.16		Cy duties withdrawn and working parties reduced. R.E. work suspended from 10 p.m. 21.7.16. till 8 p.m. 22.7.16.	
	22.7.16		O.C. Coy visited mined dugouts in K1. All work in full swing again during evening.	

Army Form C. 2118.

WAR DIARY or INTELLIGENCE SUMMARY

(Erase heading not required.)

Instructions regarding War Diaries and Intelligence Summaries are contained in F. S. Regs., Part II. and the Staff Manual respectively. Title Pages will be prepared in manuscript.

68 (FIELD) COMPANY
31 JUL. 1916
ROYAL ENGINEERS

Place	Date	Hour	Summary of Events and Information	Remarks and references to Appendices
23.7.16. ARRAS	23.7.16		Nothing particular to record, except slow persistent shelling of ARRAS all day and evening.	
	24.7.16		C.R.E. 16th D., C.R.E. at Adj 21st D., & O.C. Coy visited redoubt line. Work going well in R. Sector.	
	25.7.16.		C.R.E. and Adj visited ARRAS and gave warning of probable date of relief.	
	26.7.16.		O.C. 98th Fd Coy R.E. & O.C. Coy visited works in hand in R Sector, it covered 15 miles. 2nd Lieut Boyd Carpenter promoted Lieut.	
	27.7.16.		2nd Lieut M. L. MOWBRAY awarded Military Cross.	
	28.7.16.		Day spent in handing over jobs, work ceased at 12 noon. 98th Fd Coy arrived.	
	29.7.16		Handing over complete by 4 p.m. Coy marched out of ARRAS in half sections from 2 p.m. at 15 minute intervals. Forage carts marched out at 9.30 p.m. Remainder of transport under 2nd Lt LLEWELLYN left WARLUS 7 p.m. Whole company billetted at BRIQUETERIE in WARLUS-WANQUETIN road for night of 29/30.7.16	

C.A. I. BENSKIN, D.S.O. Major, 29th Fd Coy, at BRIQUETERIE

Army Form C. 2118.

WAR DIARY
or
INTELLIGENCE SUMMARY

(Erase heading not required.)

Instructions regarding War Diaries and Intelligence Summaries are contained in F.S. Regs., Part II. and the Staff Manual respectively. Title Pages will be prepared in manuscript.

69 (FIELD) COMPANY
8 -1 JUL 1916
ROYAL ENGINEERS

Place	Date	Hour	Summary of Events and Information	Remarks and references to Appendices
	30.7.16		Coy. paraded at 7.45 am, & was clear of The BRIGUETTERIE by 8 am and marched in ease to SOMBRIN arriving at 10.30 am. Good billets, plenty of room. Hot Roads dear. 2nd THOMAS proved an Interpreter.	
	31.7.16		Left SOMBRIN at 8.15 am. Touring 41st Bgde. Column & arrived at BARLY about 4.30 pm. suffering from want of steel helmets & packs. Excessively hot & trying march. The men fell out, Infantry had been given transport for packs - men falling out all the way. Passed Guards in billets at LE SOUICHE & NEUVILLETTE. Quite a ceremonial march as every horse had an armed guard which prevented arms, causing the men to have to march to attention!	

14th Division.

89th FIELD COMPANY,

ROYAL ENGINEERS.

AUGUST 1916.

Attached: Appendices.

WAR DIARY
or
INTELLIGENCE SUMMARY

Army Form C. 2118.

AUGUST 1916

Place	Date	Hour	Summary of Events and Information	Remarks and references to Appendices
BARLY	1.8.16		Company marched to LE BRETEL, suburb of DOULLENS - arrived about 11 a.m. Good billets, all in one farm. Hot. No men fell out.	
LE BRETEL	2nd		Kit inspection at 9.30 a.m., and cut down loads as far as possible. Farriers cart returned by C.R.E's permission. Rest day for men.	
"	3rd		Physical training 9 a.m. Lectured to Coy on Bayonet fighting. Tested Smoke helmets. Lectured to N.C.O's on map reading. Spr BOYENS accidentally drowned in R. AUTHIE at 7.30 p.m. Whilst bathing with men of A.S.C. & is been attached to No 2 Coy A.S.C of 30t Train. Body could not be found.	
"	4th		Physical training 9 a.m. Sappers housed at marching on to a task, & skirmishing. Lecture to N.C.O's on Tactics. Sports in evening.	
"	5th		Erected & tested lengths of HEM. Trained Coy at rapid wiring - & laying out Supporting post. O.C. attended C.R.E. Conference at 9.15 a.m., & Conference with Sgt 41st Bgde at 5 p.m. with Searched for body again. It could not be found.	
"	6th		All company transport & bicycles & horses marched at 11.30 a.m to 41st Bgde Transport under Capt. Alabaster. Dismounted men continued to train at wiring - field drainage. Left billets for Spr BOYENS with Town Major - DOULLENS.	

WAR DIARY or INTELLIGENCE SUMMARY

Army Form C. 2118.

AUGUST 1916.

Place	Date	Hour	Summary of Events and Information	Remarks and references to Appendices
LE BREYEL	7th		Dismounted men marched at 2.15 pm to CANDAS railway station to entrain with 4'th Inf Byde (actual train). About 5 mile march. Not all very late. Left Candas about 10.30 p.m.; arrived MERICOURT on R. ANCRE at early being met by guides from Mounted Section who had the previous evening (7th) arrived at DERNANCOURT. Men 10 in a carriage.	
DERNANCOURT	8th		Company rested in the morning. Check parade 3.30 p.m. - followed by training for N.C.O's at putting up wire rapidly - without use of French wire.	
"	9th		Returned to AOD several blankets which should have been returned previously. At 8.30 am Coy trained at rapid wiring - without use of French wire. Straightened up strength of Sections & distribution of N.C.O's.	
"	10th		O.C. & Capt. Alabaster went round work done by 78th & 3rd Coy (17th Div.) on the floor between LONGUEVAL and HIGH WOOD. Consisted of a Support line (with Inf. Labour) and Bode traps dugouts. Sappers to live at dugouts between MAMETZ and FRICOURT. Transport close to BECORDEL. Company continued training at rapid wiring.	
"	11th		Capt. Alabaster showed No. 1 & 3 Section officers round trench Gatiespal Line & Section Spt. Points - also advanced dugouts. field dressing, physical training & handling of arms. Sp. Dailey transferred sick. O.C. showed Coy trained at	

WAR DIARY
or
INTELLIGENCE SUMMARY

Army Form C. 2118.

Place	Date	Hour	Summary of Events and Information	Remarks and references to Appendices
DERNANCOURT	12	—	Some Service in morning. Physical training. Coy. moved at 7.30 under Capt Alabaster to advanced dugouts & new horse lines. Lt. Bag. Coopersh went in advance to take over dugouts. Received orders from CRE to continue work done by 78th Fd. Coy. Horse Thomas - found dugouts evacuated sick. Horse lines close to BECORDEL. Coy. advanced billets in old German dugouts (v. good) between FRICOURT & MAMETZ	
FRICOURT	13		Coy. ordered to continue work of 78th Fd Coy. Nos 2 & 3 worked on Brigade H.Qrs in BEETLE alley, between MAMETZ & MONTAUBAN. Nos 1 & 4 wired YORK trench between RE Alley & Y.L. Alley. Satisfactory progress - no casualties about 300 yds. were contributed by CRE to make good CARLTON trench through LONGUEVAL with the assistance of 1 Coy. of 11th Wings (Pioneer batn.) and to continue CRUCIFIX alley towards LONGUEVAL Church, using coal inf. working parties. Both very bad jobs as the whole area in question is one German rubbish & work had been repeated as impossible by 175 Tyd. RE	
	14		OC + Lt. MOWBRAY, Sgt MUIR, with Spr. DUNN & HAINES (carrying) went out at 3 am to lay out CRUCIFIX trench. Laid out 260 yds. through range. Sgt MUIR killed. Arranged for 2 Coys to work at 7.30 & 9.30 pm respectively. Capt. ALABASTER took charge of pioneers (Lt. CRANDALL) & Nos 3 & 4 Sections on CARLTON 3 am. Unipile while in making a way through rumaged in trench. Capt. Alabaster Sgt. WHITE slightly wounded, Spr. SOAMES badly wounded in wrist (shattered) & head dzzyjn.	89

Army Form C. 2118.

WAR DIARY
or
INTELLIGENCE SUMMARY

(Erase heading not required.)

Place	Date	Hour	Summary of Events and Information	Remarks and references to Appendices
FRICOURT MAMETZ	14		During night 14th-15th, Lt. Mowbray & Lt. Llewellyn controlled 300 Inf. & then 2 Section R.E. at digging the french laid out in morning. 3 of "men"'s bodys recovered. O.C. put first 150 Inf. on to their Tasks, then laid out a further 300 yds. trench, upon which the second 150 Inf. worked. Progress very good, & night quiet. Lt. Mowbray continued during the night at-laying out work for next night. 600× dug average 4'.6" by 2'.6" Meanwhile Nos. 3 & 4 Sections & the Coy. 11th Kings worked at occupying of CARLTON trench (old German 2nd Line trench). Useful work done in clearing a way & commencing Firesteps & fire bays. N.S. Emp. was fitted by Lt. Alexander at dawn. Construction of a tarpaulin tank at Snaroy S.21.D satisfactorily finished & provided with taplinth proof roof to hold 1500 gallons.	
"	15		O.C. visited Carlton area in the afternoon. During night 15th-16th Nos. 1 & 2 Sections continued Work on CRUCIFIX alley with 150 Inf. Good progress up to S.17.B.10.2. Average 4' by 2'. Previous night's work improved. Occasional Shelling. Rain. Dark. 4 Inf. wounded. Nos. 3 & 4 Sections with only 2 platoons 11th Kings. continued on Carlton. Reconstructed. 10 Firebays nearly finished.	
"	16th		Nos. 1 & 2 continued CRUCIFIX trench. MONTAUBAN alley was tour-shelled & shrapnelled so commencement of work was delayed by O.C.	

WAR DIARY or INTELLIGENCE SUMMARY

Army Form C. 2118.

Place	Date	Hour	Summary of Events and Information	Remarks and references to Appendices
FRICOURT Dug out	16		making the 250 yds working party (9th R.B.) keeps to the trenches & work will tough had ceased. Work resumed at 12 noon, very satisfactory. French communication area pushed through to LONGUEVAL. French being 5' deep by 3' wide. Side of craterholes were developed. Inspected was an undesirable debris of craterholes & dead. Work was not disturbed. Nos. 3 & 4 Section continued on recovery of CARLTON trench. 2 O.R. Spr. SMITH touched by a piece of shrapnel bang, but proven avoidable - not wounded. 3 men down with high fever.	
	17		In view of enemy events & bombardment as well. Made various notice boards for 61st x 62 - 2d Coy.	
	18		41st & 43rd Inf. Bgde. attacked E & W of DELVILLE WOOD. 2nd 89th 3d Coy. in reserve. 61 & 62 made supporting point. 2-Lt WALKER joined the Coy.	
	19		R.E. resting	

WAR DIARY or INTELLIGENCE SUMMARY

Army Form C. 2118.

Place	Date	Hour	Summary of Events and Information	Remarks and references to Appendices
FRICOURT	20	—	Ordered to put 2 Section at disposal of 42nd Bde. Got verbal Supply Point at junction of HOP & BEER alley in front line. Endeavoured with 3 officers to reconnoitre that night – & to employ 1 Section after 12 p.m. Chaos in trenches by the wood, with swarms of working parties, no guide available on arranging parties. Sent Section back. Lt. B. CARPENTER made all definite plans for work on night of 21st., employing 2 Section on the rear track about 4 p.m.	
"	21	—	Went to 42 Bde Hqrs at noon. Found everything changed & Bde going into left Sector of Divn. (Delville Wood) Whole Coy under 42 Bde. O. Dwelt out alone & reconnoitred 5 days, & submitted programme of work to G.O.C., approved & sent out officers at night to reconnoitre & lay out for work an night of 22nd–. No emplacement for men.	

WAR DIARY or INTELLIGENCE SUMMARY

Army Form C. 2118.

(Erase heading not required.)

88 (FIELD) COMPANY * 8 SEP. 1916 * ROYAL ENGINEERS

Place	Date	Hour	Summary of Events and Information	Remarks and references to Appendices
FRICOURT	22		OC arranged with Byde working parties for Coy. & work for near Brigade reconstruction. See appendix A. Progress made was satisfactory. Spr. CROSS wounded in leg.	
	23		Continuation of programme of work arranged & carried out, employing 300 Inf. dy. S. heavy air raids that on the aft. of 24th, the attack would take place, & that 69th would have 16 candidates & make various supporting points. Went to CRE & Div. obtained 90 men of 43rd Byde to carry up wire to dumps in front line in DELVILLE WOOD. Then to OC. 11 J.C. King's Liverpools & arranged for meeting at 11.50 am on 24th in order to finally allot parties for these points. The digging & carrying parties out partially did their work — had. King's did well that night.	
	24		See appendix attached, giving diary of events. The attack by the 42nd Byde was successful in clearing Delville Wood of Germans. No 2 Section 89- (Lt. Boyd Carpenter) were able to successfully make & consolidate their point. 3 platoons of	[signature]

Army Form C. 2118.

WAR DIARY
or
INTELLIGENCE SUMMARY
(Erase heading not required.)

68 (FIELD COMPANY) ROYAL ENGINEERS
8 SEP 1916

Place	Date	Hour	Summary of Events and Information	Remarks and references to Appendices
Fricourt or Mametz	24 25		King's also did good work in repairing Inner Trench. The remainder of the Coy. were not employed. OC went round at dawn & arranged for work with an night of 25. after finding out that front line day work was not practicable.) 43rd V Bde relieved the 42nd that night & only 2 Section 69th and 2 Coy. 11th King's were available for work – consisting of communication & Reserve (consolidating) The captured German line. No 1 Section did useful work. No 4 Bed – being totally cld. King's did good work. mainly according to the programme.	
"	26		Arranged for 2 platoons of King's to improve trench from Devil's Trench to Inner trench. 1 Coy King's to improve Eucipie Trench. 2 Section 69th. 2 Platoon King's. 100 yds to make a new Trench from S.12.c. central to front line, going NNE.	

WAR DIARY or INTELLIGENCE SUMMARY

Army Form C. 2118.

Place	Date	Hour	Summary of Events and Information	Remarks and references to Appendices
Sheet 62.D. F.4.c.8.4 near MAMETZ	26 cont?		Work done by King's good. Spr. Vanyard. 1½ Section 89. pnt.? Delville Wood continually shelled.	
	27.		Nos 1 & 4 Sections with Lt. Alexander in charge, and 1 Section 61st. helping endeavoured to put up wire in front of "Inner trench." Previous rain congestion of troops & shelling made work impracticable. Only 60 yds done. L/Cpl. DEACON wounded. O.C. rowed of down & satisfied that work could not have been done.	X. There is of course a difficult largely over-looked by afford afterwards placed to wild surprise Delville Wood &c. CME 14 Sept.
	28		No.2 Section were to wire No.3 Section in charge of 100. S.L.I. to collect men were in "Inner trench" for further work. Both Section caught in very heavy shelling in the wood. Casualties Lt. 15 cpl. Carpenter, Dunlop (injured?) L. Cpl. Matthews. Cpl. Adams. 2/Cpl. Bryan. Spr. Bowen. Hackett. Burgoyne. Ellerton. Brooker. Spr. Klingard. V. seriously wounded. killed } wounded } # Apparently 43.- Bryde returned by 42. 1 no intimation being given to 89th. S.L.I. part suffered - numbers not known.	

Apparently 43

Army Form C. 2118.

WAR DIARY
or
INTELLIGENCE SUMMARY

(Erase heading not required.)

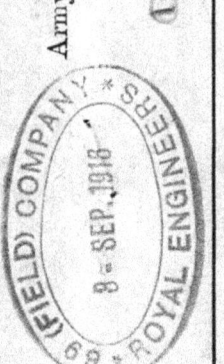

Place	Date	Hour	Summary of Events and Information	Remarks and references to Appendices
Somme	29	—	Company did not go out. Very heavy bombardment in view of coming up of 4th Army attack. Sent a party to recover Lt Boyd Carpenter's body without success. Capt. Neath of 103rd Field Coy arrived in the evening with a view of taking over on 30th. Said he would bury body. Heavy rain.	
BERNAN-COURT	30.		Company moved at 10.30 am to transport lines at BECORDEL, on relief by 103rd Fd Coy. There to an open patch of country N.W. of DERNANCOURT. Very heavy rain. Tarpaulin erected as shelter after considerable trouble was done, was informed that billets could be provided in the village after all. Too late to move.	
move	31		Dismounted parts moved to tactical train at 10.40 am to AIRAINES, thence marched 7 miles to FRETTECUISSE. Mounted portion of Coy. & Cyclists moved by road to W. of AMIENS. O.C. went ahead to find billets.	
FRETTE-CUISSE	Sept 1st		Resting, cleaning up & endeavouring to truck up H.Co's & men, who were in rather a bad way; due to loss of 3 officers & many NCOs.	

Appendix for 24.8.16

B & C Coys. 11th Kings & 4
Sections 89 9th Coy arrived
N.E. end of MONTAUBAN at
3 p.m. waited in trenches.

B & C Coys & Nos 1. 2. & 3
Sections 89th arrived YORK
trench at 5 p.m.

No. 3 Section with 1 platoon Kings
proceeded to consolidate point
S. 12. A. Central at 9.10 p.m.

Two platoons B. Coy went to
consolidate INNER trench at
10.5 p.m.

Lt Mowbray (No 2 Section) went
to reconnoitre at about 11.30 p.m

One platoon C. Coy put at
disposal of Col. MORRIS. 9th R.B.
at 11.15 p.m.

No news from Mowbray or
anyone until 2 am.

O.C. 2nd Bucks reported that
No. 3 Section reported at his
Batt'n H'qrs at 10 for A
and second party of Kings at
10.30 p.m. to digging trench
from S.C.12 onward to trench
on N.W. edge of wood - to fire
N.E. - Received 2 a.m. 25th.

Lt Mowbray wired at 1.10 am
that he was starting point C.
Also that B and D were
not possible. Wire received
at 2.45 AM.

O.C. went up 4.30 am 25th
returned 10.15 am after
finding out requirements of
Col's Martin & Webb.
(R.B. & O×B's).

Obtained permission of O.C.
to send all Kings & R.E.
back to billets, & made
out scheme of work.
/2 am.

A.
22-8-16

TABLE OF WORKING PARTIES NIGHT OF 22/23rd AUGUST

Party	Unit	Strength of party	Rendezvous	Time	Tools	Work	Remarks
A	9th Rif Brig.	150	Battalion H.Q. S.27.b.4.4½	7.30 p.m.	150 shovels 75 picks	Support line to DEVIL Trench from S.18.b.7.1 N.West	
B	5th Oxf & Bucks L.I. 200		Battalion H.Q. S.27.b.2.0	7.45 p.m.	200 shovels 100 picks	Continuation of LONGUEVAL ALLEY from S.13.c.5.4 Northwards.	
C	5th Oxf & Bucks L.I. 70		—do—	8 p.m.	70 shovels 20 picks	C.T. from SOUTH Street at S.13.b.1½.0 to DEVIL Trench at S.13.b.6.3.	
D	5th Oxf & Bucks L.I. 200		—do—	8.15 p.m.	200 shovels 50 picks	C.T. through DELVILLE WOOD from about S.13.a.6.2 to S.13.a.1.5	

WAR DIARY or INTELLIGENCE SUMMARY

Army Form C. 2118.

88 (FIELD) COMPANY ROYAL ENGINEERS
30 SEP. 1916

SEPTEMBER 1916

Place	Date	Hour	Summary of Events and Information	Remarks and references to Appendices
FRETTE CUISSE	1		The Mounted party arrived 6.30 pm no casualties and fit. Rations due have been dumped at FRETTE CUISSE as night of 31st. Men came until 9pm a.m. 1st Oct authorised. Exemption of "Iron Ration".	
"	2		Commenced training to-wards men and NCO's up. Physical training and Squad Drill with rifles. 2/Lt WHITE, 2nd Cpls BRYCE & HIND rejoined the Company. Afternoon men free to rest. Arranged with Mayor to avoid terms if required.	
"	3		Sunday. Divine Service at 9" R.B. LE FAY. Remainder of day resting. 2nd Lt. HARVEY R.E. (T.O.) joined Coy from No 4 G.B.	
"	4		Continued training as on 2nd. Capt BENSKIN R.E. left the Coy on apptt. as Brigade Major 4th Infantry Brigade. Lt. ALEXANDER in command of Coy. Lt. Llewellyn proceeded to LE TREPORT on 48 hours leave	

Army Form C. 2118.

WAR DIARY
or
INTELLIGENCE SUMMARY

(Erase heading not required.)

SEPTEMBER.

Place	Date	Hour	Summary of Events and Information	Remarks and references to Appendices
FRETTE CUISSE	5		Continued training. Squad drill & company drill. 2nd LIEUT S. H. KING R.E. (T.C.) joined Coy from No 4. G.B. Sapper PETTIE A. found dead on road from OISEMONT to FRETTE CUISSE; evidence conclusive death caused by fall from bicycle on night of 4/9/16.	/S2
"	6		Continued training. Squad drill, Smoke helmet drill. Knotting and lashing.	/S2
"	7		7 reinforcements arrived from No 4. G.B. 7/Lt. Llewellyn returned from leave.	/S2
"	8		Company inspected and addressed by C.R.E. 14th Division + congratulated on work done in DELVILLE WOOD. 2nd LIEUT. I. E. HARVEY R.E. (T.C.) sent to Hospital by M.O. 14th Div. Engineers as unfit.	/S2
" and AILLY-SUR-SOMME	9		Continued training. Company drill, first aid &c. Transport + cyclists moved to AILLY-SUR-SOMME with 41st Infy. Bde Group. Left FRETTE CUISSE at 9 a.m. under Lt LLEWELYN.	/S2

Army Form C. 2118.

WAR DIARY
or
INTELLIGENCE SUMMARY

(Erase heading not required.)

SEPTEMBER

Stamp: 68 (FIELD COMPANY) ROYAL ENGINEERS 30 SEP. 1916

Place	Date	Hour	Summary of Events and Information	Remarks and references to Appendices
DERNANCOURT	10		Transport and cyclists marched to billets in DERNANCOURT. Dismounted personnel conveyed from FRETTE COISSE to DERNANCOURT by French lorries: left 4 p.m., arrived 8.30 p.m.	/JS
FRICOURT CAMP	11		Coy. marched from DERNANCOURT at 3.30 p.m. and arrived at camp F.13.b. (ALBERT Contoured Sheet 1/40,000) 5 p.m. & bivouacked. Sgt. Matthews went to hospital sick.	/JS
do	12		Section Officers reconnoitred bivouac find DELVILLE WOOD. O.C. visited H.Q. 41st Bde, 164th Bde, 2/2 and 2/1 W. Lancs Field Coys R.E. and arranged accn. for camp at FRICOURT WOOD. Sgt Matthews returned to Coy.	/JS
FRICOURT WOOD	13		Dismounted personnel guarded Transport moving from Square E6 central. No.1 and part of No.2 Section worked at night on ammunition Pack advance. Batt. Hqrs in GREEN TRENCH at 5.12.d.73, under M.T. Llewellyn. O.C. arranged work with 4.D. Inf. Bde EGR. & OC. 11th Kings. 2nd Lt. King, 2 NCOs + 2 men of No.3 Section laid at new trench from S.18.B 5.5. S.12.d.88. 6 a.m. in DELVILLE WOOD: handed day to 1 Coy. 11th Kings 2nd Lt. WALKER 2 NCOs + 2 men of No.4 Section laid at new trench from S.18.a.10.10. to S.18.b.7.10 in DELVILLE WOOD: handed day to 1st Coy. 11th Kings. 2nd Lt B. MARGARSON reported for duty from No.4 G.B. 3 O.R. joined Coy from No. 4 G.B.	/JS

Army Form C. 2118.

WAR DIARY
or
INTELLIGENCE SUMMARY

(Erase heading not required.)

SEPTEMBER

Place	Date	Hour	Summary of Events and Information	Remarks and references to Appendices
FRICOURT WOOD	14		O.C. reconnoitred previous nights work in DELVILLE WOOD. Dismounted Gun/met mine dump to a point 200 yds N. No FRICOURT WOOD. Nº 1 & 2 Sections under 2/Lt Margesson completed construction of advanced Batt Hqrs in GREEN TRENCH. 2/Lt MARGESON wounded: 3 O.R. killed & O.Rs wounded 2 O.R. missing 1 O.R. gassed.	/A.S
FRICOURT WOOD	15		3 pontoon wagons + 1 trestle wagon complete with gear handed over to C.R.E.3 outside Park. Nº 3 & 4 Section left camp 4 a.m. & proceeded to mount 35th Bde R.F.A. & advance batteries after electing infantry lat proceeded. Work incomplete. Completed by 3 Sec. Canadians. 1 O.R. killed 9 wounded 1 missing. Section returned to Camp at 6.30 pm. Remain still-for very heavy; position looking worst R-17 central. Spr. G. GIBSON (Nº 3 Sec⁽ⁿ⁾) awarded Military Medal.	/A.S
FRICOURT WOOD	16		Resting and making implements; and loading parties by R.E. Park.	/A.S
FRICOURT WOOD TO RIBEMONT	17		Coy marched to RIBEMONT, leaving 1 p.m. arriving 4.45pm; billeted in village. 2 Pontoons + 1 trestle wagons rejoined Coy from C.R.E.'s outside Park	/A.S

Army Form C. 2118.

WAR DIARY
or
INTELLIGENCE SUMMARY

(Erase heading not required.)

SEPTEMBER.

Instructions regarding War Diaries and Intelligence Summaries are contained in F.S. Regs., Part II. and the Staff Manual respectively. Title Pages will be prepared in manuscript.

89 (FIELD) COMPANY
ROYAL ENGINEERS
8 0 SEP. 1916

Place	Date	Hour	Summary of Events and Information	Remarks and references to Appendices
RIBEMONT	18		No 4 Section started work for 43rd Infy Bde. Red Army Fatigue. Coy moved into Huts in RIBEMONT.	See
do	19		No 3 Section building men's cookhouse for G.O.C. 14th Division at BUIRE camp. No 1, 2, & 4 erecting bunks in trees at RIBEMONT. LIEUT P.G. NOTTAGE joined Coy from No 4 G.B. Coy paid.	See
do	20		Coy erecting bunks in trees.	See
do	21		Coy transport moved to TALMAS enroute to Llewellyn. 20 reinforcements arrived from No 4 G.B. Coy bathed.	See
P do	22		No 2 Complete bunks left for previous day. No 4 dismantled huts. Dismounted personnel moved to SUS ST. LEGER by bus arriving at 1.30pm. Transport annexe to SUS ST LEGER arriving 2 pm.	See
SUS ST. LEGER.	23		Coy route march in morning. Resting remainder of day.	See

Army Form C. 2118.

WAR DIARY
or
INTELLIGENCE SUMMARY

(Erase heading not required.)

SEPTEMBER

Instructions regarding War Diaries and Intelligence Summaries are contained in F. S. Regs., Part II. and the Staff Manual respectively. Title Pages will be prepared in manuscript.

Place	Date	Hour	Summary of Events and Information	Remarks and references to Appendices
SOS ST LEGER	24		Training: physical training, squad drill with and without arms. O.C. reconnoitred H Sector with a view to relief of 69th Coy. 12th Div.	A/A
do				A/A
do	25		Training as for 24th	A/A
do	26		Training as for 25th. Advance party proceeded to ARRAS. Advance party proceeded to BERNEVILLE 2 O.R. : 3 Officers 12 O.R.	A/A
do and HAUTVILLE	27		Coy moved to HAUTVILLE and billeted. Capt E.O. ALABASTER rejoined Coy from No 4 G.B. and took command.	A/A
HAUTVILLE and ARRAS	28		Coy moved to ARRAS arriving at billets at 9.30 pm. Transport lean loticuts, three pontoon wagons + 1 forge cart moved to BERNEVILLE.	A/A
ARRAS	29		O.C. arranged work in H sector with B.G.C. 43rd Inf. Bde. Distribution of work between R.E. Pioneers arranged with Prudpath, wired dugouts, trench mortar emplacements and "New Pattern" fire steps.	A/A
do	30		Work commenced in afternoon. Work continued as for 29th.	A/A

J. C. Alabaster
Captain
O.C. 88th Fld. Coy R.E.

Army Form C. 2118.

Instructions regarding War Diaries and Intelligence Summaries are contained in F. S. Regs., Part II. and the Staff Manual respectively. Title Pages will be prepared in manuscript.

WAR DIARY
or
INTELLIGENCE SUMMARY
(Erase heading not required.)

OCTOBER 1916

89 (FIELD) COMPANY ROYAL ENGINEERS
81 OCT. 1916

Place	Date	Hour	Summary of Events and Information	Remarks and references to Appendices
ARRAS	1.10.16		Quiet day. Work proceeding in H. Sector mainly dugouts for garrison and emplacements for Trench Mortars. Work on installing new pattern fire steps for "recesses" also in hand. Shortage of labour seriously affecting work. B.G.C. 43rd Bde, C.R.E. 14th Divn and O.C. Coy inspected whole of H. Sector. Three platoons B. Coy 11th King's (Pioneers) reported for duty, to replace infantry working parties.	
	2.10.16		O.C. Coy visited trenches with O.C. 43rd Bde M.G. Coy & noted requirements. Advice in concealment given to A/166 & B/166 Batteries R.F.A. C.R.E. directs that 1 Section 89th Fd Coy be employed on work for him. Work in preparing ACHICOURT–BEAURAINS road for movement of artillery started.	
	3.10.16		O.C. Coy visited trenches north B.M. 43rd Bde, particularly the secret defences of RONVILLE.	
	4.10.16		All D.A.C. men withdrawn. Casualties in 89th Fd Coy while in SOMME offensive Aug 12th to Sept 18th were 1 officer killed, 1 3 officers wounded; other ranks 6 killed in action, 1 accidentally killed, 2 died of wounds, 3 missing, 29 wounded, 1 gassed, I shall shortly	

Army Form C. 2118.

WAR DIARY
or
INTELLIGENCE SUMMARY

(Erase heading not required.)

1/7

Instructions regarding War Diaries and Intelligence Summaries are contained in F. S. Regs., Part II. and the Staff Manual respectively. Title Pages will be prepared in manuscript.

[Stamp: 68 (FIELD) COMPANY ROYAL ENGINEERS 8 OCT. 1916]

Place	Date	Hour	Summary of Events and Information	Remarks and references to Appendices
ARRAS S-10-16	5.10.16		C.R.E. came to ARRAS and discussed work in hand. O.C. visited Right Battn regarding reclamation of H₂ sector. Conference at 11.30 A.M. 43rd Bde of O.C. units in brigade. Programme of work discussed.	
	6.10.16		Work proceeding well. O.C. visited Left Battn regarding H₂ sector. All men stood to at bombardment of grenades at 9 p.m till 11 p.m.	
	7.10.16		(O) warned to be in readiness to take shelter at 1.0 a.m. and again at 8.00 p.m. Instructions received to prepare sector or accommodation H1 sector front line for storing of bombs. Brigade direct battalions to put in hand. O.C. R.E. Special Bde. R.E. undertake to supply new pattern force stops for storing of necessaries.	
	8.10.16		Gas liberated North of H sector 8.25 p.m accompanied by artillery fire. Very little hostile retaliation.	
	9.10.16		Enemy put a few shells round C.s billets 9 a.m. No harm done, but officers somewhat disturbed at breakfast. O.C. arranged for removal of accumulated mine spoil.	

2449 Wt. W14957/M90 750,000 1/16 J.B.C. & A. Forms/C.2118/12.

118.

Army Form C. 2118.

WAR DIARY
or
INTELLIGENCE SUMMARY

(Erase heading not required.)

69 (FIELD) COMPANY
31 OCT. 1916
ROYAL ENGINEERS

Place	Date	Hour	Summary of Events and Information	Remarks and references to Appendices
ARRAS	10.10.16		B.G.C. 43rd Bde and O.C. 69 reconnoitred roads suitable for hand cart traffic in H.2. Sector.	
	11.10.16		H1 front line trenches to trench mortars. Work delayed. Supr TOMLINSON awarded Military Medal for gallantry.	
	12.10.16		O.C. Coy visited H1 with Special Bde officer, who is satisfied with boxes now erected. B.G.C. located left Battn H.Q.	
	13.10.16		2/Lt RAWKENCE and 6th D.C.L.I. and parties of 1 NCO and 10 men per Battn report for duty. This is nucleus of 43rd Bde Sapping Coy for instruction under 89th FldCoy. Bde Sapping Coy employed for half day on dugouts in hand.	
	14.10.16		Bde Sapping Coy started on preparating work for new left Battn H.Q., a new garrison dug out for centre company, right Battn, each party in two reliefs under a Sapper working on its own face. O.C. Coy reconnoitred detailed roads and arranged details re sites for completion of each to be suitable for hand cart traffic.	
	16.10.16		Bde antitank commencement of a steady frend.	

6/22

Army Form C. 2118.

WAR DIARY
or
INTELLIGENCE SUMMARY
(Erase heading not required.)

Instructions regarding War Diaries and Intelligence Summaries are contained in F. S. Regs., Part II. and the Staff Manual respectively. Title Pages will be prepared in manuscript.

[Stamp: 88 (FIELD) COMPANY ROYAL ENGINEERS 81 OCT. 1916]

Place	Date	Hour	Summary of Events and Information	Remarks and references to Appendices
ARRAS	17.10.16		O.C. Coy visited work in H2 Sector. Progress satisfactory. New pattern fire step explained to O.C. 6th D.C.L.I. Lt. E.D. ALEXANDER proceeded on leave with matrimonial intent.	
	18.10.16		Nothing special to report.	
	19.10.16		C.R.E. visited work in H1 Sector. B.G.C. 43rd Bde. in gly pleased with design of left Batten H.P. in HETSAS. C.R.E. directs that all reclaimed front line trenches to prepared for gas gilandeur. O.C. Coy/Special Coy R.E. cd. O.C. 8/9th Ft. by explain scheme to G.B.G.C. 2/6 R.A.M.C. cd. 13. R.A. report for work on dug out spoil.	
	20.10.16		Noisy night and some shelling of ARRAS in early morning. Party of 13. P.P. handed over to Medium Trench Mortars. Day spent in resting, refitting and cleaning. 1 Officer and 30 n.c.o.'s By 11th KING'S. coothdown at 7.p.m.	
	21.10.16		All Pioneers withdrawn from H. Sector. Work reorganised accordingly. Report sent to C.R.E. of boys with new pattern firestep.	MA

Army Form C. 2118.

WAR DIARY
or
INTELLIGENCE SUMMARY
(Erase heading not required.)

Instructions regarding War Diaries and Intelligence Summaries are contained in F. S. Regs., Part II. and the Staff Manual respectively. Title Pages will be prepared in manuscript.

68 (FIELD COMPANY)
31 OCT. 1916
ROYAL ENGINEERS

Place	Date	Hour	Summary of Events and Information	Remarks and references to Appendices
ARRAS	22.10.16		O.C. Coy wrote B.M. 143rd Bde and O.C. Q Coy Special Bde selected suitable bays for installation of new pattern fume stops and made arrangements for work to start.	
	23.10.16		O.C. Coy visited Hr Sector and arranged with Battalion in the line to open up the blocked out portion of HETSAS ST. Lt B. LLEWELLYN. M.C. returned from leave.	
	24.10.16		B.M. 35th Inf Bde called and notified that probable working parties will be 50 Bde Miners and 150 from Reserve Battn. Summary of work done in previous month sent to C.R.E.	
	25.10.16		Report sent to C.R.E. at H.Q. 35th Bde showing condition of works in hand, in suspended animation and in rear. All attached R.A.M.C. left 10.15 p.m. Programme of work submitted to C.R.E. at H.Q. 35th Bde for about a fortnight for 3 Sections R.E., 1 Coy Pioneers, 50 Bde Miners, 150 Reserve Battn, and 500 additional labour found by Divn H.Q.	

Army Form C. 2118.

WAR DIARY
or
INTELLIGENCE SUMMARY
(Erase heading not required.)

68 (FIELD) COMPANY
31 OCT. 1916
ROYAL ENGINEERS

Place	Date	Hour	Summary of Events and Information	Remarks and references to Appendices
ARRAS	26.10.16		4 3rd Inf Bde left ARRAS, being relieved by 35th Inf Bde; 89th Fd Coy relieved.	
	27.10.16		O.C. Coy visited H.Q. 35th Bde and arranged for work as follows:— Bde Mining Section to do two dugouts; 11th Kings to do 3 dugouts, 1 Medium T.M Emplacement, and supervision of H.S. line and bomb blocks; 89th Fd Coy with permanent working party and additional labour to do 7 dug outs, 1 Heavy T.M Emplacement, 2 Medium T.M Emplacements, and defences of RONVILLE ed ACHICOURT, and gas boxes from H25 to H33. D. Coy 11th KINGS returned to H. Sector	
	28.10.16		O.C. Coy reconnoitred defences of RONVILLE ed ACHICOURT.	
	29.10.16		Organisation of stores for H. sector arranged. Notification received that 2 Sections of a Fd Coy and 2 Coys Inf will be available for a fortnight from 1.11.16; arranged with 35th Bde for 1 of these R.E. Sections and the 2 Coys Inf to work on communication trenches between H.S. and front line and the other Section R.E. to take on 2 new dug outs.	

Army Form C. 2118.

WAR DIARY
or
INTELLIGENCE SUMMARY

(Erase heading not required.)

Instructions regarding War Diaries and Intelligence Summaries are contained in F.S. Regs., Part II. and the Staff Manual respectively. Title Pages will be prepared in manuscript.

[Stamp: 88 (FIELD) COMPANY ROYAL ENGINEERS 8 OCT. 1916]

Place	Date	Hour	Summary of Events and Information	Remarks and references to Appendices
ARRAS	30.10.16		O.C. 63rd Fld Coy R.E. visited 89th Fld Coy in ARRAS and made preliminary arrangements for his 2 Sections to work in H. Sector.	
			O.C. 89th visited work in Left sector; particularly a dugout badly sited by our predecessors. A heavy T.M. shell landed in the entrance and stopped all the timbering of half the shaft, top covers &c, luckily not serious effects. Officer of 63rd Coy accompanied so as to make a tour of Left sector.	422
	31.10.16		Sapper ARTHUR admitted to hospital and will about tell what is result of slow retarded trench mortar shell.	
			O.C. 63rd Fld Coy shown over Right Sector, and jobs required of him explained.	477

J. Calverton
Capt & Adjt
O.C. 89th Fld Coy R.E.
31.10.16

Vol 15

Confidential

War Diary
of
(80) 83rd Bde. R.G.A.
from 1st November 1916 to 30th November 1916.

(Volume I).

Army Form C. 2118.

WAR DIARY
or
INTELLIGENCE SUMMARY
(Erase heading not required.)

Instructions regarding War Diaries and Intelligence Summaries are contained in F. S. Regs., Part II. and the Staff Manual respectively. Title Pages will be prepared in manuscript.

[Stamp: 89 (FIELD) COMPANY ROYAL ENGINEERS — 30 NOV 1916]

Place	Date	Hour	Summary of Events and Information	Remarks and references to Appendices
ARRAS	1.11.16		Warning received of G.S. having been installed in I Sector.	S.F.R.
	2.11.16		Arrangements made for the care of permanent working party when we go probably on 5.11.16.	S.F.R.
	3.11.16		O.C. & 2 Section Officers 69th Fd Cy R.E. arrive to see our work in hand at 2 p.m., copy sent to C.R.E. Summary of jobs given to them. Lt. ALEXANDER who arrived from leave on 30.11.16 goes to WARLUS to overhaul transport & stores accumulated.	S.F.R.
	4.11.16		Day spent in organising up jobs in hand & getting ideas out ready for relieving unit.	S.F.R.
	5.11.16		Lt. ALEXANDER & Lt. KING took on transport from WARLUS, LLEWELLYN acted as billeting officer. O.C. & remainder of Coy from ARRAS relieved at 5 p.m. by 69th Fd Cy R.E. and marched to GOUY.	S.F.R.
GOUY	6.11.16		Day of rest. O.C. at 1st Div LEDLEXANDER rode to AMBRINES to see about accommodation, but informed by 43rd Div that we are to move to new ...	S.F.R.

Army Form C. 2113.

1/24

WAR DIARY
or
INTELLIGENCE SUMMARY

(Erase heading not required.)

Instructions regarding War Diaries and Intelligence Summaries are contained in F. S. Regs., Part II. and the Staff Manual respectively. Title Pages will be prepared in manuscript.

69 (FIELD) COMPANY * ROYAL ENGINEERS
8 NOV. 1916

Place	Date	Hour	Summary of Events and Information	Remarks and references to Appendices
GOUY-EN-ARTOIS	7.11.16		Gas helmet drill and general instructions of Sections under Section Officers. Heavy rain prevented proper programme being carried out.	app
ditto	8.11.16	9.30 a.m.	Company paraded 9.30 a.m. and marched via FOSSEUX, BARLY, AVESNES, AMBRINES, MAIZIERES, GOUY-EN-TERNOIS to MONTS-EN-TERNOIS. Heavy rain, gale, and hail, but no casualties.	app
MONTS-EN-TERNOIS		3.30 p.m.	a blanket lorry was between 13 and 14 hours late in reporting at GOUY-EN-ARTOIS. Men and animals were finally bedded down at 2 a.m. 9.11.16.	
do	9.11.16		Owing to delay in receipt of blankets last night, training was not started till 10.30 a.m. This consisted of Physical Training, Squad drill and Rifle exercises. O.C. arranged with Staff Captain 43rd Bde for reconnaissance of villages with regard to accommodation.	app
	10.11.16		G.O.C. 14th Divn visited MONTS-EN-TERNOIS and returned O.C. by to direct cleaning of teams. C.R.E. took O.C. by to HESDIN for lecture on R.E. Work in the Field.	app

Army Form C. 2118.

WAR DIARY
or
INTELLIGENCE SUMMARY

(Erase heading not required.)

Place	Date	Hour	Summary of Events and Information	Remarks and references to Appendices
MONTS-EN TERNOIS	11.11.16		Reconnaissance of MONTS EN TERNOIS completed. Other villages in hand. Ot. by Lt. NOTTAGE arranged with B.M. 43rd Bde for opening Brigade School of Fieldworks on 13.11.16. Company continued training in infantry work	V.P.R
	12.11.16		Church parade on MONCHEAUX. Rest day. Recommendation sent to C.R.E. for commissions for Sjt. MATTHEWS and a/Sjt. G. CHANNING. A.D.V.S. visited village & decided that men could occupy farms but not the stables or outhouses where (explain or range now made) could animals must not be taken where notices have been erected.	V.P.R
	13.11.16		Bde School started. Repairs to MONCHEAUX & MONTS-EN-TERNOIS started by No 3 & 4 Sections No 1 & 2 Section Training	V.P.R
	14.11.16		Work & training as on 13". Arrangements made for turnshurval clearing North of TREBREUVIETTE.	V.P.R

Army Form C. 2118.

WAR DIARY
or
INTELLIGENCE SUMMARY

(Erase heading not required.)

Instructions regarding War Diaries and Intelligence Summaries are contained in F. S. Regs., Part II. and the Staff Manual respectively. Title Pages will be prepared in manuscript.

126.

*Stamp: 89 (FIELD) COMPANY * ROYAL ENGINEERS, 8 NOV 1916*

Place	Date	Hour	Summary of Events and Information	Remarks and references to Appendices
MONTS-EN-TERNOIS	15.11.16		Work and training as before. Brushwood clearing started North of REBREUVIETTE & timber felling at LE CAUROY.	
	16.11.16		Site for baths selected in SERICOURT. Military Medal awarded for work prior to 30.6.16. to Corpl. SEPPISTON (since killed in action), Corpl C. SHAW, Sapr H. DUNN.	
	17.11.16		Work in MONTS-EN-TERNOIS, HOUVIN, SERICOURT, REBREUVIETTE, LE CAUROY, and farming in MONTS-EN-TERNOIS. No tracing.	
	18.11.16		Frost, sleet and rain. Farming continued. Arrangements made for 3 travelling saw mill in FREVENT.	
	19.11.16		S/C MATTHEWS & F/S/C CHANNING interviewed by G.O.C. 14th Divn with view to obtaining infantry commissions. Instructing of Sections on worked out tracing arranged. Company on a 5 mile run at urged walk.	

2449 Wt. W14957/M90 750,000 1/16 J.B.C. & A. Forms/C.2118/12.

Army Form C. 2118.

WAR DIARY
or
INTELLIGENCE SUMMARY

(Erase heading not required.)

Instructions regarding War Diaries and Intelligence Summaries are contained in F. S. Regs., Part II. and the Staff Manual respectively. Title Pages will be prepared in manuscript.

89 (FIELD) COMPANY
8 NOV. 1916
ROYAL ENGINEERS

Place	Date	Hour	Summary of Events and Information	Remarks and references to Appendices
MONTS-EN-TERNOIS	20.11.16		Nos 3 and 4 on Training. Nos 1 and 2 on work. Most of No 1 at LIENCOURT.	App.
	21.11.16		2Lt G. WALKER went on leave.	App.
	22.11.16		C.R.E. authorises suspension of training if necessary to carry out work in villages of 43rd Bde area.	App.
	23.11.16		Arrangements made with 43rd Bde unit for work to be carried out by units with R.E. assistance. C.R.E. visited MONTS-EN-TERNOIS. Orders received to take over DENIER, BERLENCOURT, SARS-LEZ-BOIS from 62nd Fd Coy R.E.	App.
	24.11.16		Lt E.D. ALEXANDER authorised by G.O.C. 14th Divn to wear badges of rank as a Captain while 2nd in command of 89th Fd Coy R.E. (C.R.E. E.145/1). Training and fatigues in morning. To AVESNES ~~cinema~~ in afternoon.	App.
	25.11.16		Warned that Coy may move to SERICOURT on 28th	App.

2449 Wt. W14957/M90 750,000 1/16 J.B.C. & A. Forms/C.2118/12.

Army Form C. 2118.

WAR DIARY
or
INTELLIGENCE SUMMARY

(Erase heading not required.)

Instructions regarding War Diaries and Intelligence Summaries are contained in F. S. Regs., Part II. and the Staff Manual respectively. Title Pages will be prepared in manuscript.

89 (FIELD) COMPANY * ROYAL ENGINEERS
8 NOV. 1916

Place	Date	Hour	Summary of Events and Information	Remarks and references to Appendices
MONTS-EN-TERNOIS	26.11.16.		Collecting and making up materials for horse troughs at BERLENCOURT & SARS. Otherwise no work.	VPP
	27.11.16		160ft of horse troughs erected at above places. Arrangements for men met by tea 115 in Divisional Cross country race.	VPP
MONTS-EN-TERNOIS and SERICOURT	28.11.16		No 1 Section remains at LIENCOURT. No 2 " marches to BERLENCOURT 1.30p.m. No 3 " remains at FREVENT ½ No 4 " " Remainder of Coy marches to SERICOURT 1.45 p.m.	VPP
	29.11.16.		No 1 Section working near LIENCOURT No 2 " working at BERLENCOURT, DENIER, SARS-LEZ-BOIS No 3 " working at FREVENT No 4 " " SERICOURT Box respirators in bulk received in the evening	VPP
	30.11.16		Nos 1 & 2 Sections T.A.B. Inoculation. Capt ALEXANDER instructs Nos 1 & 2 in respirator drill. Arrangements made for Nos 3rd & 4 & H.Q. to be inoculated & drilled on 1.12.16.	VPP

J.O. Alexander
Capt R.E.

OC. 89: Fd Coy R.E.

2449 Wt. W14957/M90 750,000 1/16 J.B.C. & A. Forms/C.2118/12.

Army Form C. 2118.

WAR DIARY
or
INTELLIGENCE SUMMARY
(Erase heading not required.)

Instructions regarding War Diaries and Intelligence Summaries are contained in F. S. Regs., Part II. and the Staff Manual respectively. Title Pages will be prepared in manuscript.

68 (FIELD) COMPANY ROYAL ENGINEERS — 11 JAN. 1917

Vol 16

Place	Date	Hour	Summary of Events and Information	Remarks and references to Appendices
SERICOURT	1.12.16		No 1 Section at LIENCOURT, tree felling.	
			No 2 " BERLENCOURT, repairing barns.	
			½ No 3 " PREVENT, ".	
			Remainder of Coy at SERICOURT, repairing barns.	
			T.A.B. Inoculation carried out.	6???
	2.12.16		Lt NOTT & Lt [Innocent] on leave.	
			2/Lt WALKER returns from leave.	
			No 1 Section ordered by C.R.E. to H.Q. Section.	
			Work on cinema theatre at HOUVIN started.	8???
	3.12.16		Box respirators issued to H.Q. and No 3 and 4 Sections not later.	
			Orders for trenching DENIER, BERLENCOURT, SIBIVILLE, SERICOURT received.	9???
	4.12.16		Schemes for increasing accomodation including test of officers prepared.	
			Box respirators issued to No 1 and 2.	8???
	5.12.16		No 1 and 2 took their gas test.	
			O.C. Coy sees C.R.E. about Corps laundry.	
			Sgt Midworth trains D.L.I. in expat wiring.	8???

2449 Wt. W14957/M90 750,000 1/16 J.B.C. & A. Forms/C.2118/12.

WAR DIARY
or
INTELLIGENCE SUMMARY

Army Form C. 2118.

Place	Date	Hour	Summary of Events and Information	Remarks and references to Appendices
SERICOURT	6.12.16		Arrangements made for resuming General will at night as work as do. Arrangements made to contact all officers at Mess 9 P.M. in rotation.	
	7.12.16		C.R.E. visits company and Honores of new magazine in cellars of Coptelands. Supports to away troops at forms of 2 stage at HOUVIN crown employer. L.t. E.D. ALEXANDER proceeds Retro Copter 18.9.16 by tot 11.00 ds 24.11.16.	622 6010
	8.12.16		C.E. Third Army visits FREVENT ecounts, it is satisfied with program.	622
	9.12.16		Lt. P.G. NOTTAGE ordered by C.R.E. to join 61st Fld Coy on return from leave on 21st November. Lt. KINAGINE to HESDIN to give technical advice on Canadian Forms hops as the huts	622
	10.12.16		Rest for whole company. Box respirator drill.	622
	11.12.16		B.G.C. 43rd Bde offers O.C. Coy sent to his car to H.Seats on 12.12.16	622
	12.12.16		O.C. Coy goes to ARRAS and finds out work on hand.	622
	13.12.16		Operations Orders for relief of 69th Fld Coy R.E. received. Work on village wards eg. Suggested distribution of work sent to H.Q. 43rd Bde.	622

Army Form C. 2118.

WAR DIARY
or
INTELLIGENCE SUMMARY

(Erase heading not required.)

131.

Place	Date	Hour	Summary of Events and Information	Remarks and references to Appendices
SERICOURT	14.12.16		Handing over reports and receipts sent to C.R.E. Outlying sections return to Coy H.Q. 2nd Lt KING with D.R.M.S. & Lt AUBIN to report on site for Divisional laundry.	App.
SOMBRIN	15.12.16		Company marched at 9.30 a.m. from SERICOURT via FREVENT, REBREUVIETTE and IVERGNY to SOMBRIN arriving 3.00 p.m. No particular incident to record.	App.
DUISANS	16.12.16		Company marched at 8.30 a.m. from SOMBRIN via AVESNES-LE-COMTE, HABARCQ to DUISANS, arriving 1.30 p.m. Lt P.G. NOTTAGE rejoined from leave.	App.
ARRAS	17.12.16		2nd Lt WALKER & Lt LLEWELLYN and advanced parties took over work in H. Sector from 69th F.W.Coy R.E. Lt NOTTAGE left to join 61st F.W.Coy R.E. 2nd Lt S.H.KING proceeded on leave. Capt ALEXANDER took heavy transport to WARLUS by day. OC. marched company at 4.30 p.m. direct to ARRAS. Settled in 7.00 p.m.	App.

Army Form C. 2118.

132

Instructions regarding War Diaries and Intelligence Summaries are contained in F. S. Regs., Part II. and the Staff Manual respectively. Title Pages will be prepared in manuscript.

WAR DIARY
or
INTELLIGENCE SUMMARY
(Erase heading not required.)

68 (FIELD) COMPANY ROYAL ENGINEERS
11 JAN. 1917

Place	Date	Hour	Summary of Events and Information	Remarks and references to Appendices
A.R.R.A.S.	18.12.16.		Company employed on clearing up dumps, general fatigues in barracks, inspections, and reconnaissance of work. O.C. obtained approval by B.G.C. 43rd Bde for distribution of work, and arranged with 11th KINGS, 5th NORTHANTS, Medium T.M.B and M.G. Coy for various jobs to be undertaken. Capt. ALEXANDER prepared details of scheme for continuing Heavy T.M. trolley line through H.1 sub-sector.	S.P.P.
	19.12.16.		Work by 89th Field Coy and 43rd Bde M.G. Pioneer Coy started, dugouts for various purposes. Party left behind at WARLUS work on horse lines pending our return.	S.P.P.
	20.12.16.		C.R.E. 14th Divn. visited by H.Q. and saw some of work in hand. 5th NORTHANTS and 11th KINGS having relieved each other got under way. Capt. ALEXANDER arranged with D/Q R.E. for Compiègne horse transport to keep dumps full.	S.P.P.
	21.12.16.		O.C. inspected work in centre of H. Sector, and arranged for gas curtains to be erected in H.2 sub-sector by 203rd Field Coy.	S.P.P.

WAR DIARY
or
INTELLIGENCE SUMMARY

Army Form C. 2118.

Place	Date	Hour	Summary of Events and Information	Remarks and references to Appendices
ARRAS	22.12.16		2nd Lt. J.C. ALLAN Indian Army Reserve reported for duty.	
	23.12.16		Work commenced on laying Decauville track in H.T.M Tramway trench.	
	24.12.16		O.C. went to Conference of Coy. Commanders at C.R.E.'s	
	25.12.16		Christmas Day. Work as usual till 3 p.m. Christmas dinner and distribution of presents afterwards.	
26.12.16			Awards given by G.O.C. 14th Division for O.C. Capt. E.D ALABASTER to wear the badge of the rank of Major, for which he had been recommended under C.O.S 384(a) para 6.	
			C.R.E. visited Coy. HQrs and various works in hand. O.C. left for England on leave. CAPT. E.T.D. ALEXANDER in command.	
	27.12.16		O.C. visited works in H2 Subsector, and arranged for additional working parties from 43rd Bde. one 1000 for shell frontline AREAS during night; no casualties in coy.	
	28.12.16		O.C. and O.C. V/2 H.T.M. Bty selected sites for emplacements + orderly for H.T.M Tramway.	
	29.12.16		O.C. visited works in H1 Subsector. took series of working parties arranged with Brigade.	
	30.12.16		C.R.E. inspected H.T.M Tramway + other work. Lt. KING reported from leave.	
	31.12.16		O.C. visited H2 Subsector - arranged details for employment of Sgt McKean + Sapper Vickers with Explosives in operations with O.C. 10th D.L.I. for New Years Day.	

WAR DIARY
or
INTELLIGENCE SUMMARY
(Erase heading not required.)

Army Form C. 2118.

Vol 17

89 (FIELD COMPANY) ROYAL ENGINEERS
31 JAN. 1917

89 - ARMY R E

JANUARY 1917

Place	Date	Hour	Summary of Events and Information	Remarks and references to Appendices
ARRAS	1.1.17		Operations in H Section performed. Work as usual.	
	2.1.17		Work in hand:- Trench tramway (ex Henry Trench Minlars, Bryants (mined) for gunners, Lewis Gunners, Machine Gunners; connecting cellars by tunnels for evening Stalins; Camouflaged O.P.s in front & support lines. Work as usual.	
	3.1.17		ditto.	
	4.1.17		Gas shells fired into ARRAS between 10.70 pm & 12 midnight.	
	5.1.17		CRE visited New Advanced Brigade Hqrs dugout in METSAS 87, and ROMVILLE evening Stalins. Gas shells into ARRAS between 9 pm -11 pm & 12.30am-1am.	
	6.1.17		Heavy bombardment & raid on German trenches opposite H 40; bombardment started 11.15 am; highly successful; raid by 150 men 10th D.L.I. at 3.8 pm acty Cpl S.F. MATHESON and L/Cpl H.W. GURNETT accompanied raiders with explosives to destroy suspected minenwerfer in "FUCHSBAU"; they all made to reach their objective owing to heavy counter-attack but both distinguished themselves in the fighting, particularly Cpl MATHESON and were congratulated by Col NORANT commanding 10th D.L.I. Both Sapper attended but remained at duty. Cpl MATHESON used at again a/k return for raiding parties & helped to bring in wounded. No word in minute.	
	7.1.17		Work resumed as usual.	

Army Form C. 2118.

WAR DIARY
or
INTELLIGENCE SUMMARY

(Erase heading not required.)

135.

Instructions regarding War Diaries and Intelligence Summaries are contained in F. S. Regs., Part II. and the Staff Manual respectively. Title Pages will be prepared in manuscript.

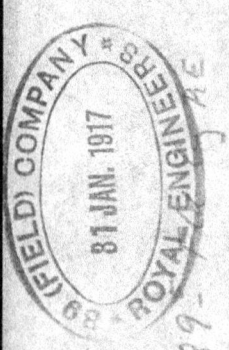

89 (FIELD) COMPANY
31 JAN. 1917
ROYAL ENGINEERS

89 — JAE

Place	Date	Hour	Summary of Events and Information	Remarks and references to Appendices
ARRAS	8.1.17		Work as usual.	/5/a
	9.1.17		do	/5/a
	10.1.17		do	/5/a
	11.1.17		do	/5/a
	12.1.17		do. New M.T.M. emplacement adjacent commenced in HAZEBROUCK ST.	/5/a
	13.1.17		Transport moved to BETONVILLE. Work that usual. O.C. arranged for starting R.E. Engineering School for recruiting & rapid wiring with B-M.	/5/a
	14.1.17		O/C R.E. inspected work in H.1 Subsection.	/5/a
	15.1.17		R.E. Engineering School started. 2Lt. MOWBRAY rejoined Coy from No 4 G.B.D.	/5/a
	16.1.17		Lt LLEWELLYN and No 1 Section attached 61[?] R.E.M Coy for special work in F Sector.	/5/a
	17.1.17		Work as usual.	/5/a
			do	/5/a
	18.1.17		Reports on site & materials for labor material submitted to CRE for 53 M.T.M. emplacements and 16 M.T.M. emplacements with dugouts, in H2 Subsection.	/5/a
	19.1.17		Reports on work on 14 Section submitted to CRE. Major E. O. ALABASTER rejoined and took over command of Coy.	/5/a
	20.1.17		O.C. to inspect tubes in ROMNEY, BEAUVRAINS Rec. and O.C. N.Z Tunnelling Coy. Further examination necessary.	/5/a

2449 Wt. W14957/Mg0 750,000 1/16 J.B.C. & A. Forms/C.2118/12.

Army Form C. 2118.

WAR DIARY
or
INTELLIGENCE SUMMARY

(Erase heading not required.)

Instructions regarding War Diaries and Intelligence Summaries are contained in F. S. Regs., Part II. and the Staff Manual respectively. Title Pages will be prepared in manuscript.

89 (Field) Company Royal Engineers
31 JAN. 1917

Place	Date	Hour	Summary of Events and Information	Remarks and references to Appendices
ARRAS	21.1.17		H.T.M. Emp. d. BANQUET cancelled. Two men 11th KINGS killed, one all ranks except injury. Firing shaft, entrance & tunbay destroyed. Mortar, ammunition at post safe. 1/L.S. H.KING, transferred to 62nd Fld Coy R.E.	App
	22.1.17		L. LLEWELYN & No1 Section return from F. Sects. 2L MOWBRAY signs company. O/Cpl MATHESON, S.F. (67106) awarded Military Medal. *Capt ALEXANDER recommended for appointment as G.S.O.3.	App
	23.1.17		*Capt ALEXANDER proceeds on leave. Capt E.B. ALABASTER promoted Acting Major. List 118 by Cmd 13.1.17 dated 30.11.16.	App App
	24.1.17		Work proceeding normally. Report on subsidences in RONVILLE-BEAURAINS road sent to C.R.E.	App
	25.1.17		Scheme for work on battle Hqs. & H2 Sents prepared & submitted	App
	26.1.17		Railway, I.W.T., & Dock Services regets sent in.	App
	27.1.17		S/t MAYSTED warned to replace S/t PETERS, transferred to ENGLAND.	App
	28.1.17		Work proceeding normally. Warned that 30th Divn will take over all tramways soon.	App

Army Form C. 2118.

WAR DIARY
or
INTELLIGENCE SUMMARY

(Erase heading not required.)

68 (FIELD) COMPANY * ROYAL ENGINEERS
31 JAN. 1917
89 -

Instructions regarding War Diaries and Intelligence Summaries are contained in F. S. Regs., Part II. and the Staff Manual respectively. Title Pages will be prepared in manuscript.

137

Place	Date	Hour	Summary of Events and Information	Remarks and references to Appendices
ARRAS	29.1.17		CAPT P.G. NOTTAGE arrived to take over temporary command of 89th F&Cg R.E. during absence of MAJOR ALABASTER at R.E. School, until return of CAPT ALEXANDER from leave	
	30.1.17		C.R.E. visited ARRAS; B.G.'s commanding battle fronts will be responsible for all preparations, but any suggested departures from normal in design must be referred to C.R.E.	
	31.1.17		Arrangements made for work for next week or more. Sections concentrated on a small number of dugouts in 43rd Bde. front.	

J. O. Alabaster
Major RE

O.C. 89th F.U.Cg RE
31.1.17

2449 Wt. W14957/M90 750,000 1/16 J.B.C. & A. Forms/C.2118/12.

WAR DIARY or INTELLIGENCE SUMMARY

Army Form C. 2118.

FEBRUARY 1917

[Stamp: 69 (FIELD) COMPANY * ROYAL ENGINEERS * 28 FEB. 1917]

Place	Date	Hour	Summary of Events and Information	Remarks and references to Appendices
ARRAS	1.2.17		C.R.E. visited ROE H.Q. HETSAS, a hut in RONVILLE ROAD. Major ALABASTER left n/k. C.R.E. to R.E. School near HESDIN. CAPT. R.G. NOTTAGE tok on temporary command of Coy. Work in hand, enlarging dug out in HARDY ST. T.M. dug out in RONVILLE-BEURAIN ROAD. Garrison dug outs in HARDY ST. & HARRINGTON ST. again M.T.M.E.P. in HARRINGTON ST. dug out in S.L. near HOLBORN. H.T.M. TRAMWAY.	/a
	2.2.17		} n/k as usual.	/a
	3.2.17			/a
	4.2.17			/a
	5.2.17		Handed over work in H.2 Sector to the 61st Field Coy. R.E. Commenced filling in Motoria RONVILLE-BEURAINS ROAD. & new dug out in RAILWAY STATION YARD.	/a
	6.2.17		Coy. moved into new billets in the RUE JEANNE D'ARC. n/k as usual. Soho for her M.T.M.E.P. again visited n/k as usual Div. M.T.M.O.	/a
	7.2.17		C.R.E. visited AREAS. Coy. recommenced work on Bath H.Q. dug out near HOLBORN n/k in which party from 143rd Inf. Bde. attho' in 42nd Inf. Bar. Coca Soho for n/k. H.T.M.E.P. again visited n/k Div. H.T.M.O. Captain Alexander returned from leave to England. to take on command of the Company. H.T.M. ammunition called for in HAYMARKET.	/a
	8.2.17		Captain Alexander took on command of the Company. Arrangements made with O.C. 44th Field Ambulance for commencement of work on new RONVILLE dressing station, and ambulance road across railway on 9.2.17. Work on new dugouts in Railway station yard stopped - no labour or material available.	/a

Army Form C. 2118.

WAR DIARY
or
INTELLIGENCE SUMMARY

(Erase heading not required.)

89th Field Coy R.E.

Place	Date	Hour	Summary of Events and Information	Remarks and references to Appendices
ARRAS	9.2.17		Commenced work in Ambulance Road across Railway and Ronville Dressing Station.	A/G
	10.2.17		O.C. arranged for shingling 2 cellars & making 1 dugout for 14th Divn Signals.	A/G
	11.2.17		Work commenced as above. O.C. arranged for commenced work on 4 M.T.M. Battery positions + 6 H.T.M. gun positions with A Coy 11th Kings (Pioneers) and T.M. officers concerned.	A/G
	12.2.17		Work commenced as above. Major E.O. Alabaster returned from course and took over Command of Coy. New communication trench (HORNE ST) taped out with B.G.C. 43rd Inf. Bde.	A/G
	13.2.17		Work as usual.	A/G
	14.2.17		O.C. arranged for commenced trench as to full 4 M.T.M. Battery position with B Coy 11th Kings Pioneers.	A/G
	15.2.17		Work commenced as above.	A/G
	16.2.17		Major E.O. Alabaster evacuated sick from Divn area. Capt E.D Alexander in command. C.R.E. visited Station.	A/G
	17.2.17		Work as usual.	A/G
	18.2.17		ditto	A/G

Army Form C. 2118.

WAR DIARY
or
INTELLIGENCE SUMMARY
(Erase heading not required.)

89th Field Coy R.E.

89 (FIELD) COMPANY
28 FEB. 1917
ROYAL ENGINEERS

Place	Date	Hour	Summary of Events and Information	Remarks and references to Appendices
ARRAS.	19.2.17		Work in hand: Rest Bays dugout in support line: 9 M.T.M. Battery position; work in Patrol Line; 13 H.T.M. positions: advanced dressing station Ronville; Narrow gauge on Railway yard: Strengthening cellars & making dugout on Cable line for signals; filling in 3 collapsed caves in Ronville-Beaurains Road: Returning 2 tunnels under abutments of Rly bridge on Ronville-Beaurains Road.	
	20.2.17		Work continued as above	
	21.2.17		Ditto.	
	22.2.17		Ditto.	
	23.2.17		Ditto. Chief Engineer VII Corps & C.R.E. inspected various work in hand.	
	24.2.17		Work as usual	
	25.2.17		do	
	26.2.17		do	
	27.2.17		All T.M. positions in H₁ subsector handed over to O.C. 466th Field Coy R.E. 46th Division.	
	28.2.17		Relief of 14th Division by 46th Division in H₁ subsector cancelled.	

WAR DIARY or INTELLIGENCE SUMMARY

Army Form C. 2118.

89 (FIELD) COMPANY ROYAL ENGINEERS — 31 MAR. 1917

89th Field Coy (A.S.) — March 1917

Vol 19

Place	Date	Hour	Summary of Events and Information	Remarks and references to Appendices
ARRAS	1.3.17		Coy working on Reutel Hqrs dugout in support line; Ronville Baumann Rd; Ambulance Roadways; Railway Yard; Advance Dressing Station in Ronville and at Huilerie; Achicourt Road; Signal Dugouts on Bruised Cable line. Machine & Heavy Trench Mortar Positions on H Sector. Reinforced concrete slab over bridge at Achicourt. Ammunition in ARRAS	
	2.3.17		Work continued as above	
	3.3.17		Do.	
	4.3.17		Do.	
	5.3.17		Do. Major E.D. Alabaster R.E. returned from hospital & took over command of Coy.	
	6.3.17		Work proceeding normally. C.R.E. visited by & arranged for special explosive charges for use in a raid. O.C. visited work on Ambulance Road, HUILERIE at RONVILLE D.S.A.	
	7.3.17		Orders received to take on T.M. work from HOPE ST & HULLUCH ST. Arrangements made & estimate of time with exact labour to do. O.C. visited Bn Battle Hr. Centre at night Bn Hr.; Caves and running T.M. between HAVANNAH ST & METSOS ST.	

Army Form C. 2118.

WAR DIARY
or
INTELLIGENCE SUMMARY

(Erase heading not required.)

Instructions regarding War Diaries and Intelligence Summaries are contained in F. S. Regs., Part II. and the Staff Manual respectively. Title Pages will be prepared in manuscript.

[Stamp: 88 (FIELD) COMPANY ROYAL ENGINEERS 31 MAR. 1917]

Place	Date	Hour	Summary of Events and Information	Remarks and references to Appendices
ARRAS	8.3.17.		Work progressing on T.M. positions, Signal Stations, Batt. HQ, and Dressing Stations, at Road bridges.	EOM
	9.3.17.		Party of 6th KOYLI instructed in the method of firing Bangalore torpedoes. 2Cpl GRIERSON, a/2Cpl SLAUGHTER, Spr DOVER, LEADBITTER, STAMP, STOCKTON volunteers for raid at gun Coy of KOYLI. to be engaged. Instructions received regarding procedure of work on T.M. positions.	EOM
	10.3.17.		Work proceeding normally.	OM
	11.3.17.		O.C. visited T.M. positions in H1 Sector with O.C. 11th KINGS. Arrangements made for employing 20 men from 2nd Div. M.T.M. Battery at 68th H.T.M.B. Plouvière shelled.	OM
	12.3.17.		Spr STAMP killed, Spr DOVER deafened, Spr STOCKTON wounded, in raid. Capt LEATHAM 6th KOYLI i/c raid wrote acknowledging splendid work of R.E. party. C.R.E. calls for hands in own report of H.1. Sector by 6th –. ARRAS shelled at intervals. Instructions received to be prepared to demolish PENICOURT Mill. No 19473 Corpl J. EVANS awarded ITALIAN Bronze Medal for Military Valour.	OM

Army Form C. 2118.

WAR DIARY
or
INTELLIGENCE SUMMARY
(Erase heading not required.)

143.

Instructions regarding War Diaries and Intelligence Summaries are contained in F. S. Regs., Part II and the Staff Manual respectively. Title Pages will be prepared in manuscript.

[Stamp: 68 (FIELD) COMPANY * ROYAL ENGINEERS * 81 MAR. 1917]

Place	Date	Hour	Summary of Events and Information	Remarks and references to Appendices
ARRAS	13.3.17.		Work proceeding normally. Hostile shelling changed zone finished T.M. position.	072.
	14.3.17.		B.G.C. 43rd Bde congratulates party of 89th Fld Coy who took part in raid.	60p.
			C.R.E. 14. Divn. visits Company at warns us to be prepared to hand over our work in H1 Sector on 16.3.17.	
	15.3.17.		O.C. & Lt Col EGAN. R.A.M.C. reconnoitred additional requirements in the way of dressing stations.	50p.
			C.R.E. warns that 1 Section of 89th on Divisional work will be relieved by 1 Section of 61st in a few days.	
	16.3.17.		Work in H1 Sector handed over to 513th F.d.Coy.	
			O.C. 61st undertakes to carry on work demolition of ACHICOURT mill &c.	52p.
			D.T.M.O. & C.T.M.O. ask for extra work on T.M. positions, informed that we must find labor if R.E. may assist.	
	17.3.17.		Arrange for maintenance of T.M. positions.	52p.
			Lt Q.M. PRESCOTT arrived	

Army Form C. 2118.

WAR DIARY
or
INTELLIGENCE SUMMARY
(Erase heading not required.)

Instructions regarding War Diaries and Intelligence Summaries are contained in F.S. Regs., Part II. and the Staff Manual respectively. Title Pages will be prepared in manuscript.

144

Stamp: 89 (FIELD) COMPANY ROYAL ENGINEERS 31 MAR. 1917

Place	Date	Hour	Summary of Events and Information	Remarks and references to Appendices
ARRAS	18.3.17.		Heavy shelling by our guns early. No reply.	
		11 a.m.	Warned not to send out any more parties.	
		1 p.m.	Company concentrating at billets and standing to, preparing to work on roads.	
		2.15 p.m.	No. 3 Section sent to complete ACHICOURT bridge.	
		9.00 p.m.	No. 4 Section sent to bridge trenches on RONVILLE - BEAURAINS up to our front line under 2/Lt WALKER.	
		11.30 p.m.	No 1 and 2 Sections sent to assist No. 4, without officers.	App.
	19.3.17	5.00 a.m.	Bridges on RONVILLE - BEAURAINS road complete in spite of very heavy shelling. S/t WHITE, 2/Lt SIMS, Saprs. GODDARD, FRY, BROOKER, Pnr GRAHAM wounded.	
		6.30 a.m.	No. 3 Sect sent to ACHICOURT bridge.	
			Officers reconnoitre roads of BEAURAINS and brickfields during the day. 2/Lt G. WALKER recommended for immediate award.	
		5.00 p.m.	No. 2 Sect sent to complete visual station in HETSAS and Reserve Line, and entrances to dugout in support line near HOLBORN	App.
	20.3.17.		Company employed on RONVILLE - BEAURAINS road. Lt MOWBRAY reconnoitres wells in BEAURAINS. O.C. and Lt ALLAN remove German mines placed near dugout entrances. Sapr LEADBITTER awarded Military Medal.	App.

WAR DIARY or INTELLIGENCE SUMMARY

Army Form C. 2118.

Place	Date	Hour	Summary of Events and Information	Remarks and references to Appendices
ARRAS	21.3.17		Nos 1 and 2 Sections with P. Coy Special Bde R.E. salvaging material from Trenchwork on hill near MAISERSTELLUNG and PRUSSIAN WAY.	
			Nos 3 and 6 Sections took 2 parties of 80 men each from 1st & 2nd East Lancs near ARRAS front BEAURAINS.	EOP
			S/C WHITE reconnoitred for immediate work.	
	22.3.17		Work the same as on 21st except:	
			Lt. PRESCOTT and LLEWELYN made NET bayonets near front line.	
			No. 4 Section caught by shellfire in RONVILLE. Shelled(?) by enemy, casualties: Lc.Cpl MITCHELL, L.Cpl COLEY, Sprs ANDERSON, E.DURSTON, J.JONES, LITTLE killed. Sprs PASSMORE, ACKRILL, ROBINSON wounded. Sprs LYNN, HIGGINS shell concussion.	EOP
	23.3.17		No 2 and P. Coy and battalion pioneers complete Rackebonding PRUSSIAN WAY to front line, and start trenchboard factory at Bde dump in RONVILLE.	
			No 3 & two reliefs of No 80 men each cleaning BEAURAINS road.	
			No 4 & two parties of 42 & 83rd start preparing footpath from front across to new front line in order to shell RONVILLE.	
			No 1 & Lt PRESCOTT & LLEWELYN topped out more assault trenches. Work also on Bde HQ in CHRISTCHURCH CAVE and dugout for RAMC on old German front line. Spr PASSMORE died of wounds received on 22nd.	EOP

WAR DIARY or INTELLIGENCE SUMMARY

Army Form C. 2118.

Place	Date	Hour	Summary of Events and Information	Remarks and references to Appendices
ARRAS	24.3.17		Infantry back from front trenches RONVILLE to top end of RONVILLE completed. Road for guns in No MAN'S LAND from road to road made. BOUDHA & CHRISTCHURCH CAVE completed. Work on BERCORIN'S Road and trackhead fully continuing. Lts LLEWELLYN and PRESCOTT before out on rds coming parties. Tramcars & Presents shunted up Bouchavesnes trackway from new shaft where Capt WARREN & Sgt ROSE who operate Bouchavesnes & Sgt GRIERSON who takes the air to the Sylvan camps arrived.	
	25.3.17		O.C. sent 4/5 Inf Bn about work. No one thing is worth note. tracks, roads, trackheads, dugouts are complete. B shafts started from new pit 3ft – No 1 talent to Bhs.	
	26.3.17		Work continuing as on 25th. up RONVILLE BEAURAINS Rd Trackway is making naturals extension approach track to shaft RONVILLE. Sjt J S WHITE awarded Military Medal. Orders received to take over R. E. Park.	

Army Form C. 2118.

WAR DIARY
or
INTELLIGENCE SUMMARY
(Erase heading not required.)

Instructions regarding War Diaries and Intelligence Summaries are contained in F. S. Regs., Part II and the Staff Manual respectively. Title Pages will be prepared in manuscript.

88 (FIELD) COMPANY
31 MAR 1917
ROYAL ENGINEERS

Place	Date	Hour	Summary of Events and Information	Remarks and references to Appendices
ARRAS	27.3.17		Handed over RONVILLE - BEAURAINS C.6.2.F&G. up to this point.	
			Road practically labour work.	
			Arranged to complete trench boards KRIEGERSTELLUNG + 28.3.17.	
			up for 81st F.Co to take over schedules of Engineer work	
			on 29.3.17.	
	28.3.17		No.4 Section made up to full strength by taking skilled men from	
			other Sections so as to take on R.E. Park on 28.3.17	
			Company having suffered heavier % of casualties than any other unit	
			in Division is to be taken out of the line to refit.	V.G.O
			O.C. takes C.R.E. to see Decauville track near GROUPE DESMAISONS, BUCQUOY ROAD, BARRUME	
			Road through BEAURAINS, Infantry track West of RONVILLE.	
			2/Lt G. WALKER with No.4 Section take over DAINVILLE R.E. Park.	
ARRAS cont.			Neighbourhood of billets heavily shelled during evening. Sjt EVANS & Sjt WEBB did very	S.O.P
			good work in attending to wounded under fire. None of our men hurt.	
DAINVILLE	29.3.17		Wagons left at Riding School on previous night loaded up by means of hand cart.	E.G.O
			All men & vehicles clear of ARRAS by 4.30 p.m. No casualties.	
			Company in billets in DAINVILLE by 5.30 p.m.	

Army Form C. 2118.

No 48.

WAR DIARY
or
INTELLIGENCE SUMMARY
(Erase heading not required.)

Instructions regarding War Diaries and Intelligence Summaries are contained in F. S. Regs., Part II. and the Staff Manual respectively. Title Pages will be prepared in manuscript.

68 (FIELD) COMPANY 68 * ROYAL ENGINEERS *
31 MAR 1917

Place	Date	Hour	Summary of Events and Information	Remarks and references to Appendices
DAINVILLE	30.3.17.		No 4 Section moving R.E. Park. Remainder of company fixing up billets in the morning, kit and equipment inspection & respirator drill in afternoon.	EOA.
	31.3.17.		Physical Training, Squad drill, guard duties, rifle exercises, musketry. Sjt WHITE interviews G.O.C. 14th Divn with a view to R.E. commission.	EOA.

F. O. Alabaster
Major R.E.
O.C. 89th Fld Cy R.E.

14/W.
14 JU 20
(FIELD) COMPANY
30 APR. 1917
ROYAL ENGINEERS

Army Form C. 2118.

WAR DIARY
or
INTELLIGENCE SUMMARY

(Erase heading not required.)

89th Fld Coy R.E.

April 1917

Place	Date	Hour	Summary of Events and Information	Remarks and references to Appendices
DAINVILLE	1-4-17.		Company resting	E29
	2.4.17		No. 4 Section R.E. Park.	
			No. 1 " Bombing } in morning. First aid in afternoon.	
			Nos. 2 + 3 " Pontoon drill }	
			O.C. takes NCO's and runners in map reading.	
			2/Lt. G. WALKER awarded Military Cross	
			O.C. sees C.R.E. and is informed of general situation. 89th Coy to be in reserve in DAINVILLE works out harbour officer work and assembly Brigade	
	3.4.17		No. 4 Sect RE Park	E29
			No. 2 " Bombing	
			No. 1+3 " Taping out strong points } Also infantry covering	
			O.C. visits B.G.RE 42nd & 43rd Inf Bdes concerning harbour officers	
	4.4.17.		Bombardment commences 7. a.m.	E29
			No. 4 Sect R.E. Park	
			No. 1 " Pontoon drill	
			No. 2 " Taping out strong points	
			No. 3 " Bombing	
			2.T. MOORE arrived 11.30 p.m.	

WAR DIARY
or
INTELLIGENCE SUMMARY
(Erase heading not required.)

Instructions regarding War Diaries and Intelligence Summaries are contained in F.S. Regs., Part II. and the Staff Manual respectively. Title Pages will be prepared in manuscript.

Place	Date	Hour	Summary of Events and Information	Remarks and references to Appendices
DAINVILLE	5.4.17.		Nº 4. R.E. Park.	
			Nº 1 } Weldon trestle drill	
			Nº 2 }	
			Nº 3. Hutting.	
		3.00 p.m.	Nº 2 proceeds to ARRAS to fix up wiring for R.A. Horses.	
	6.4.17.		Nº 4. R.E. Park.	
			Nº 1 & 2. Making of charges.	
			3. Weldon Trestle drill	
			C.R.E. warns that Sappers and some transport will certainly move to bivouac near GROUPE DES MAISONS for Y, Z, Z+1, Z+2, Z+3 days.	
			A few shells in DAINVILLE on CCS entering.	
	7.4.17.		62nd Fld Coy start taking over R.E. Park.	
			62nd Fld Coy take over R.E. Park.	
	8.4.17		2nd Lt ALLAN proceeds to 42nd Fld. Hqrs as R.E. Liaison Officer.	
			2nd Lt WALKER " " 43rd " " "	
		6 p.m.	O.C. + 2 Lts LLEWELYN + MOWBRAY, 10 sections and 1 tool cart, 1 Forge cart + 3 Pedr. Wagons proceed to bivouac near GROUPE DES MAISONS. Remainder of Coy + transport arrived at DAINVILLE. Bivouac shelled at night, transport somewhat.	

… (FIELD) COMPY
Army Form C.N.2118.
30 APR 1917
ROYAL ENGINEERS

WAR DIARY
or
INTELLIGENCE SUMMARY
(Erase heading not required.)

Instructions regarding War Diaries and Intelligence Summaries are contained in F.S. Regs., Part II. and the Staff Manual respectively. Title Pages will be prepared in manuscript.

Place	Date	Hour	Summary of Events and Information	Remarks and references to Appendices
GROUPE DES MAISONS	9.4.17		Zero hr 14th Divn 7.34 am. Coy in reserve. Arthurson killed during morning; 1 driver wounded (at duty); 2 Spr HAMILTON badly wounded; 2/Lt ALLAN & WALKER act as Liaison officers with attacking brigade.	S.T.R.
	10.4.17		Company employed on Sunken Road, making track passable for enemy. O.C. ad L. MOWBRAY endeavours to enter WANCOURT to reconnoitre water supplies; village however not captured.	S.T.R.
	11.4.17		Company concentrates at bivouacs near Groupe des Maisons.	S.T.R.
	12.4.17		Company employed on Sunken Road. Orders received regarding relief; Lt MOWBRAY proceeds to DAINVILLE & DAINVILLE for billets.	S.T.R.
		6.00 p.m.	Work handed over to 7th FLD COY R.E., and whole company withdrawn to DAINVILLE.	S.T.R.
DAINVILLE	13.4.17	9.30 am	Company marched out of DAINVILLE.	S.T.R.
		1.30 p.m.	Company arrived at GIVENCHY LE NOBLE.	S.T.R.
GIVENCHY LE NOBLE	14.4.17	7.45 am	Company marched out of GIVENCHY LE NOBLE.	S.T.R.
		10.00 am	Company arrived SUS ST LEGER	S.T.R.
SUS ST LEGER	15.4.17		Overhauling kits, and cleaning up. C.R.E. visits company and directs overhaul of equipment. BGC RA of 42nd Inf Bde & ADMS. thank R.E. Coys for good work.	S.T.R.

WAR DIARY or INTELLIGENCE SUMMARY

(Erase heading not required.)

Place	Date	Hour	Summary of Events and Information	Remarks and references to Appendices
SUS ST LEGER	16.4.17		Physical Training, Sanitation, and overhaul of vehicles and tools.	/es
	17.4.17		Overhaul of equipment and packing up by H.Q. & Sections. Weather bad.	/es
	18.4.17		Section training under Section Officers, particular attention to discipline.	/es
	19.4.17		No 1. Taping, No 3 Drill, No 2 Welden trestle, No 4 Ponton.	/es
	20.4.17		Half holiday. G.O.C. 14th Divn visits Company.	/es
	21.4.17		No 1 & 3. Welden trestle and Ponton. No 2 & 4 Taping and Drill.	/es
	22.4.17		No 1 Drill, No 3 Taping, No 2 Ponton, No 4 Welden Trestle. Half holiday, football enter ½ Company.	/es
	22.4.17.		Church Parade and painting.	/es
BAVINCOURT	23.4.17		Coy moved to huts at BAVINCOURT in afternoon	/es
	24.4.17		Coy moved to billets at BASSEUX in morning	/es
BASSEUX	25.4.17		Coy took over from 447th Field Coy R.E. in line. Coy marched from BASSEUX at 4.30 p.m. Transport and No 4 Section bivouaced in Gully at BEAURAINS. O.C. and Nos 1, 2, 3 Sections bivouaced at TELEGRAPH HILL.	/es

WAR DIARY
or
INTELLIGENCE SUMMARY

(Erase heading not required.)

Army Form C. 2118.

Instructions regarding War Diaries and Intelligence Summaries are contained in F.S. Regs., Part II and the Staff Manual respectively. Title Pages will be prepared in manuscript.

No. 153

Stamp: 9 FIELD COMPANY, 30 APR. 1917, ROYAL ENGINEERS

Place	Date	Hour	Summary of Events and Information	Remarks and references to Appendices
TELEGRAPH HILL	26.4.17		Nos 1, 2 & 3 Sections constructing shelters for infantry in Square N.15 (W of WANCOURT). No.4 Section Salving materials in BEAURAINS.	
	27.4.17		Nos 1 & 2 Section working on shelters in N.15. Nos 3 & 4 on Advanced Divn Hqrs and W² Bdl Hqrs in N.7.d.	
	28.4.17		Nos 1 & 2 Sections working on shelters in N.15. No. 3 Section on Adv. Divn Hqrs in N.7.d. No. 4 Section with 1 Battn Infantry constructing duy weather tracks along TILLOY BEAURAINS Road and from Adv. Divn Hqrs forward towards WANCOURT. Transport carting stores from dump to RONVILLE SCIERIE & from Divn R.E. dump on TILLOY - WANCOURT Road at N.15.b.4.3.	
	29.4.17		Nos 1, 2 & 3 Sections as above. No. 4 and 100 Infy continuing track towards WANCOURT Transport as above.	
	30.4.17		Work on 6.ᵗʰ 29.4.17	

[Signature] Capt. RE
for O.C. 9ᵗʰ Field Coy
30.4.17

WAR DIARY
INTELLIGENCE SUMMARY

89th Field Coy R.E.

MAY 1917

Place	Date	Hour	Summary of Events and Information	Remarks and references to Appendices
TELEGRAPH HILL	1.5.17		Nos 1, 2 & 3 Section working on Infantry Shelters in N.15.	R.E.
			No 4 Section making a Infantry Track from Telegraph Hill to Copse Ravine near WANCOURT.	
	2.5.17		Nos 1-3 Sections working on Shelters.	R.E.
			No 4 Section completed Infantry Track.	
			No 2 Section with 5" Porlons & 20 pack animals took barbed wire + pickets and formed dump at O.19.c.7.7 ready for operation on following day. Concertina shelters including gas shelters in casualties bays were slightly affected by gas.	
	3.5.17		Zero 3.45 a.m. 4th & 12th Divn B'des attacking.	R.E.
			O.C. at Advanced Hd Qrs Hqts 1 P.m.	
			Coy moved to black at N.14.d.9.5. at 2 P.m.	
			Coy moved off by Sections at above intervals at 10.30 P.m. to start a wire in front of PANTHER Trench in O.19.b. Very heavy Shelling due to renewed attacks on right + left. Sgt Peel came in from valley. Work completed. Casualties 1 OR Killed 3 ORs wounded. Section returned to dugouts independently	

1577 Wt.W10791/1773 500,000 1/15 D.D.&L. A.D.S.S./Forms/C. 2118.

Army Form C. 2118.

WAR DIARY
or
INTELLIGENCE SUMMARY.
(Erase heading not required.)

Place	Date	Hour	Summary of Events and Information	Remarks and references to Appendices
TELEGRAPH HILL	4.5.17		Coy resting.	
	5.5.17		Nos 1 and 2 Sections reconnoitring & pegging out new communication trench above COJEUL VALLEY West and south of WANCOURT.	
			No 3 Section laying out new front line trench.	
			No 4 Section salving material in BEAURAINS.	
			Sgt Evans wounded.	
	6.5.17		No 4 Section and 104 infantry salving trench stores from PREUSSEN WEG, collecting material. Smoking trench boards near WANCOURT.	
			Nos 1 and 2 Sections and infantry laying out and digging new C.T. across COJEUL VALLEY.	
			No 3 Section resting.	
	7.5.17		Nos 1 and 2 Sections and infantry continuing digging of new C.T.	
			No 3 Section constructing advanced Batt. H.Q.	
			No 4 Section salving trench boards in BEAURAINS with 80 infantry.	

Army Form C. 2118.

WAR DIARY
or
INTELLIGENCE SUMMARY.
(Erase heading not required.)

Place	Date	Hour	Summary of Events and Information	Remarks and references to Appendices
TELEGRAPH HILL	8.5.17		Nos 1, 2, 3 and 4 Sections on C.T. for 7.5.17.	R/a
	9.5.17		2/Lt. WALKER taped out new C.T. SHIKAR LANE.	R/a
			Nos 1, 3 and 4 Sections on for 8.5.17.	
			No 2 resting	
			2/Lt G WALKER left Coy to take up duties of Assistant Adjutant to C.R.E.	
	10.5.17		Nos 1 2 3 + 4 continue works	R/a
	11.5.17		do.	R/a
	12.5.17		do.	R/a
	13.5.17		do. Spr. BIDDICK (No 2) Killed.	R/a
	14.5.17		do.	R/a
			Coy relieved in front line by 61st Field Coy R.E. Coy taken over work on CORPS LINE West + South of HANCOURT.	
	15.5.17		No 4 Section working on removal of 18"town Hqrs to new site for 14 "train. Remainder of Coy reconnoitring new works.	R/a
	16.5.17		Nos 1 and 2 Sections constructing dugouts in CORPS LINE. No 3 Section erecting low wire in front of CORPS LINE No 4 Section as for 15.5.17	R/a

1577 Wt.W10791/1773 500,000 1/15 D.D.&L. A.D.S.S./Forms/C. 2118.

Army Form C. 2118.

WAR DIARY
or
INTELLIGENCE SUMMARY.
(Erase heading not required.)

Place	Date	Hour	Summary of Events and Information	Remarks and references to Appendices
TELEGRAPH HILL	17.5.17		As for 16.5.17 except No 2 Section detailing wire in front of CORPS LINE in addition to No 3.	
	18.5.17		Do.	
	19.5.17		Do. Lc Brooks & Spr Carter killed.	
	20.5.17		Do. CAPT. E. D. ALEXANDER and Sergt J. EVANS "mentioned in despatches".	
	21.5.17		Work as for 20.5.17	
	22.5.17		Do.	
	23.5.17		Do.	
	24.5.17		No 2 Section taken on R.E. Park DAINVILLE from 62nd Field Coy RE. Remainder of Coy as for 23.5.17	
	25.5.17		Do.	
	26.5.17		Do.	
	27.5.17		Do.	
	28.5.17		Do.	
	29.5.17		Do.	
	30.5.17		Do.	
	31.5.17		Do.	

CONFIDENTIAL.

14th Division "A".

      Herewith the War Diary for the month of June '17 of the 89th Field Coy. R.E.

3.7.17.

                       Lieut-Colonel. R.E.
                       C. R. E. 14th Division.

Army Form C. 2118.

WAR DIARY
or
INTELLIGENCE SUMMARY.

(Erase heading not required.)

156

JUNE 1917

Place	Date	Hour	Summary of Events and Information	Remarks and references to Appendices
TELEGRAPH HILL	1.6.17		No 1 Section working on strong points & in CORPS LINE.	
			No 3 Section ditto	
			No 2 Section at RE workshops DAINVILLE	
			No 4 Section working on new R.E. Park, Divn Hqrs. Baths VC	A/c
	2.6.17		ditto	
	3.6.17		Coy moves to billets in old trenches near at N20.b.6.6. Sheet 51.B.S.W.	A/c
			East of NEUVILLE VITASSE. Transport remains at BEAURAINS.	
			Cap. returns 52nd Seed Coy R.E. in front line & is attached to 45th Divn Retn.	
NEUVILLE VITASSE	4.6.17		Sgt Moxted, D.C.M. & D/W. Williams killed by shellfire in BEAURAINS.	E/22
			Day-spent chiefly in reconnaissance.	
			Lt. Col. COLLINS, D.S.O., new C.R.E. visits camp.	
	5.6.17		Company employed as infantry & 2 two sections in the line, relieving reserve line & others in support line.	E/22
			O by 4 B.M. 43rd Bde sent round all the Bde front	
	6.6.17		not progressing normally.	E/22
			Warning order about probable move received.	

1577 Wt.W10791/1773 500,000 1/15 D. D. & L.   A.D.S.S./Forms/C. 2118.

Army Form C. 2118.

WAR DIARY
or
INTELLIGENCE SUMMARY.
(Erase heading not required.)

Place	Date	Hour	Summary of Events and Information	Remarks and references to Appendices
NEUVILLE VITASSE	7.6.17		O.C. Coy takes C.R.E. 18th Divn round front, support and reserve lines.	
	8.6.17		Work proceeding normally	
			Work continuing on dugouts in support line and reclaiming of reserve line. C.R.E. gives general instructions about coming rest. Training in morning drill, gymnastics at Weldon trestle.	
"	9.6.17.		Advance party of 56th Divn Fld Coy arrive. Transport move from BEAURAINS to NEUVILLE-VITASSE.	
	10.6.17		O.C. takes 56th Divn officer round left sector. 14th Divn handed over left sector by 6 a.m.; O.C. select site for bivouac from 11:15 till 13:5, near BEAURAINS. All work opened up by 11.30 p.m. and parties return to bivouac.	
	11.6.17		Coy move to AGNY and bivouacs.	
AGNY	12.6.17		Coy resting	
"	13.6.17	4.30 am	Coy moves with 43rd Infy Bde Group to BEAUMETZ.	

Army Form C. 2118.

WAR DIARY
or
INTELLIGENCE SUMMARY.
(Erase heading not required.)

Instructions regarding War Diaries and Intelligence Summaries are contained in F. S. Regs., Part II. and the Staff Manual respectively. Title pages will be prepared in manuscript.

"60"

Place	Date	Hour	Summary of Events and Information	Remarks and references to Appendices
BEAUMETZ	14.6.17	4 am	Coy moves to SAULTY.	
SAULTY	15.6.17	4 am	Coy moves to AUTHIE	
AUTHIE	16.6.17		Coy parade in full marching order. R.E. Inspection CRE took Coy. Major E.O. ALABASTER proceeds on leave to ENGLAND. CAPT. E.D. ALEXANDER in command. Fatigues - cleaning vehicles &c.	
	17.6.17		Range practice at THIÈVRES	
	18.6.17		do	
	19.6.17		Close order drill	
	20.6.17		do	
	21.6.17		do	
	22.6.17		Full marching order inspection by CRE	
	23.6.17		Church Parade	
	24.6.17		Range practice at THIÈVRES.	
	25.6.17			
	26.6.17		Divisional Horse Show	

Army Form C. 2118.

WAR DIARY
or
INTELLIGENCE SUMMARY.

(Erase heading not required.)

16/

Place	Date	Hour	Summary of Events and Information	Remarks and references to Appendices
AUTHIE	27.6.17		Preparing to move. Lt. MOORE & advance party leave for BEAUQUESNES	/Px
	28.6.17		Coy marches to SAULTY. Entrained at 12.15 p.m. Left at 4 p.m. MAJOR B.O. ALABASTER returns from leave	/Px
BAILLEUL	29.6.17		Coy detrained at midnight, marches to CLARE CAMP near LOCRE. CRE IX Corps visits Coy & gives instructions for work. Coy to work on Corps Line between and in front of MESSINES and WYTSCHAETE. Lt. J.C. ALLAN I/AR. left for England on leave for India Coy marches to Aysette. Transport at BUS FARM nr. KEMMEL - NEUNEEGLISE Road.	/Px /Px
SHAMUS DUGOUTS on WOLVERGHEM - WYTSCHAETE Road	30.6.17	10 am	Reconnaissance in evening	

WAR DIARY
or
INTELLIGENCE SUMMARY.
(Erase heading not required.)

89th FLD COY R.E.   Army Form C. 2118.

JULY 1917.   Vol 23

Place	Date	Hour	Summary of Events and Information	Remarks and references to Appendices
SHAMUS DUGOUTS WULVERGHEM — WYTSCHAETE ROAD	1.7.17		Nos 1 & 2 Sections under Lt MOORE and Nos 3 & 4 Sectn under Lt MOWBRAY working on CORPS LINE on east slope of MESSINES Ridge. Work:- draining, levelling & handshaking section of the line.	ktr
	2.7.17		BD. Company canteen started.	ktr
	3.7.17		AOD:- Five Officers and 120 O.R. of 8th EAST LANCASHIRE Regt reported as a permanent working party. (37 train.) Two platoons detailed for work with LT MOORE and two with LT MOWBRAY.	ktr
	4.7.17		Work continued on Ridge Defences in two sections of about 200' each.	op
	5.7.17		O.C. & O'i/c Working /parts reconnoitre Corps Line & decide to make one front line before starting support line.	op
	6.7.17		C.R.E. 14" Divn & C.R.E. IX Corps Troops visit company, former will try hand to obtain more officers.	op
	7.7.17		O.C. selects Southern strong front & reconnoitres were generally. St LOCKE wounded.	op
	8.7.17		O.R.'s conference of Fld Cy C.O's regarding redistribution of work. Shortage of officers to be taken up by C.R.E.	op

Army Form C. 2118.

WAR DIARY
or
INTELLIGENCE SUMMARY.
(Erase heading not required.)

No. 163.

Instructions regarding War Diaries and Intelligence Summaries are contained in F. S. Regs., Part II. and the Staff Manual respectively. Title pages will be prepared in manuscript.

Place	Date	Hour	Summary of Events and Information	Remarks and references to Appendices
SHAMUS DUG-OUTS	9.7.17		2/Lt PAGET joined by 62nd & 89th.	App.
	10.7.17		Work on new sector started. Noisy night.	App.
	11.7.17		Work continued; 2/Lts SCALES, SYDENHAM, SMITH, LORD wounded.	App.
	12.7.17		2/Lt (acting Capt) L.G.M. LYON, R.E.T.F. wounded, being posted as Lieut.	App.
	13.7.17		CAPT. E.D. ALEXANDER proceeded on leave.	App.
	14.7.17		Work continued normally.	App.
	15.7.17		2/Lt DEVERAL R.E.T.C. reported for duty.	App.
	16.7.17		8th EAST LANCS working party relieved by 7th R.B.	App.
	17.7.17		Work proceeding normally.	App.
	17.7.17		A.D.W.S. Corps inspected animals. Satisfactory.	App.
	18.7.17		Very little work done owing to heavy rain.	App.

Army Form C. 2118.

WAR DIARY
or
INTELLIGENCE SUMMARY.
(Erase heading not required.)

Instructions regarding War Diaries and Intelligence Summaries are contained in F.S. Regs. Part II. and the Staff Manual respectively. Title pages will be prepared in manuscript.

Place	Date	Hour	Summary of Events and Information	Remarks and references to Appendices
SHRAPNEL Dugouts	19.7.17.		Work proceeding normally.	App.
	20.7.17.		ditto	App.
	21.7.17.		Baths for whole company at 62nd Fd. Coy H.Q.	App.
	22.7.17		C. Coy 7th R.B. relieved by A. Coy 7th R.B. Work unaffected.	App.
	23.7.17.		Work proceeding normally. After new employed work traces by day on finishing touches.	App.
	24.7.17		Capt. ALEXANDER returns from leave	App.
	25.7.17.		Work proceeding normally	App.
	26.7.17		Lt. MOWBRAY proceeds on leave. Warning order regarding reconnaissance of work nearer HOLLEBEKE received. Front line & Ridge Defences connected through; but a lot of work remains to be done.	App.
	27.7.17.		List of names recommended for awards sent in; L/ALLAN (I.RR) Capt. ALEXANDER, Sergt. LOOSEMORE, Corpl. GRIERSON, 2Corpl. STOCKTON	App.
	28.7.17		A. Coy 7th R.B. relieved by B. Coy 7th R.B. O.C. at Capt. ALEXANDER reconnoitre work which may be taken over from 41st Divn near THE BLUFF	App.
	29.7.17.		No infantry working; owing to early departure on 30th. Sappers employed on trimming work	App.

Army Form C. 2118.

WAR DIARY
or
INTELLIGENCE SUMMARY.
(Erase heading not required.)

165.

Place	Date	Hour	Summary of Events and Information	Remarks and references to Appendices
SIRMUS Dugouts	30.7.17		R.B. party returned to join battalion.	
WULVERGHEM			Final report on RIDGE DEFENCES, work ceasing at 4 a.m.	
			Report sent to C.R.E. on foundations of a bridge being erected near the BLUFF.	E/22
	31.7.17		Warned at 10 a.m. to get ready for a move at short notice.	
			C.R.E.'s conference 2.30 p.m. 89th Field Coy will be employed probably on back area work	E/22

J.D. Coletri
Major R.E.
O.C. 89th F.Coy R.E.
4.25 a.m. 31.7.17

Army Form C. 2118.

WAR DIARY
or
INTELLIGENCE SUMMARY.   89th FLD COY R.E.

(Erase heading not required.)

Vol 24

August 1917

Place	Date	Hour	Summary of Events and Information	Remarks and references to Appendices
SHAMUS Dugouts WULVERGHEM.	1.8.17.		Nothing special to record. Company standing by ready to move at short notice.	APP.
	2.8.17.		Heavy rain and light shelling of shelters	APP.
	3.8.17.		as for 1.8.17.	APP.
	4.8.17.		O.C. & 2/c MOORE reconnoitred site for camp near KEMMEL. 1 Rider at 1 Mate returned to Mobile Vet. going to reduction in establishment. No. 1 Section drawing RIDGE DEFENCES. Tunnel had stood well, but shows were clothed	APP.
	5.8.17.		Machine order inspection at gas helmet drill.	APP.
	6.8.17.	11.15am	Company concentrated at BUS FARM near LINDENHOEK at 10.30 a.m; no interference from enemy shelling en route Marched via DRANOUTRE, BAILLEUL, STRAZEELE & BORRE to LA BREARDE ex HAZEBROUCK – STEENWOORDE Road; camp made of tarpaulins and bridging material.	
LA BREARDA (27.V.Se.73)		8.30pm	Settled in and all ranks had a hot meal.	

Army Form C. 2118.

WAR DIARY
or
INTELLIGENCE SUMMARY.

(Erase heading not required.)

167 COMPANY ROYAL ENGINEERS

Instructions regarding War Diaries and Intelligence Summaries are contained in F.S. Regs., Part II. and the Staff Manual respectively. Title pages will be prepared in manuscript.

Place	Date	Summary of Events and Information	Remarks and references to Appendices
LA BREARDE	7.8.17	Fighting order parade. Gas helmet drill. Washing vehicles.	app
	8.8.17	Fighting order parade. Gas helmet drill. Cleaning all transport.	app
	9.8.17	Kit inspection. Gun inspection.	app
	10.8.17	Nº 1+2 Sections. Trestle bridging, gas helmet drill, rifle exercises. Nº 3+4 Sections. Route march.	app
	11.8.17	Nº 1+2 Sections. Route march. Nº 3+4 Sections. Trestle bridging, gas helmet drill, rifle exercises.	app
	12.8.17	Arms inspection and church parade.	app
	13.8.17	Practice in demolitions	app
	14.8.17	Pontoon drill in water	app
	15.8.17	Marched & bussed to RENINGHELST	app
RENINGHELST	16.8.17	Rested	app
	17.8.17	Marched to CHATEAU SEGARD, near DICKEBUSCH, took over from 5/12 F.C.Coy	app
	18.8.17	Reconnaissance of tracks near ZILLEBEKE	app
	19.8.17	Working parties cancelled owing to bombardment in early morning. Company employed on infantry track from ZILLEBEKE to ZOUAVE WOOD and on aid post in HOOGE	app

Army Form C. 2118.

WAR DIARY
or
INTELLIGENCE SUMMARY.

(Erase heading not required.)

Instructions regarding War Diaries and Intelligence Summaries are contained in F.S. Regs., Part II. and the Staff Manual respectively. Title pages will be prepared in manuscript.

169th COMPANY ROYAL ENGINEERS

Place	Date	Summary of Events and Information	Remarks and references to Appendices
CHATEAU SEGARD	20.8.17	Company employed as on 19th. Route for traffic in HOOGE reconnoitred	E/22
	21.8.17	Aid Post, HOOGE, finished. Track moved under made possible for stretchers, and esparto for infantry to frontline.	E/22
	22.8.17	Started by day owing to threat of 4.22 + 4.35"? of Gasshell.	E/22
	23.8.17	Bath house started near the RIDGE. Men shelters direct HOOGE Ridge Park. 2nd Lt. MOWBRAY, M.C. killed by shell fire in HOOGE	E/22
	24.8.17	Heavy attack by the enemy in afternoon; barrage put down on HOOGE, SANCTUARY WOOD and westward of ZILLEBEKE LAKE. Lt. MOORE with 5 of walking wounded East of ZILLEBEKE before going down at once, had for huts for ZILLEBEKE & 150 J wounded. Envy HOLLEBAY HOUSE. Parties of Parties of Parties, at night, at walk to fire on. Running up guard comping to HOOGE, front line now was not under rifle fire only while.	E/22
	25.8.17	Work on Bath Rod, HOLLEWAY HOUSE, tramways, Z.Gcave Wood as usual. 2nd Lt. McKENNA wounded by aeroplane bomb	F/22

A.5834. Wt.W4973/M687. 750,000. 8/16. D.D. & L., Ltd. Forms/C.2118/13.

Army Form C. 2118.

WAR DIARY
or
INTELLIGENCE SUMMARY.
(Erase heading not required.)

Place	Date	Hour	Summary of Events and Information	Remarks and references to Appendices
CHATEAU SEGARD	26.8.17		Coy marched to WIPPENHOEK area and camped. Coy in 42nd Bde Group.	A/A
WIPPENHOEK AREA	27.8.17		Coy raining, high wind & heavy rain - Camp flooded.	A/A
do	28.8.17		Rush work. Lt LYON & advance party proceed to new area BERTHEN. Major E.D. ALABASTER took over charge of C.R.E. Capt. R.D. ALEXANDER took Command of Coy. 2Lt L.T. MOOTE proceeds to ENGLAND on leave.	A/A
do	29.8.17		Coy marches to new area near BERTHEN & encamped at R 33 c 1.3. 217 B. OTTEWELL joined Coy from R.E. Base depot in reinforcement.	A/A
BERTHEN AREA	30.8.17		Coy inspected vehicles cleaned. Coy warned we leaving to reconnu's farm R 32 d 9.6. 7 animals done with influenza.	A/A
	31.8.17		Coy's public clean not quiet. Bernard Band played in evening at Coy HQrs.	A/A

Army Form C. 2118.

WAR DIARY
or
INTELLIGENCE SUMMARY.
(Erase heading not required.)

89TH FIELD COY R.E.

Place	Date	Hour	Summary of Events and Information	Remarks and references to Appendices
BERTHEN AREA	1.9.17		Lecture by M.O. and unpacking in toweling by Divn Bombing Officer	App
"	2.9.17		Coy moved into line - bivouacs near NEUVE EGLISE 28 T 16 a 7.8. Coy to work under C.R.E. 41st Bde in the line. Transport in NEUVE EGLISE — DRANOUTRE Road. 28 T.B.C.8.4.	App
NEUVE EGLISE	3.9.17		Officers & NCOs reconnoitred the Divn sector which comprises area between BLAUWEPOORTBEEK and RIVER DOUVE. Coy working on Mule Track from LA PETITE DOUVE FARM to WHITE SPOT COTTAGE and O.Ps. at BLAUWEN MOLEN and O 33 c.3.3	App
	4.9.17		Working party of 100 from 41st Arty Bde: work as for 3.9.17. Tramway diversion near BLAUWEN MOLEN reconnoitred.	App
	5.9.17		Work as for 4.9.17.	App
	6.9.17		Work as for previous day.	App
	7.9.17		Work on O.Ps. completed.	App
	8.9.17		Work started on repairs to Strong Points in CORPS LINE. Materials from CORPS LINE taken up.	App

WAR DIARY or INTELLIGENCE SUMMARY

Army Form C. 2118.

Place	Date	Hour	Summary of Events and Information	Remarks and references to Appendices
NEUVE EGLISE	9.9.17		Work as for previous day. Wiring of CORPS LINE interfered with by steel pins. Strengthening of Right Battn. Hqrs. at U.10.a.0.7. (Concrete construction) and construction of new Regt. Aid Post at U.10.a.1.5. (3 cwt & Corr. dugouts) taken on from 62nd Field Coy. R.E. 2nd Lt. T. MOORE returned from leave in England.	A/c
	10.9.17		MAJOR ALBASTER rejoins company from A/CRE. Work on Mule Track, Wiring Corps Line, R.A.P. and Batn. H.R. Camp shelled at 10 p.m. — 10.15 p.m. 12.15 a.m., 1.15 a.m. No harm done.	S22
	11.9.17.		O.C. took C.R.E. and C.E. VIII Corps to MESSINES RIDGE. Work as on 10.9.17, except more on wiring and more on Mule Track owing to relief of Brigade stopping working parties.	S22
	12.9.17.		Work as on 10.9.17. B.A.P. knocked by shelling.	S22
	13.9.17.		Shifted ST QUENTIN dump to LA PETITE DOUVE. Mule Track repaired and extended. Other work held up owing to storm.	S22

Army Form C. 2118.

WAR DIARY
or
INTELLIGENCE SUMMARY.

(Erase heading not required.)

172

Place	Date	Hour	Summary of Events and Information	Remarks and references to Appendices
NEUVE EGLISE	14.9.17		Work on Mule Track, Rt R.A.P., Rt Bn H.Q.	E.P.M.
	15.9.17		Work started on R.A.O.P's, one for each battery of 47" Bde R.F.A., and on shelter for R.A.M.C. personnel at relay post near Swayne's F.M. No infantry parties available except 12 men from Bn. in line. But work carried out on Mule Track and Rt R.A.P.	E.P.M.
	16.9.17		Work continued on O.P's, Relay post, R.A.P., Batt HQ, Mule Track, and C.o/s Line	E.P.M.
	17.9.17		Work as on 16.9.17.	E.P.M.
	18.9.17		Work as on 17.9.17 but rather interfered with owing to artillery activity	E.P.M.
	19.9.17		Work continued normally. Some shelling near our camp, nothing damaged.	E.P.M.
	20.9.17		Relay Post and Rg.Lt R.A.P. practically finished. Recommendation of N.C.O's for New Years Honours :- Sjt LOOSEMORE, Cpl GRIERSON, Cpl GARRATT, Sjt STENT, 2nd Cpl STOCKTON.	E.P.M.

Army Form C. 2118.

WAR DIARY
or
INTELLIGENCE SUMMARY.
(Erase heading not required.)

173.

Instructions regarding War Diaries and Intelligence Summaries are contained in F. S. Regs., Part II. and the Staff Manual respectively. Title pages will be prepared in manuscript.

Place	Date	Hour	Summary of Events and Information	Remarks and references to Appendices
NEUVE EGLISE	21.9.17		Continued work on R.F.B. H.Q., with O.P.'s North of MESSINES, CORPS LINE wires and Mule Track	622
	22.9.17		As for 21.9.17. but stopped wiring. Started clearing CORPS LINE between Mule Track and HUNS WALK so as to give covered approach to sites of proposed O.P.s near HUNS WALK.	622
	23.9.17		As for 21.9.17.	622
	24.9.17.		As for 23.9.17. Officers of 62nd Fld Bg shown details of our work which they are to take over.	622
	25.9.17.		As for 23.9.17. Section Officers reconnoitred work to be taken over from 62nd Fld Bg	622
	26.9.17		No 1 Section in FANNY'S C.T. van GAPPARD.) GAPPARD GANAWAY coupled by order of No 2 } " " NEW CROSS AVENUE) Division. 4 } 3 " " Reserve line North of FANNY.	622
	27.9.17.		As for 26.9.17. Camp bombed and machine gunned by aeroplane during the evening. No harm done	622

A5834. Wt.W4973/M687. 750,000. 8/16. D. D. & L. Ltd. Forms/C.2118/13.

Army Form C. 2118.

WAR DIARY
or
INTELLIGENCE SUMMARY.
(Erase heading not required.)

174.

Place	Date	Hour	Summary of Events and Information	Remarks and references to Appendices
NEUVE EGLISE	28.9.17		Brigade relief. Attention ruits [routes] forward and of NEWCROSS AVENUE reconnoitred.	SEE
	29.9.17		Work continued as usual except one party who were caught by shelling at the dump at where Spr. PRICE was wounded.	SEE
	30.9.17		Site for two bridges over R. DOUVE reconnoitred. Work on FANNY C.T. interfered with by shelling at night fire. Cpl. GRIERSON killed, Spr. AUSTIN wounded.	SEE

J.D. Alabaster
17yr RE.
OC. 89th F.W.C, R.E.

Army Form C. 2118.

175

WAR DIARY
or
INTELLIGENCE SUMMARY.

(Erase heading not required.)

"OCTOBER, 1917"

8th (FIELD) COMPANY R.E.

Place	Date	Hour	Summary of Events and Information	Remarks and references to Appendices
NEUVE EGLISE	1-10-17		C.R.E. and G.S.O.1 visited company in afternoon and decided that (1) existing foot bridge near MOA FARM would do and (2) bridge between front lines need only be 18" wide and able to take one man at a time.	app
			Work on forward end of FANNY C.T., Reserve line North of FANNY, NEW CROSS AVENUE.	app
	2.10.17		Work as on 1.10.17., and also repairs to Signal dugout.	app
	3.10.17		Work as on 1.10.17.	app
	4.10.17		Light bridge thrown over R. DOUVE in NO MAN'S LAND, by N°4 Section under supervision of O.C. and 4th EN DEVERELL. Not a hitch or a casualty.	app
	5.10.17		Work staircase as on 1.10.17. Orders received at 4.30p.m. to be ready to move at 12 hrs notice. All working parties cancelled.	app
	6.10.17		Capt. ALEXANDER and about 17 men left behind to do maintenance work at hand over to incoming unit. Remainder of company marched to WESTOUTRE.	app
DICKEBUSCH	7.10.17		Marched to DICKEBUSCH, & took over work at camp from 222nd Fld Co. Orders were to shift camp to near BELLEGOED FM; but weather if falling out to shift was not made.	app

Army Form C. 2118.

176

WAR DIARY
or
INTELLIGENCE SUMMARY.

(Erase heading not required.)

OCTOBER 1917

89 (FIELD) COMPANY
31 OCT 1917
ROYAL ENGINEERS

Place	Date	Hour	Summary of Events and Information	Remarks and references to Appendices
DICKEBUSCH	8.10.17		Work on PLUMER'S DRIVE, plank road. Quiet morning, but kind of afternoon. CAPT. ALEXANDER and party arrived in the afternoon.	6/22
	9.10.17		Work cancelled. Started preparing forward billets. Act/Lt LYON (R.E.T.F) to be Lt. and retain temp rank of CAPTAIN	6/22
	10.10.17		Work as on 8.10.17. Sappers CHRISTIAN & COOPER wounded.	6/22
	11.10.17		Took over work from 491st Fld Coy to the line. Work consisting of duckboard tracks near STIRLING CASTLE.	6/22
	12.10.17		Nos 1 & 2 Sections working with 43rd Inf Bde.	6/22
			Nos 3 & 4 " " making accommodation for a battalion at BEDFORD HOUSE	6/22
	13.10.17		As for 12.10.17. Sgt STENT wounded.	6/22
	14.10.17		As for 13.10.17. Nos 1 & 2 finished work just before heavy shelling started. Arrangements made with 43rd Inf Bde & C.R.E about distribution of work between us & Pioneers	6/22
	15.10.17		As for 14.10.17. Heavy shelling started early. Spr PITTS killed & Spr BARTRAM wounded.	6/22

WAR DIARY
or
INTELLIGENCE SUMMARY.

Army Form C. 2118.

59 (FIELD) COMPANY
31 OCT 1917
ROYAL ENGINEERS

Place	Date	Hour	Summary of Events and Information	Remarks and references to Appendices
DICKEBUSCH	16.10.17		Nos 1 & 2 on duckboard tracks in SANCTUARY WOOD.	EPR
			Nos 3 & 4 on hutting at BEDFORD HOUSE.	EPR
	17.10.17		As on 16.10.17.	EPR
	18.10.17		As on 16.10.17. Officers and N.C.O's reconnoitring jobs of Nos 1 & 2 sections.	EPR
			Nos 3 & 4 go to advanced billets on YPRES-COMINES CANAL near WITHUIS CABARET after work & remain there.	
	19.10.17		Nos 1 & 2 on BEDFORD HOUSE.	EPR
			3 & 4 on duckboard tracks in SANCTUARY WOOD. JERK track at G. Back continuous	
			from ZILLEBEKE to JERK HOUSE near POLYGON WOOD.	
	20.10.17		As on 19.10.17, small switches made to avoid congestion of traffic.	EPR
	21.10.17		As on 20.10.17. A wonderfully quiet morning reminds one of DCNY in the	EPR
			Spring of 1916.	
			33 illuminated signs made for use on the tracks	

Army Form C. 2118.

WAR DIARY
or
INTELLIGENCE SUMMARY.
(Erase heading not required.)

178

Instructions regarding War Diaries and Intelligence Summaries are contained in F. S. Regs., Part II. and the Staff Manual respectively. Title pages will be prepared in manuscript.

68 (FIELD COMPANY) ROYAL ENGINEERS
31 OCT. 1917

Place	Date	Hour	Summary of Events and Information	Remarks and references to Appendices
22.T DICKEBUSCH	22.10.17		Illuminated signs erected. Repairs to duckboard tracks continued. Lively morning. 2/Lt. E.V. DEVERALL wounded, remaining at duty.	S22
	23.10.17		Arrangements made for handing over all work to 527th Fd Coy, 5th Dvn.	S22
	24.10.17		Clean arms, kit, and box respirator parade. Vehicles washed. Improvements to shelters.	S22
	25.10.17		Company employed on repairing PLUMER'S DRIVE.	S22
	26.10.17		As for 25th, but work practically impossible owing to shell fire. Coy. called out at 9 pm to repair PLUMER'S DRIVE.	S22
	27.10.17		Major F. O. ALABASTER R.E. proceeded to England on 30 days leave. Capt. E. D. ALEXANDER in Command.	S22
	28.10.17		Repairing PLUMER'S DRIVE. Casualties 2 O.R. wounded.	S22
	29.10.17		Repairing PLUMER'S DRIVE	S22
	30.10.17		ditto	S22
	31.10.17		ditto	S22

Ashman Capt. M.R.

O.C. 89th Field Coy. R.E.

REPORT ON THE CROSSING OF THE RIVER LYS
ON THE 14th. & 15th. OCT. 1918.
BY
89th FIELD COY. R.E.

****

For some days prior to the attack on Oct. 14th. it was evident that the Field Coy. working with the Brigade in the line holding the RIVER LYS front would be required to negotiate the passage of the River. Everything possible was therefore done to obtain as much information as possible about the forward area, without interfering with ordinary work. Until the night before the attack the Coy. had been engaged on the important work of screening communication Roads. Particularly screening from view of the enemy, the long forward slope of the Messines Ridge as far east as GAPAARD. Also the construction of a Horse transport Road from MESSINES to GAPAARD to be used as an alternative Road if the MESSINES-WARNETON ROAD was at any time shelled. In the forward portion of the Brigade area all enemy pill boxes were examined and reported on, and they proved very useful for accommodating troops.

During the 14 days before the attack I arranged for all Officers of the Coy. with their section N.C.Os to make a thorough reconnaisance of the front area, both behind our outpost line and as far in front as the ground and enemy's watchfulness would allow. This work was invariably carried out in conjunction with the Infantry holding the Line.

The outpost line held by us was at least 900 yds. from the river bank and the enemy, throughout, was very nervous firing intermitting bursts from Machine Guns, all through the night. Under these conditions the progress in examining bridges with a view to repair, was very slow. It was decided that in the event of an enemy retirement it would be necessary to have some bridging material at hand. A dump was therefore formed for material at a point in the centre of the Brigade Front and by the night of Oct. 12th barrels, trench bridges and spruce poles had been taken down within 1200 yds. of the RIVER LYS.

Before/

(2)

Before Oct. 12th. the Divisional Front had been extended. To the west it included BAS WARNETON running to a point midway between WERVICQ and COMINES known as HOOGEMOTTE.

At the C.R.E's conference on the afternoon of Oct. 12th. information was received that there would have to be 4 Bridges constructed across the RIVER LYS during the forthcoming operations and that it was likely the Bridges would be required within 48 hours. As there were two Battalions holding the front line each would require two Bridges. One Bridge on the right Battalion front which the enemy had not demolished beyond repair was to be quickly repaired for Field Guns.

The positions of the Bridges are as follows:-

No. 1 Bridge at 28.V.9.a.2.0
No. 2   "   " 28.V.9.b.9.9
No. 3   "   " 28.P.35.d.0.5
No. 4   @   " 28.P.30.a.2.7
No. 5   "   " 28.V.9.b.9.9 for Field Guns.

At this time the approaches to Nos. 1 & 2 bridges had been well reconnoitered but it was impossible to get a nearer view of them.

On the night of Oct. 12th. I made the following arrangements:-

No. 1 Bridge to be erected by 2nd Lt. G.H.R. Oldfield.R.E. with No. 2 Section.

No. 2 Bridge to be erected by 2nd Lt. E.V. Deverall.M.C.R.E. with No. 4 Section.

No. 3 Bridge to be erected by 2nd Lt. F.H.C. Hollowell.R.E. with No. 3 Section.

No. 4 Bridge to be erected by 2nd Lt. A.J. Nairn.R.E. with No.1 Section.

Bridges Nos 3 & 4 had not been reconnoitred, therefore,2nd Lts. Nairn and Hollowell and reliable N.C.Os went out at once to do this and to take up stores required to forward dump. It was arranged that each party should take up 6 - 15 ft. Trench Bridges,a certain number of 20ft Poles with laths nailed across forming a strong ladder,a number of Trench Boards and sufficient timber to make a more permanent footbridge after the Bridgehead had been secured.

The/

(3)

The stores for Nos 3 & 4 Bridges that night were finally carried to within 250 yds of the point to be crossed. Notwithstanding the enemy's gas shelling and machine gunning of the approaches, the stores were taken into position without heavy loss.

In the case of No. 4 Bridge I proposed not to erect a new floating bridge at the side but to repair the existing partly demolished bridge using the wreckage superstructure as a foundation for the new Bridge. The old structure had been built for heavy traffic and for carrying a Light Railway.

On the evening of Oct. 12th, 2nd Lt. Nairn proceeded to reconnoitre the Bridge but was unable to get near enough to gain a satisfactory sight. He, however, waited until dawn and from a house in COMINES he obtained an excellent view of the Bridge, this enabled him to make an accurate estimate of stores required to complete a footway over the River.

At No. 3 Bridge it was proposed to use the old Railway Bridge consisting of 6 heavy twin piled trestles and to span the gaps caused by the demolition with Trench Bridges or strong ladders. The approach to the Bridge was a very dangerous one, the only way being along the top of the embankment 25 ft. above ground level. The land at the foot of the embankment was very wet and marshy.

It was not deemed advisable to bridge the River at any other point away from the Railway Bridge owing to the open nature of the ground on each side of the River. Once the crossing had been effected, troops could assemble west of the embankment and have cover from enemy's O.P's on the high ground at PAUL BOCK.

Our photos revealed a considerable amount of wreckage on the Bridge and it was considered quite possible and likely that by arrangement of this wreckage a temporary crossing could be secured. 2nd Lt. Hollowell, R.E. attempted to approach the Bridge on the night of Oct. 12th. He, however, only reached a point 30 yds. from the Bridge as the enemy was holding the

opposite/

opposite bank in considerable force.

West of the Railway Embankment the enemy had fortified the buildings of the DISTILLERY, with concrete Pill Boxes, Machine Guns and Trench Mortar emplacements. From these positions the enemy opened a very heavy fire and from Bombing Posts on each side of the embankment and threw many Hand Grenades on to the wreckage of the Bridge. After many attempts he got to the Bridge. As dawn was coming on Lt. Hollowell returned to Coy. Headquarters, having patrolled the Bridges for nearley 7 hours and getting vauable bridging material near to the point where the Bridge would be required on the day of the attack.

The site of No. 2 Bridge was close to a German Horse Transport bridge, the two centre bays being hinged for lifting in order to allow the passage of river traffic. Every effort possible had been made to examine this Bridge but as the only approach was by means of a "trestleway" some 250yds. long and the enemy having machine gun posts on the North Bank of the River, others on the South Bank, in the Chateau and in LAMLASH FARM; a close survey was impossible. A distant view, however, in daylight revealed a complete bridge fit for Horse Transport.

It was considered likely that the enemy would make further efforts to destroy the bridges and as it was proposed to erect a bridge for Field Guns at this point, sufficient timber was taken to the advanced dump to repair 3 bays.

Also to meet the possibility of a complete destruction, a light petrol tin float bridge in 6 sections was taken forward with a few spare poles, trench boards and lashings so that Infantry could cross the River.

At No. 1 Bridge 2nd Lt. Oldfields Section carried down 6 petrol tin floats to the North edge of the trestleway which was the only means of approach to the site selected.

The enemy was very active throughout and as I afterwards observed had put down heavy concentration of shells on to the only approach road.

During the night of Oct. 13th, the enemy sent out

strong/

strong patrols across the River to cover their bridge demolition party on No. 2 Bridge where they made a very good demolition. These patrols undoubtedly observed our carrying parties.

The site of No. 1 Bridge was that of a landing stage for barges on the river and the approaches were swept by fire from a series of pill boxes in a group of buildings called BLANCHE FARM. Several ingenious sniper posts also commanded the bridge from the South Bank.

Reconnaissance of No 1 Bridge proved impossible by both Royal Engineer patrols and by the infantry in the line, attempts met with casualties to the patrols.

It had been arranged that in the event of the enemy's retirement attempts to cross the river should be made on Oct. 14th. after the attack by the Division on our left had attained objectives: also in the event of strong enemy resistance a series of Artillery barrages were arranged according to the estimated time required to bridge the river.

Nos. 1,2 & 3 Bridges were allotted a shrapnel barrage of 10 minutes duration from Zero hours to cover the carrying parties getting the bridges on to the Bank. This barrage was intense and swept the South Bank of the River. After Zero plus 10 minutes the barrage lifted to a line 200 yds. further south where it was to remain for 20 minutes, after that a slow rate of fire was to be maintained on all known targets whilst heavy artillery carried out counter battery work on all guns likely to fire on the bridges.

No. 4 Bridge was to be allowed only 5 minutes intense barrage on the river and afterwards 15 minutes barrage fire 200 yds. from the bank. This was considered ample as the Sappers and their Stores were under cover only 150 yds. from the bridge.

The 4 Sections proceeded to their allotted stations in the forward area on the night of Oct. 13th. at 20-00 hours.

No. 4 Section took its Tool Cart and Limber Wagon also 6 Pack Mules and stabled them in old German Huts near WAI CORNET just off the main COMINES WARNETON road (28/V.2.b.80:90). It was intended that this transport would be invaluable after the river had been crossed for getting up heavy stores, e.g. trench boards, heavy baulks for repairing the Medium Bridge near No. 2 Bridge and for taking 30 gall. barrels down for the more permanent footbridge. Each/

Each Section Commander on arrival at forward billets visited the Coy. Commanded responsible for the Infantry Crossing and made all arrangements for a combined effort.

On Oct. 14th. in the course of the morning the different covering patrols allotted to the bridges went forward to see if they could draw fire.

At Bridges 1,2 & 3 the enemy opened heavy fire on our troops.

On No. 4 Bridge the Infantry patrol was not apparently observed, 2nd.-Lt. R.J. NAIRN, therefore proceeded at once to Bridge the river. At first his party was not observed but the enemy who had been temporarly blinded by our Smoke Screen in COMINES suddenly opened fire from 2 pill boxes near CHATEAU HAZEBROUCK near WERVICQ-SUD. Point blank Field Gun fire was also opened on them from PAUL BUCQ a prominent hill south of WERVICQ. For 2½ hrs. the enemy shelled and machinegunned the bridge. Notwithstanding this Lt. Nairn succedded in getting to the other side of the River, 3 men of his Section had then to swim back across the river owing to the shelling and machine gun fire. When the situation had calmed down a strong force of Infantry crossed the river. Lt. NAIRN then withdrew his party, leaving 2 Sappers to keep the Bridge in repair.

The Infantry patrol were only able to maintain their bridge head for a few hours as the enemy put down an exceptionally heavy barrage on their positions and they were obliged to retire, having sustained considerable casualties. R.E. casualties were very light having only 2 men wounded by Machine Gun fire.

On No. 3 Bridge 2nd. Lt. P.W.C. Hollowell (No. 3 Section) was informed by the Infantry patrol leader that his patrol had exposed themselves and had not been fired upon. He therefore proceeded with his Section, less 6 Sappers in reserve along the Railway Embankment to the dump of stores, these were picked up and Lt. Hollowell with his Section Sergeant went straight to the bridge. The enemy at once opened fire with machine guns from the DISTILLERY and from the M.G. Pill Boxes near CHATEAU HAZEBROUCK. Field Guns also put down a barrage; after lying lying between between the rails for a few minutes Lt. Hollowell got up and with his Section Sergeant proceeded in spite of the fire to construct the bridge. Immediately the Section Sergeant was killed, the next Sapper behind carrying material was also killed instantly and Lt. Hollowell received no less than 10 wounds from M.G. bullets and bombs: the enemy were seen to be

patrolling/

patrolling the South Bank and the remainder of the Sappers carrying stores further back, dropped their stores and opened a heavy fire on the enemy several of whom were killed whilst running for cover.

The enemy by this time concentrated all available weapons on No. 3 Bridge and put out of action all but 3 of the bridging detachment; the Infantry patrol leader and his Sergeant were both killed. The Sappers under L/Cpl. Harley. R.E. kept up a steady fire on the DISTILLERY which was filled with Germans. At 05-30 the Coy. Commander sent a message through to L/Cpl. Harley to withdraw, this he did, at the same time rescuing Lt. Hollowell from the wreckage of the Bridge: all wounded were subsequently evacuating. Fire had at this time died down.

On Nos 1 & 2 Bridges every effort to reach the bridge approaches drew heavy fire from all weapons and the Infantry Coy. Commanders in the line decided to pospone the crossing until an artillery barrage could be arranged.

On learning that Lt. NAIRN with No. 1 Section had completed bridge No. 4, I ordered him to withdraw his Section into reserve and as Lt. Hollowell had become a casualty, to get into touch with No. 3 Section and their Infantry Coy. to whom they were attached, ready to recommence operations with a barrage the following morning. Learning later that No. 3 Section had 75% of their bridging detachment out of action, I sent up No. 1 Section from Reserve to reinforce No. 4 Section: they reported to Lt. Nairn at 04-30 hours just in time for the operation which was to be carried out at 05-30 hours.

I visited Nos 2 & 4 Sections between noon and dusk and found them in good spirits and arranged with them to get their stores down nearer the river bank if the enemy would allow them to do so, and to send me a wire to this effect reporting completion.

I returned to Bde. Hqrs. and at 22:00 hrs. received a wire stating that all stores had been taken down to the position decided upon.

At 05:30.hrs. on October 15th. all sections were at their store dumps, from 400 to 500yds. from the bridges 2Lt. Oldfield's No. 2 Section carried their petrol tin bridge sections down to the water's edge to No. 1 Bridge and a few minutes before the barrage had lifted from the line 200 yards beyond the enemy's bank of the river, succeeded in crossing .

A party/

A party of Sappers at once went across and anchored the last section to the River Bank. Several of the enemy who had been compelled to take cover from the barrage and the garrison of the BLANCHE-FARM Pill Box surrendered and were handed over to the Infantry Commander.

Enemy resistance was comparatively slight the barrage accounting for many of them.

At 07:00 hours 2 Companies of the Rifle Brigade had crossed the River and were "mopping" up the country well in advance of the River LYS.

At No. 2 Bridge 2nd. Lt. Deverall with No. 4 Section and an Infantry patrol followed under the barrage down to the river bank but were at once met by heavy rifle and machine gun fire, both R.E. and Infantry suffering casualties. They at once took cover and proceeded to engage the enemy with rifle and Machine Gun fire: after an engagement lasting over 30 minutes the enemy who suffered heavy losses, gave up the fight, some attempted to escape by running towards bridge No. 1. There they were here captured by the Infantry who covered the crossing at that point.

At 07:15 hours I received a message from Lt. Nairn to say that he had secured the crossing over the Railway Bridge (No. 3 Bridge) and then by 06:45 hours 2 Companies of Infantry had crossed to the opposite bank.

Throughout the night No. 4 Bridge had remained intact and the 2 Sappers kept there for maintenance, reported that 2 Companies had successfully crossed at that point.

At 05:30 hours I proceeded with Brigade Major, 41st. Infy. Brigade to advanced Brigade Headquarters at GARDE DIEU CABARET (28/O.36.b.2:7.) thence I proceeded to visit works, arriving No. 1 Bridge at 07:00 hours.

I here met Lt. Oldfield. R.E. and told him to proceed at once with the construction of a strong barrel pier bridge. Following the Tow-path of the River I reached No. 2 Bridge and found that Lt. Deverall had succeeded in getting over the River. The Horse Transport bridge at this place, reported to be in existence, had been completely destroyed on the night of Oct. 14/15th and its repair was out of the question.

A wire was therefore sent to Headquarters R.E. for Pontoon and Trestle bridging equipment, a good site for this having been found some little distance from the old German Trestle Bridge.

In the afternoon all footbridges being in good condition, works were handed over to 61st. Field Coy. R.E. who erected a Bridge for Field Guns at the side of No. 2 Bridge, traffic crossing at 20:00 hours.

The/

The success of the operation was largely due to the determination before the attack of all ranks on getting the Stores as far forward as possible: little damage was done to the Stores, only one petrol tin Floatbridge being put out of action by Machine Gun bulets perforating the tins.

The Artillery barrage was in the case of Bridges 1 & 3 very adequate and perfectly accurate.

The transport taken forward proved to be of tremendous value.

Infantry footbridges of 15 ft. span with petrol tins attached proved excellent for getting the first batches of Infantry quickly across the river. Apart from inadequate freeboard at the joints the bridge was erected quickly and gave every satisfaction.

The Infantry in the line did everything humanly possible to make the work of bridging a success.

28/10/18.

S. Snell.
Major. R.E.
OC 89 Field Coy R.E.

WAR DIARY
or
INTELLIGENCE SUMMARY

Army Form C. 2118.

Vol 27

89th FIELD COY. R.E.

NOVEMBER 1917

Place	Date	Hour	Summary of Events and Information	Remarks and references to Appendices
DICKEBUSCH	1.11.17		Arrangements made with CRE X Corps Troops for work on hutting at CAFÉ BELGE. Reports of Coy. finds cleaning up work on Stables & camp improvement.	Pte
do	2.11.17		Nos 1 & 2 Sections erecting Nissen Huts at CAFÉ BELGE. Gr X Corps. Nos 3 & 4 Sections erecting Huts at advanced Billets for accommodation of 100 infantry to be attached to Coy. 2nd Lieut G.H.R. OLDFIELD joined Coy. from R.E. Base Depot. Return received to reat with an Infantry accommodation at 4pm	Pte
do	3.11.17		Nos 1, 2 & 3 Sections erecting Nissen Huts at CAFÉ BELGE. No 4 Section cleaning transport, painting pontoons & making gospel roadway out of Camp.	Pte
do	4.11.17		Nos 2, 3 & 4 Sections erecting Nissen Huts at CAFÉ BELGE. No 1 Section engaged washing out of Camp & cleaning gas masks & hutch equipment.	Pte
do	5.11.17		Nos 1, 2, & 3 Sections hutting. No 4 Section erecting stables at ANZAC CAMP.	Pte

Army Form C. 2118.

WAR DIARY
or
INTELLIGENCE SUMMARY.
(Erase heading not required.)

Place	Date	Hour	Summary of Events and Information	Remarks and references to Appendices
DICKEBUSH	6.11.17		Capt. L.G.M. LYON proceeded to England on 14 days leave. Coy. working on hutting & stables at ANZAC CAMP	
do	7.11.17		Coy. working as on 6.11.17	
do	8.11.17		3 Sections working on hutting at ANZAC CAMP. 1 Section working on trench tram. from ZILLEBEKE to JACKDAW JUNCTION (taken over from 6th Field Coy. R.E.) Orders received from 52.F.S. that Coy. was to transferred to 1st Canadian Corps. No more work from X Corps.	
do	9.11.17		Coy. concentrated at H.Q. Orders received relative to KRAMMERTINGHE area together with advance Party proceeded to KRAMMERTINGHE - KLAMMERTINGHE Road	
do	10.11.17		Coy. moved in afternoon to huts in CAFE BELGE - KLAMMERTINGHE Road	
KLAMMERTINGHE AREA	11.11.17		Arrangements made as to relief of 3rd Canadian Field Coy. on its O.C. Coy. in road construction of FRANK ROAD near ABRAHAM'S HEIGHTS. within No.3 Section needed to BZRETHEN + formed w.3 w.4 rd group for 1 recces and arrangements made as to site for next section bivouac at rear not with divisions near ST OMERS.	
do	12.11.17		No 1 & 2 Sections proceeded to billets at POTIJZE and took over work on NORTH ROAD.	

Army Form C. 2118.

WAR DIARY
or
INTELLIGENCE SUMMARY.
(Erase heading not required.)

Instructions regarding War Diaries and Intelligence Summaries are contained in F.S. Regs., Part II. and the Staff Manual respectively. Title pages will be prepared in manuscript.

181

Place	Date	Hour	Summary of Events and Information	Remarks and references to Appendices
POTIJZE	13.11.17		No 4 Sec & HQ moved to POTIJZE at 9 am. Transport moved to Trinquillrius nr. VLAMERTINGHE. No 1 & 2 Secs working on Plank Road; shelled off and thus hour 2 O.R. wounded	[sig]
do	14.11.17		No 2 & 4 Secs working on Plank Road. Practically no work possible. Heavy shelling in trolley orders; in R.E. casualties: several among working parties.	[sig]
do	15.11.17		No 1 & 4 Secs working on duckboard across murdered ravine forming new Plank Road with 120 parties working party. Completed 300 yds. duckboards also enquired work up to duckboard. Shelled off & on for 3½ hrs.	[sig]
do	16.11.17		No 1 & 2 Secs completed duckboards & repaired & employed on Plank Road. Intermittent shelling but not enough to interfere with work.	[sig]
do	17.11.17		No 2 & 4 Secs working on Plank Road. Enemy putting on barrage, repaired 5 camp tubes - started driver road 21 and tod Plank Road. about 3 hours.	[sig]
do	18.11.17		No 1 & 4 Secs working on Plank Road. 40 yds double road laid.	[sig]
do	19.11.17		No 1 & 2 Secs working on Plank Road. 30 yds double road laid. Heavy shelling stopped work at 3.15 pm.	[sig]

Army Form C. 2118.

WAR DIARY
or
INTELLIGENCE SUMMARY.

(Erase heading not required.)

Place	Date	Hour	Summary of Events and Information	Remarks and references to Appendices
POTIJZE	20.11.17		Pilots kits & vehicle cleaned at Transport Camp	
do	21.11.17		Cleaning & kit inspection. Coy paid	
do	22.11.17		Coy transport concentrated at KRUMBEERTINGHE and marched to WATOU under 2/LT T. MOORE. Remainder under OC entrained at 3.30 p.m. & detrained at KUMBRAS at 12 midnight. Not men & mens arrived at dumps by 4.2 wt Bde. Marched to billets at QUELMES arriving 2.30 am 23.11.17	
QUELMES	23.11.17		Coy parade at 12 noon – cleaning up equipment &c. Transport marched from WATOU to ST MOMELIN	
do	24.11.17		Coy parade 9 am. Close order drill. Baths in afternoon. Transport arrived at 3 p.m. CAPT LYON returned from leave.	
do	25.11.17		Sunday: parade 10 am. Close order drill & vehicles cleaned	
do	26.11.17		Parade 9 am. Close order drill, route march & baths. Football match in afternoon.	

Army Form C. 2118.

WAR DIARY
or
INTELLIGENCE SUMMARY.

(Erase heading not required.)

183

Place	Date	Hour	Summary of Events and Information	Remarks and references to Appendices
QUELMES	27.11.17		Pay parade & route march.	BM
do	28.11.17		Sports, football match & horse took over nr St Omer in evening. Major E.O. ALABASTER returned from leave in England and took over command of Coy.	Sme
	29.11.17		Company drill in morning. Horses took men into ST OMER in evening	S.R.R
	30.11.17		Clean arms parade for all ranks. Rain on and off the [?] and continued all day.	S.R.R

E.O. Alabaster
Major R.E.
O.C. 89th Fld Coy, R.E.
30.11.17.

Army Form C. 2118.

WAR DIARY
INTELLIGENCE SUMMARY.
(Erase heading not required.)

89th FLD COY R.E.

December 1917

Place	Date	Hour	Summary of Events and Information	Remarks and references to Appendices
QUELMES	1.12.17		O.C. & 2Lt DEVERALL proceeded to YPRES to take over work from 15th Field Coy R.E. Coy. cleaning vehicles, bicycles etc.	
	2.12.17		Work taken over from 15th FLD COY; maintenance of N° 5 D.B. Track, other work finished. Billets of 2nd Fld Coy at CANAL BANK taken over. Transport at VLAMERTINGHE. Transport marched from QUELMES to WINNIZEELE.	SOP
CANAL BANK KAAI. YPRES	3.12.17		Transport marched to VLAMERTINGHE, arrived 3 p.m. Company by tactical train to ST JEAN siding; arrived 11 a.m. 89th to de horse lines in YPRES at accommodation at D.H.Q. C.R.E.'s conference; work re-allotted.	SOP
	4.12.17		Work as allotted carried out. Capt ALEXANDER goes on leave.	SOP
	5.12.17		Work as on 4.12.17. Most of pill boxes in Divn area reconnoitred.	SOP
	6.12.17		Work as on 4.12.17 and at ST JEAN bomb store.	SOP
	7.12.17		O.C. & Lt MOORE visited VAUXHALL CAMP and reported on requirements.	SOP
	7.12.17		Work as on 6.12.17 and also and parts WATERLOO and SOMME REDOUBT. Lt MOORE & N°1 section proceed to VAUXHALL camp for work, all remain there.	SOP
	8.12.17		Work as on 7.12.17	SOP
	9.12.17		Work as on 7.12.17. CRE's conference 5.30 p.m. re allotting work.	SOP

Army Form C. 2118.

WAR DIARY
or
INTELLIGENCE SUMMARY.
(Erase heading not required.)

89ᵗʰ F(ld Cy) R.E.

Place	Date	Hour	Summary of Events and Information	Remarks and references to Appendices
CANAL BANK.	10.12.17		Nº 1 Section at VAUXHALL CAMP, working at Divn Depot Bn.	
			Nº 2 " " on Pack Transport Lines YPRES.	
			Nº 3 " " " , shelter at A.D.S. SOMME REDOUBT, and Nissen Huts at WIELTJE.	
			Nº 4 " " Divn H.Q.	
			C.S.M. and odd men shelters in CAPRICORN TRENCH.	
			O.C. accompanied C.R.E. at O.C.61, visiting work of 61ˢᵗ Fld Cy R.E. Heavy shelling at SOMME REDOUBT resulted in a shelter of 12 complete sections being lifted bodily on to the roof of another shelter. Company started fresh work of maintaining forward roads in November near PASCHENDAELE.	6/22
	11.12.17.		Work as on 10.12.17., except Nº 2 on Nº 5 Track, the Pack Transport Lines being handed over to 62ⁿᵈ Fld Cy R.E.	6/22
	12.12.17.		Work as on 11.12.17. with addition of New A.D.S. at BRIDGE HOUSE.	6/22
	13.12.17.		Work as on 12.12.17. That at SOMME REDOUBT A.D.S. being finished, except for extra sandbagging to be done by R.A.M.C.	6/22
			O.C. reconnoitred road in hand by 61ˢᵗ Fld Cy next in order to change over on 13.12.17.	6/22

Army Form C. 2118.

WAR DIARY
or
INTELLIGENCE SUMMARY.
(Erase heading not required.)

December 1917

Place	Date	Hour	Summary of Events and Information	Remarks and references to Appendices
CANAL BANK	14.12.17		Work as on 13.12.17.	S22
	15.12.17		No. 2 Section wiring No. 6 Post (AVIATIK FM) of ABRAHAM SWITCH	
			3] " repairing No. 6 Track.	
			4] "	
			Details on G.O.C. hut.	S22
	16.12.17		Work as on 15.12.17.	
	17.12.17		No. 2 Section wiring No. 7 Post (WURST FM) of ABRAHAM SWITCH.	
			No. 3 & 4. Repaired No. 6 Track from CAPRICORN to WOODLAND PLANTATION, including switches to PLANK RD near KANSAS CROSS and to BELLEVUE.	
			Details started switch from SPREE DUMP to No. 6 Track.	
			Arrangements made for taking over supervision of a new road for R.R. near GRAVENSTAFEL.	S22
	18.12.17		No. 2 Section wiring No. 7 Post (WURST Pn) of ABRAHAM SWITCH.	
			No. 3 Repaired No. 6 Track from PLANK Rd to PETER PAN "	Int
			No. 4 Repaired No. 6 Track from PETER PAN to VINE COTTAGES loaft hym tak on detail as or Engr. Major Nekmoracky to C.R.E.	
	19.12.17		No. 2 Section connecting No. 7 Post (WURST) to No. 6 Post (AVIATIK)	
			No. 3 Repairing No. 6 Track from PETER PAN to KRONPRINZ	
			No. 4 Dwelling track from PETER PAN to ISER JUNCTION.	Int

Army Form C. 2118.

WAR DIARY
or
INTELLIGENCE SUMMARY.
(Erase heading not required.)

Instructions regarding War Diaries and Intelligence Summaries are contained in F. S. Regs., Part II. and the Staff Manual respectively. Title pages will be prepared in manuscript.

Place	Date	Hour	Summary of Events and Information	Remarks and references to Appendices
Camel Bush	20/12/17		No 2 Section – Improving WURST to AVIATIK	Nil
			No 3 Section – Repairing & Improving No 6 Track PETER PAN to ISER	
			No 4 Section – Repairing No 6 Track from PETER PAN to PLANK ROAD.	
	21/12/17		No 2 Section – Improving AVIATIK (POST 6) & BOETLEER (POST 5)	Nil
			No 3 Section – Improving BOETLEER (POST 5) to DUMP HOUSE (POST 4)	
			Cpl Cruickshank & Sapper May injured by Enemy mm trench mortar	
			No 4 Section – Improving No 6 Track PETER PAN to ISER	
	22/12/17		No 2 Section – Erecting strengthening tilt fence at BOETLEER	Nil
			No 3 Section – do	
			No 4 Section – Repairing No 6 TRACK	
			Lt Moore & new draft from Div. Depot Batt.	
	23/12/17		No 1 Section – Wiring at BELLEVUE	Nil
			No 2 & 3 Sections – Erecting strengthening tilt fence at AVIATIK	
			No 4 Section – Repairing No 6 TRACK & Improving from ISER & PETER PAN	
	24/12/17		No 1 Section – As on 23rd	Nil
			No 4 " – As on 23rd	
			No 3 " – Strengthening WURST	
			No 2 " – Working for CRE at Headquarters.	

Army Form C. 2118.

188

WAR DIARY
or
INTELLIGENCE SUMMARY.

(Erase heading not required.)

Instructions regarding War Diaries and Intelligence
Summaries are contained in F. S. Regs. Part II.
and the Staff Manual respectively. Title pages
will be prepared in manuscript.

Place	Date	Hour	Summary of Events and Information	Remarks and references to Appendices
CANAL BANK	25.12.17		N° 1 Section – Barded wiring at BELLEVUE	
			N° 2 Section – Working at C.R.E	
			N° 3 Section – Strengthening POST 7 (WURST)	
			N° 4 Section – Repairing N° 6 TRACK standing between ISER & PETER PAN	Knick
			Capt Lyon went out work of 2nd Field Coy RE will assist on taking our Capt ALEXANDER returned from leave & took over command of Coy.	
do	26.12.17		N° 1, 2 & 4 Secs making good N° 6 Track for relief of 14th Div by 6th Div. N° 3 Sec working on Bn. H.Q.	F.E.
do	27.12.17		Coy working on plank road from BRIDGE HOUSE to KANSAS CROSS on maintenance of road. Road broken in 6 places during night by shell fire.	F.E.
do	28.12.17		Coy repaired damage during morning & afternoon. Heavy shelling near KANSAS CROSS from 12 noon to 8.30pm. Road badly broken in 10 places. Coy turned out in two reliefs 12 – 10pm 2nd 3am 29th.	F.E.
	29.12.17		Road repaired for single traffic at 7.30am. Dense traffic at 8am	

A5834 Wt.W4973/M687 750,000 8/16 D. D. & L. Ltd Forms/C.2118/13

Army Form C. 2118.

WAR DIARY
or
INTELLIGENCE SUMMARY.
(Erase heading not required.)

189

Place	Date	Hour	Summary of Events and Information	Remarks and references to Appendices
CANAL BANK	30.12.17		Coy working on PANET ROAD. Rations drawn & vehicles cleaned.	
do.	31.12.17		Coy ceased to be responsible for maintenance of PANET ROAD at 6 a.m. Transport marched to ZERMEZEELE under Capt LYON.	

Redwards
Captain
O.C. 258th Army Tps. Coy. R.E.

A5634. Wt.W4973/M687. 750,000. 8/16. D.D.&L.Ltd. Forms/C.2118/13.

WAR DIARY
or
INTELLIGENCE SUMMARY.

Army Form C. 2118.

JANUARY 1918.

Place	Date	Hour	Summary of Events and Information	Remarks and references to Appendices
CANAL BANK YPRES	1.1.18		Coy marched out of camp at 8.10 a.m. entrained at VLAMMERTINGHE, detrained at WIZERNE'S and marched to ST. MARTIN-AU-LAERT near ST OMER. Transport marched from ZERMEZEELE to ST. MARTIN-AU-LAERT.	
ST. MARTIN AU-LAERT	2.1.18		Cleaning up and pay. Men given leave to ST. D. MER.	
do	3.1.18		Coy marched to ST. OMER Station at 7 p.m. and entrained: detrained at EDGEHILL: marched to BRAY-SUR-SOMME. arriving 3.30 p.m. Coy took 45 minutes to detrain: men worked splendidly.	
BRAY-SUR-SOMME	4.1.18			
do	5.1.18		Route march in morning: needles to cool for drill	
do	6.1.18		Sunday. Coy parade. Company cinema in evening: very successful. Sgt LOOSEMORE No 1 Sec awarded D.C.M. in Honours Gazette 1.1.18. 2Lt OTTEVELL proceeded to ENGLAND on 14 days leave.	

Army Form C. 2118.

WAR DIARY
or
INTELLIGENCE SUMMARY.
(Erase heading not required.)

19/

Place	Date	Hour	Summary of Events and Information	Remarks and references to Appendices
BRAY-SUR-SOMME	7.1.18		Coy Parade. Ceremonial and close order drill. Lecture to NCOs on general duties. Field works school started for 43rd Q.F. Bde.	
do	8.1.18		Coy Parade. Ceremonial section drill: General mounting. Coy taken to 14th Divisional Theatre in afternoon. NCOs continued in Field Works School. Major E.O ALABASTER appointed S.O. R.E. XXII Corps.	
do	9.1.18		Coy Parade. Ceremonial and coy drill. Route march. Baths. NCOs continued in Field works School. Work very difficult owing to frost and snow.	
do	10.1.18		Coy Parade. Ceremonial. Coy drill & bar upgrade drill. Numerous inspections. NCOs completed in Field works School. CAPT R.D. ALEXANDER appointed to command of Coy.	
do	11.1.18		Coy Parade. Ceremonial, Coy drill. Lignes and trench & facing work. Heavy Parties. Lecture to NCOs on Army Grenade. Field works School completed with Lt Crayfield commenced instruction 6th KOYLI in afternoon. 6th DCLI in morning.	

Army Form C. 2118.

WAR DIARY
or
INTELLIGENCE SUMMARY.
(Erase heading not required.)

192

Place	Date	Hour	Summary of Events and Information	Remarks and references to Appendices
BRAY-SUR-SOMME	12.1.18		Coy parade Ceremonial drill. Trickle drill. Bn responds column of route. 43rd M.G. Coy & 43rd T.M.B. attended Field Engineering Course in morning	
do	13.1.18		Church parade. T/Capt. R.W. ORMSTON appointed to command of Coy.	
do	14.1.18		Capt. E.D. ALEXANDER proceeded a rate on course of Capt. Coy. Major TEMPERLEY Capt. L.G.M. LYON is command.	
do	15.1.18		Coy parade. Ceremonial drill. Evening lecture at MERICOURT-SUR-SOMME for Div. Cross Country Race. Coy drill. Field Engineering Course.	Limit
do	16.1.18		Coy parade. Ceremonial drill. Route march	Lunt
do	17.1.18		Coy parade weather very wet. Lecture by Lt. MOORE on Discipline etc. Coy breek in every - great success	Limit
do	18.1.18		Ceremonial drill, Section drill, Knotting & lashing	Lunt
do	19.1.18		Ceremonial drill. Captains LEFEBVRE & LYON judging Brigade wrong competition. T/Capt. E.W. ORMSTON joined Coy.	d.mb
do	20.1.18		Divisional Cross Country Race. Coy team finished 11th. Church parade.	

A.5534 Wt.W4973/M687. 750,000 8/16 D.D. & L. Ltd. Forms/C.2118/13.

Army Form C. 2118.

WAR DIARY
or
INTELLIGENCE SUMMARY.
(Erase heading not required.)

193

Place	Date	Hour	Summary of Events and Information	Remarks and references to Appendices
BRAY SUR SOMME	21.1.18		CAPT E D ALEXANDER rejoined Coy. Loading vehicles, cleaning up &c. No 1 and 4 Sections left on detachment, personnel proceeding by train and transport by road to UGNY-LE-GAY to exit huts & for III Corps H.Q. 2nd LT. L.T. MOORE proceeded on leave to ENGLAND.	R/I
do	22.1.18		Coy moved to HARBONNIERRS, marching with 43rd Bde Group.	R/II
HARBONNIERES	23.1.18		Coy moved to GRUNY	R/III
GRUNY	24.1.18		Coy moved to QUESMY	R/IV
QUESMY	25.1.18		Coy moved to FLAVY-LE-MARTEL. Capt ALEXANDER proceeded to REMIGNY to take over work and billets of 12/63 at 6th Regt de Genie, French army.	R/V
FLAVY-LE MARTEL	26.1.18		Coy moved into billets at REMIGNY.	R/VI
REMIGNY	27.1.18		Coy (less two section on detachment at UGNY-LE-GAY) working with 43rd Bde. O.C. & L. OLDFIELD reconnoitred sector.	R/VII

WAR DIARY
or
INTELLIGENCE SUMMARY.

(Erase heading not required.)

Army Form C. 2118.

Place	Date	Hour	Summary of Events and Information	Remarks and references to Appendices
REMIGNY	28.1.18		Further reconnaissance of lines and laying and drainage of front line posts. Section working on water pond, RESTIGNY; Dugouts. Road to MOY; Reserve to SOREUN on REMIGNY — LY FONTAINE Road, making wire bands. S.A.A. loads &c.	Rds
do	29.1.18		Work as for 28.1.18; in addition work started on clearing BOYAU D.12 LA SEINE from ST QUENTIN-VENDEUIL Road forward.	Rds
do	30.1.18		Ditto. 2/Lt OTTEWELL returned from leave. Remainder of front line posts located for drainage.	Rds
do	31.1.18		Work as for 30.1.18. In addition work commenced on new baths at REMIGNY; and clearing communication trench forward from R.E. Batt Hq.	Rds

E W Dwelin R.E.
Major
O.C. 89 F.Coy R.E.

3/4/18.

WAR DIARY
or
INTELLIGENCE SUMMARY.

Army Form C. 2118.

89 Fd Coy R.E.
Vol 30

Place	Date	Hour	Summary of Events and Information	Remarks and references to Appendices
REMIGNY	1-2-18		Work continued on communication trenches, Baths etc. No 3 Section at Advanced billets near CAPOGNE FARM. Reports on left Batt? front reconnoitred.	B.O.
do.	2-2-18		Training of T.R. de RENNES and Reserves of B. de la SEINE. Staff Capt. left NEUVILLE-EN-SEINE. No.4 Section rejoined Coy at REMIGNY. No.1 Section (Capt. Kyn R.E.) proceeded to JUSSY for Divisional Work.	B.O.
do.	3-2-18		Work as for 2-2-18.	B.O.
do.	4-2-18		-do-	B.O.
do.	5-2-18		-do-	B.O.
do.	6-2-18		-do- Capt. Alexander R.E. left for course at Fifth Army School of Instruction for Officers. Work commenced on left Batt? Gun front lines.	B.O.
do.	7-2-18		Work on trenches continued.	B.O.
do.	8-2-18		Work on Strong Point at Junction of SEINE~NANTES commenced. Strong Point North of GUINCETTE WOOD taped.	B.O.
do.	9-2-18		Wiring of SEINE~NANTES Strong Point continued. Wiring commenced at S.P. N. of GUINCETTE WOOD. 2/Lt. MOORE RE returned from leave to England.	B.O.

Edw Onnen Major R.E.
H. Brothell Capt. R.E.

WAR DIARY or INTELLIGENCE SUMMARY

Army Form C. 2118.

Place	Date	Hour	Summary of Events and Information	Remarks and references to Appendices
REMIGNY	10-2-18		Weather continues very fine. Clearing and trenchboarding continued and cutting of firestep in CHARANTE. Work commenced on Strong Point on right (South) of CAPONNE – MOY ROAD. Laying Gas curtains to dugouts of Batts in line.	B.O.
do.	11.2.18		Work as for 10-2-18. Baths at REMIGNY completed.	B.O.
do.	12-2-18		-do- Left Batt. gun boat store completed.	B.O.
do.	13.2.18		-do- 2Lt. TAYLOR D.W. 11th KINGS LIVERPOOL REGT attached to Coy. for duty.	B.O.
do.	14.2-18		Repairing tramway CAPONNE FM. to GUINGETTE FM. Work continued on Strong Points, CHARANTE TRENCH, R. FRANCOIS and R. de la SEINE.	B.O.
do.	15-2-18		Work as for 14-2-18	B.O.
do.	16-2-18		-do- 3 Officers commanding 1 Platoon each, 9th KRRC, 9th Scottish Rifles and 6th S.L.I. report to O.C. for instructions, & are then attached to Coy. for work.	B.O.
do.	17-2-18		Work on Strong Points and forward trenches continued. 2Lt. ORR with 1 Platoon of 9th Scottish Rifles and 2Lt. MACDONALD with 1 Platoon of 9th KRRs. arrive and are accommodated near Camp at REMIGNY. 2Lt. MOORE R.E. relieved CAPT. LYON R.E. in command of No.1 Section at JUSSY.	B.O.

Army Form C. 2118.

WAR DIARY
or
INTELLIGENCE SUMMARY.
(Erase heading not required.)

Instructions regarding War Diaries and Intelligence Summaries are contained in F. S. Regs., Part II. and the Staff Manual respectively. Title pages will be prepared in manuscript.

197

Place	Date	Hour	Summary of Events and Information	Remarks and references to Appendices
REMIGNY	18-2-18		Work as for 17-2-18. Lieut. LEIVERS with 1 Platoon of 6th S.L.I. reported to 2Lt. OTTEWELL R.E. at advanced killer near CAPONNE FARM, for work. They were accommodated near No. 3 Section. No. 2 Section (CAPT. LYON R.E.) relieved No. 3 Section (2Lt. OTTEWELL R.E.) at CAPONNE FARM.	B.O.
do.	19-2-18		Deepening, draining, and revering of FRANCOIS, CHARANTE, COUESNON and RENNES trenches continued. Also firing of 900 cartouches to dugouts by Left Battn.	B.O.
do.	20-2-18		do for 19-2-18.	
do.	21-2-18		-do- C.R.E. and O.C. visited works in Left Sector. Site for new Artillery O.P. recommended.	B.O.
do.	22-2-18		In accordance with OC's instructions OC. platoon 4th KRRC. left camp at REMIGNY and proceeded to advanced billets at ABRIS CORSE. Trench works continued. Work commenced on two O.P's for 169 Bde. R.F.A. French bridge over Tr. de SARRETOCHE erected for 169 Bde. R.F.A.	B.O.
do.	23-2-18		Instructions given by O.C. and arrangements made for action in case of hostile attack. 2Lt. OLDFIELD R.E. proceeded on leave to England. Work on Stong Points and trenches continued.	B.O.

A.5834 Wt.W4973/M687 750,000 8/16 D. D. & L. Ltd. Forms/C.2118/13.

Army Form C. 2118.

WAR DIARY
or
INTELLIGENCE SUMMARY.

(Erase heading not required.)

198

Instructions regarding War Diaries and Intelligence Summaries are contained in F. S. Regs., Part II and the Staff Manual respectively. Title pages will be prepared in manuscript.

Place	Date	Hour	Summary of Events and Information	Remarks and references to Appendices
REMIGNY	24-2-18		Men at work on trenches and S.P's. Excavators for shelters at Strong Points.	B.O.
do.	25-2-18		Standing - over report forwarded to 79th Field Coy. R.E. O.C. visited new billets at BENAY. Arrangements continued for handing over trench work and BATTLE ZONE work.	B.O.
do.	26-2-18		Nos. 3 and 4 Sections left camp at REMIGNY, proceeded to BENAY. And part of H.Q. Section vacated by 79th Field Coy. R.E. the platoon of 9th Scottish Rifles accompanied Nos. 2 Section and its remaining 2 platoons of infantry attached. Reformed Coy. at BENAY. Transport proceeded to JUSSY and took over camp from 79th Field Coy. R.E. No. 1 Section remain at JUSSY. Relief completed satisfactorily. 79th Field Coy. R.E. took over camp at REMIGNY.	B.O.
BENAY	27-2-18		Coy. at work improving billets. O.C. and officers reconnoitred new work.	
do.	28-2-18	1.30 pm	Coy. received orders to take precautionary action. Standing-to in billets.	

Ed J Munch
Major RE
OC 89 Field Coy RE

14th Divisional Engineers

———————

89th FIELD COMPANY R. E.

MARCH 1918

Army Form C. 2118.

89 2nd Army R.E.
Vol 31

WAR DIARY
or
INTELLIGENCE SUMMARY.
(Erase heading not required.)

Instructions regarding War Diaries and Intelligence Summaries are contained in F. S. Regs., Part II. and the Staff Manual respectively. Title pages will be prepared in manuscript.

Place	Date	Hour	Summary of Events and Information	Remarks and references to Appendices
BENAY.	1st		No 1 Section at Jussy Workshops working on track and work for C.R.E.	17M
"	2,3rd		No 2 " " working on Strong Point "EGYPT"	17M
			No 3 " " Battle Zone Strong Point BENAY	17M
			No 4 " " constructing Observation Post.	17M
"	4th		Ditto —	17M
"	5th		Capt. ALEXANDER rejoined Company.	17M
"	6th		Work same as 1st inst. Capt ALEXANDER appointed O.C. 92nd Field Company R.E.	17M
"	7th		Lt DEVERALL and party rehearsing raid at MONTESCOURT.	17M
"	8th		Capt ALEXANDER left Company.	17M
"	9th		Lt DEVERALL reconnoitred the Disposition of enemy's wire –	17M
			No 1 Section working on "EGYPT" and "EUROPE" Strong Points.	
"			No 2 " " at Jussy. No 4 Section on O.Ps.	
"			No 3 " " working on Battle Zone Strong Points.	
"	10th		Lt DEVERALL and a party of No 4 SECTION accompanied raiding party of 4th SCOTTISH RIFLES. Raid unsuccessful. No sapper casualties.	17M
"	11th		Front line of Defences (REAR of BENAY) started.	17M
"	12th		Company at work as on 9th. Lt OLDFIELD rejoined Company from leave	17M
"	13th		Lt DEVERALL took over work at Jussy from No 1 Section. Group to Junction of MONTESCOURT CHATEAU field	17M
"	14th		HD QUARTERS Cooks and BATMEN using Funk line at BENAY	17M
			Lt MOORE rejoined Company from JUSSY.	
"	15th		No 1 Section working on Strong Points EGYPT and EUROPE	17M
"	16th		No 2 " " " OBSERVATION POSTS BENAY	
"	17th		No 3 " " " STRONG POINTS Battle Zone	
"	18th		No 4 " " at JUSSY WORKSHOPS	
"	19th		Lt OTTEWELL left for FOREWAY COY R.E.	17M
"	20th		Company staff by —	17M

Army Form C. 2118.

WAR DIARY
or
INTELLIGENCE SUMMARY.
(Erase heading not required.)

Instructions regarding War Diaries and Intelligence Summaries are contained in F.S. Regs., Part II and the Staff Manual respectively. Title pages will be prepared in manuscript.

Place	Date	Hour	Summary of Events and Information	Remarks and references to Appendices
REMY	21st	4.30 a.m	Heavy Enemy Bombardt. Company stood to until 6 a.m. No 1 Section reported to Brigade HQ Qrs and took up position in Sunken Road. H.20.d. No 2 and 3 Sections and HQ Qrs left for Jussy. Lt OLDFIELD reported to C.R.E. No 4 Section stood to at Canal Bridge Jussy. MONTESCOURT CHATEAU Demolitions. No 2 and 3 Sections took up position on Railway embankment Jussy. Transport proceeded to FLAVY. Sappers DEXTER and DUFELL KILLED. Sappers DALLAS, MURRAY, HOUGHTON, McWILLIAMS, SMITH, GARNETT WOUNDED.	17ML
JUSSY	22nd		Bridge destroyed. Coy stood to in village, and later took up position at Railway Embankment FLAVY. Coy proceeded to LA NEUVILLE EN BEINE. One Sapper wounded.	Link
LA NEUVILLE EN BEINE	23rd		Coy proceeded to BEAUMONT EN BEINE and took up position on right of MONTALIMONT FARM, later proceeded to village taking up new position at Coopers. Transport at GUISCARD.	Link
BEAUMONT	24th		Coy took up position at MONTALIMONT FARM. SEVEN SAPPERS wounded. Transport at MURACOURT. MAJOR E.N. ORMSTON WOUNDED. LASSIGNY. Lt. Hollowell joined Coy and in the afternoon moved to	Link
ROUSSON	25th		Transport moved to ROUSSON. Party of sappers in the line attached to 61st Field Coy R.E. Capt S. SNELL appointed O.C. Coy at ROUSSON.	Link
ROUSSON	26th			Link
	27th		Coy moved to BRAISNES & MOŸ-VILLIERS	Link
MOŸ VILLIERS	28th		At MOŸ VILLIERS	Link

Army Form C. 2118.

WAR DIARY
or
INTELLIGENCE SUMMARY.

(Erase heading not required.)

Instructions regarding War Diaries and Intelligence Summaries are contained in F. S. Regs., Part II. and the Staff Manual respectively. Title pages will be prepared in manuscript.

Place	Date	Hour	Summary of Events and Information	Remarks and references to Appendices
BEAUREPAIRE	29th		Coy. moved to BEAUREPAIRE	Nil.
	30th		Coy. moved to BIZANCOURT	Nil.
	31st		Coy. moved to VELLENNES	Nil.
	1.4.18		Coy. moved to FLÉCHY	Nil.
	2.4.18		Coy. moved to VERS	Nil.
	3.4.18		Heavy transport at AMIENS. Coy. to AUBIGNY.	

Snell
Major
O.C. 89 Field Coy. R.E.

14th Div.

89th FIELD COMPANY, R.E.

A P R I L

1 9 1 8

WAR DIARY
or
INTELLIGENCE SUMMARY.

(Erase heading not required.)

Army Form C. 2118.

89 2nd Coy S^n

Place	Date	Hour	Summary of Events and Information	Remarks and references to Appendices
VELLENNES	1-4-18		Coy. moved to FLECAY	U
	2-4-18		Coy moved to VERS.	
	3-4-18		Coy moved to AUBIGNY leaving heavy transport in the suburbs of AMIENS (ST ACHEUIL) and light transport in GLISY.	U
	4-4-18		Coy. taken to reserve positions in support of the Infantry who were being heavily attacked by the enemy. After waiting some time Coy were ordered back on to a ridge running N. and S. behind VILLERS BRETTONEUX and AUBIGNY. Here the Coy dug-in and stood by for further orders. At 9 A.M. Coy were ordered back into billets in AUBIGNY.	U
	5-4-18		Coy. received reserve positions at 4.30 AM. Weather was very bad raining hard throughout the day. At 5.30 P.M. Coy was ordered back to billets in BLANGY.	U
	6-4-18 7-4-18 8-4-18 9-4-18		Coy working all day on reserve positions near AUBIGNY: laying out strong points and wiring up woods and centres of resistance. Coy ordered back to billets at 4.30 P.M. reaching them at 7 P.M. Company left for TEN marked 6. ST ACHEUIL billeting for the night in a factory. Coy remained in ST ACHEUIL until 10th inst.	U
	10-4-18		Coy bn transport entrained at SALEUX STATION at 10 P.M. arriving at the station 6 hours previously. After travelling all night arrived destination following day.	U
	11-4-18		Arrived GIMANCHES 7.30 A.M. then found lorries waiting for kits etc. Coy to be billeted in BAZINVAL 5 Kilos. distant.	U
	12-4-18		Training Programme and reorganisation of Coy immediately taken in hand.	U

Army Form C. 2118.

INTELLIGENCE SUMMARY.

(Erase heading not required.)

Instructions regarding War Diaries and Intelligence Summaries are contained in F. S. Regs., Part II. and the Staff Manual respectively. Title pages will be prepared in manuscript.

Place	Date	Hour	Summary of Events and Information	Remarks and references to Appendices
BAZINVAL	12-4-18		At 2 P.M. orders received for Coy. to move to FERRIERES (N. of AMIENS) staging night 12/13 in CITERNE. Coy packed up at once and moved off. No 1,2 and 3 sections having a BATHS PARADE some miles away rejoined the Coy later. Coy arrived in CITERNE 11 P.M. and settled into billets. Coy then left the Division, under orders of 18 Corps.	DJ
	13-4-18		Coy. ordered to move to VIGNACOURT WOOD near/FLIXECOURT a march of 25 miles. Col. Patankan Walsh the C.R.E. of the G.H.Q. LINE (A SECTOR) visiting O.C. 89 Coy and giving necessary orders. Coy. marched to destination arriving at 5:30 P.M. 8 tents given to Coy for cover. Coy Hqrs however subsequently located in BACHIMONT FARM (Shooting Box) where comfortable quarters were obtained.	DJ
	14-4-18		Works around FLIXECOURT inspected and a start on work made at once. G.H.Q. LINE extended some 5 miles from ST. ETOILE W. of FLIXECOURT to the West of VIGNACOURT.	DJ
	15-4-18		Two Chinese Labour Corps available for digging. Good progress made, but some little trouble experienced with the Chinese.	DJ
	16-4-18		Work on G.H.Q. Defences. Breastworks started in SOMME VALLEY.	DJ
	17-4-18 18-4-18		Work on G.H.Q. line carried on	DJ
	20-4-18		Work on G.H.Q. LINE (REAR DEFENCES) ceased and a new switch line from VIGNACOURT to CHABUSSEE Commenced. Coy. moved at 10 A.M. to BELLOY-SUR-SOMME.	DJ
	21-4-18		Work proceeding satisfactorily.	DJ

INTELLIGENCE SUMMARY.

(Erase heading not required.)

Instructions regarding War Diaries and Intelligence Summaries are contained in F. S. Regs., Part II. and the Staff Manual respectively. Title pages will be prepared in manuscript.

Place	Date	Hour	Summary of Events and Information	Remarks and references to Appendices
BELLOY-SUR-SOMME.	22-4-18		Coy. handed over this new line to the No6 FOREMAN'S Coy R.E. and started work on A.S.F. Sector the hour system of G.H.Q. Defence line.	I.S.
	23/4/18		Work continued on Defences of G.H.Q. line. A new map of area being commenced	I.S.
	24-4-18.		First consignment of Ordnance Stores received from Base since March 18th. State of coy being bad, boots, socks being completely worn out. Underclothing and S.D. being scarce and filthy. Work being continued with all possible speed.	I.S.
	25-4-18		Work continued on G.H.Q line between ST. SAUVEUR and BERTANGLES.	I.S.
	26/4/18.		Field Coy engaged in wiring the various lines, and the Chinese digging trenches. Tasks for Chinese coolies being 120 cubic ft. in loam and 130 cubic ft. in chalk.	I.S.
	27/4/18		Considerable trouble experienced with Chinese labour, owing to varying nature of tasks. Work however being pressed on. O.C. visited works in morning.	I.S.
	28/4/18		C.R.E. of "A" Sector G.H.Q. line visited the O.C. and discussed various points with him.	I.S.
	29/4/18		A 4th Chinese Labour Coy sent for work on G.H.Q. line.	I.S.
	30/4/18		C.O.S. "A" Sector went round the sector and visited O.C. Extra future works discussed.	I.S.

C. Mull.
Major R.E.
O.C. 89 Field Coy R.E.

Army Form C. 2118.

WAR DIARY
or
INTELLIGENCE SUMMARY.
(Erase heading not required.)

89th Coy R.E.

Vol 33

Place	Date	Hour	Summary of Events and Information	Remarks and references to Appendices
VAUX-EN-AMIENOIS.	1-5-18		New Observation Line on North Bank of River Somme near St Sauveur and ARDEURES laid out and spitlocked. OC 89 Coy R.E. visited all work on forward system. GHQ Defences. West of AMIENS.	A.
	2-5-18		O.C. visited HARBARCOWOOD near ARRAS in company with CRE "A" Sector GHQ Line for types of examining new types of obstacle.	A.
	3-5-18		2nd Canadian Tunnelling Coy R.E. Sent for work on GHQ LINE. They were employed on wiring the Obstacle Zone to a depth of 70 yds in front of Main Line of Resistance	A.
	4-5-18		Owing to Anti-Aircraft guns at Agra and Zante Corps coming into village of VAUX 89 Coy ordered to leave billets. Coy HQrs established in a copse on the VAUX-AMIENS ROAD in a small copse.	A.
	5-5-18		Coy sent to Baths in VAUX-EN-AMIENOIS. Kindly lent by OC Trench Mortar School of Army.	A.
	6-5-18		Gas Officer XIX Corps inspected Coy. ANTI-GAS appliances. Ordered received at midday that Coy was to entrain on following day and rejoin Division in LILLERS AREA. Coy ceased work at 3A.M.	A
	7-5-18		Coy left camp near Vaux at 3PM and entrained at HAZEL MESSELLES STATION 5.35 PM. Weather at this time very showery but warm.	A
	8-5-18		Coy arrived at LILLERS STATION after an all night journey at 1.30 A.M. Offloading proceeded slowly owing to bad or insufficient supply of "ramps"	A

Army Form C. 2118.

WAR DIARY
or
INTELLIGENCE SUMMARY.
(Erase heading not required.)

Place	Date	Hour	Summary of Events and Information	Remarks and references to Appendices
LE CORNET BRASSART	8.5.18.		Coy. appreciation reported to R.T.O. for orders as to future location of the coy. Nothing had been arranged owing to Coy. Turning up earlier than previously arranged by Army. Coy after a march of 9.0 minutes arrived at LE CORNET BRASSART a small HAMLET near HAM. Coy visited by CRE in afternoon, all details of our new work arranged.	
	9.5.18.		89 Coy ordered to work on the LILLERS – STEENBECQUE LINE a defensive position consisting of Breastworks, front line and support. O.C. went round the line with O.C. 61 Field Coy R.E. and arranged to take over all works from GUARBECQUE to LE ACRE. Working Parties on the new defensive system consisted of one Portuguese Labour Coy. and 4 British Labour Coy.	
	10.5.18.			
	11.5.18.		Work progressing excellently. Trouble experienced with trenches/revisions dug over - inches below water level. This country is very flat the water being almost to the surface.	
	12.5.18 – 15.5.18 16.5.18		Work continued on G.H.Q. LINE. NEW RESERVE LINE 6 coy W. of from FRONT LINE Position. Taped out Work commenced. Breastwork building first. All Bridges were drawn secretly.	
	17.5.18		Preparations made by Coy for a transport competition between the 3 Field Coys. to be held on 19th inst. Sunday on which day the Coy was to have a rest.	
	18.5.18		GOC 1st (Light) Division went round trenches, O.C. 89 Coy accompanied him. M.G. emplacements were marked out.	

Army Form C. 2118.

WAR DIARY
or
INTELLIGENCE SUMMARY.
(Erase heading not required.)

Place	Date	Hour	Summary of Events and Information	Remarks and references to Appendices
LE CORNET BRASSART	19.5.18		Coy. resting. This being the first day of absolute rest since Coy. went into the Line South of ST. QUENTIN on January 26.9.18. Transport Competition between the 3 Field Coy. RE. 14 Division 61, 62, 63, Field Coy. Judges:- G.O.C. 14 Division, O.C. 14 Div. Train Lt. Col. Richan and the A.A. & Q.M.G., Col. Corfield. Judging commenced at 11 A.M. on the in a field near HAM Village. Results 63 Coy. R.E. winners, 62 Coy. second. Cup presented by C.R.E. 14 Division Lt. Col. Allen D.S.O. P.E.	Sqh Go Cols
	20.5.18		A practice of manning the Battle Stations on the Front Line system being carried out by the Coy. took place at 9 A.M. R.E. dispose on roadways until orders to hold same & guide retreating troops into new positions. Practice satisfactory. All arrangements well in hand and satisfactory. Carried out. O.C. accompanied G.S.O.1. 14 Division in making inspection of dispositions. In afternoon O.C. went round the lines with C.R.E. 14 Division. This was continued in the evening.	
	21.5.18 - 25.5.18		Work continued on the LILLERS-STEENBECQUE LINE. Excellent progress made with the assistance of 4 Labour Companies - 63rd, 79, 712, 725. — On 24th inst. Coy. and Working Parties resting. In honour of same, General equipment inspection. At 5.30 P.M. Dinner Service at 6.30 P.M. a Concert was held. A stage consists of a bay of pontoon G.S. was erected and a most excellent Concert was given with the assistance of artists from various units.	
	26.5.18		Attached Gun emplacement started. This was built into the Trenchworks, going 6 ft. Corpl. CR. & pioneered the trenches a company of with O.C. 63 Coy. Camouflage officer 1st Corps, artistes & site of M.G. emplacements.	

Army Form C. 2118.

WAR DIARY
or
INTELLIGENCE SUMMARY.
(Erase heading not required.)

Instructions regarding War Diaries and Intelligence Summaries are contained in F.S. Regs., Part II. and the Staff Manual respectively. Title pages will be prepared in manuscript.

89 Field Coy RE

Place	Date	Hour	Summary of Events and Information	Remarks and references to Appendices
LE CORNET BRASSART.	27.5.18		Bridge over River GUARBECQUE completed. Screens also built up. Drawing of this is attached.	see attd drawing A
	28.5.18		Excellent Progress made on RIVIERS-STEENBECQUE RESERVE LINE. The working parties up to 5 offs 140 ors, a good day's work, averaging 130 c.ft. per man.	A
	29.5.18		OC reconnoitred a large tract of country with a view to following over the outfall of drains, the water level in trenches being higher than the normal, notwithstanding the fine hot weather; this was owing to brick blocking up drains to provide a supply of water.	A
	30.5.18		OC went round the Short and Reserve lines. Arrangements made to take over additional work from 61 Field Coy RE, as a certain amount of labour was being withdrawn from the works.	A
	31.5.18		OC out all afternoon with Camouflage Officer Ll Cpl. viewing Machine Gun Emplacements. Arrangements in hand for showing horse, mule, and vehicle at the 4/Divl. Horse Show on Sunday.	A

Duell
Major
OC 89 Field Coy RE

WAR DIARY or INTELLIGENCE SUMMARY

Army Form C. 2118.

VOL 34

89th Field Coy RE

Place	Date	Hour	Summary of Events and Information	Remarks and references to Appendices
LE CORNET BRASSART	1-6-18		The Readjustment of Works boundaries between 61 Field Coy and 89 Coy, the latter being given an additional piece of the line.	L.J.
	2-6-18		Sunday morning company paraded in full marching order for inspection and instruction in equipment fitting. 2 hours drill carried out under Section Officers. Same morning Company Sports held in the afternoon, the meeting was attended with great success. Prizes given to winners at Pay Parade 6 P.M.	L.J.
	3-6-18		Excavation commenced for 3 M.G. concrete emplacements. One extra platoon of labour put on to the Réserve Line.	L.J.
	4-6-18		Details of action to be taken by 89 Field Coy RE in event of hostile attacks written out and Section officers detailed to various duties in this respect. C.R.E. visited Coy HQrs.	L.J.
	5-6-18		Arrangements made for daily detailing off all important points in the line. A working party 600 strong consisting of a Battn. of Royal Irish Fusiliers available on 6th inst. for work on the Réserve Line.	L.J.
	6-6-18		5 R.I.F. Battn. placed on works at the Pire near RIVERS. Two days work completed by them.	L.J.
	7-6-18		O.C. 89 Coy. visited OC 5 Royal Irish Fusiliers with a view to fixing tasks & responsibility for a sector of the work.	L.J.
	8-6-18		A framework construction completed. As ground very hard are dug now sod cutting and digging very trying.	L.J.
	9-6-18		Usual Sunday Parade with 2 hours drill. Church Parade 6 P.M. and concert afterwards. 43 (L.N) Infantry Brigade took over defences (MILITARY STEENBECQUE LINE.)	L.J.
	10-6-18		Redistribution of labour and works front the line, formerly divided into 3 groups given in charge of N.C.O's with N.C.I. Section and a Field Section of No4 Section	L.J.

Army Form C. 2118.

WAR DIARY
or
INTELLIGENCE SUMMARY.
(Erase heading not required.)

Place	Date	Hour	Summary of Events and Information	Remarks and references to Appendices
LE CORNET BRASSART.	10-6-18		(Cont) with 3 platoons (600 men) of the 63 725 Labour Company for a working party, on a piece of the line from LE PRÉ to LE CORNET BOUDOIR. 725 Labour Coy. from Le CORNET BOUDOIR to Le CORNET BRASSART finishing that portion of the almost completed line. The northern line from Le CORNET BRASSART to the BERGUETTE — ST. VENANT RAILWAY under Lieut Hallowell with 4 Platoon 103rd Labour Coy and 1 Platoon 712 Labour Coy.	A1
	11-6-18		Drainage of the Breastwork sited by O.C. man-chain being committed. No 4 Section and 159 Labour Coy placed on BERGUETTE DEFENCES so far south as the Railway.	A.
	12-6-18		Works on all Defence Line progressing steadily. The 2 Battalion provided for workers Reserve Line departed on Saturday, staff are no longer available for works.	A
	13-6-18		Slight redistribution of labour. 1 Platoon 725 Labour Coy. being placed at disposal of No 2 Section on the Reserve Line. The odd platoon of 712 Labour Coy under Lt Hallowell placed on Reserve line for work.	A
	16-6-18		A large amount of wiring completed on the sea-wing & Inspection Trains being received.	A
	17-6-18		Front line which had been commenced on 7-5-18 by 8 & Coy R.E. about 4000-5000 yds in length completed, breastworks 6 ft of cover in proper and 5 ft of parados. Several thousand yards of wire put out.	A
	19-6-18			A
	20-6-18		No 3 section placed on Reserve line with orders to complete the wiring of the	A

Army Form C. 2118.

WAR DIARY
or
INTELLIGENCE SUMMARY.

(Erase heading not required.)

89th Field Co RE

Place	Date	Hour	Summary of Events and Information	Remarks and references to Appendices
LE CORNET BOURG BRASSART.	21-6-18		Fresh Instructions issued to Section officers in the event of Battle Stations being manned. Each section to furnish 2 figures for all roads leading into the Sector from LA MIQUELLERIE to GOARBECQUE. Seven figures in all. Duty of figures being to guide troops returning from front line into the LILLERS-STEENBECQUE DEFENCE LINE.	U.
	22-6-18		Work continued on lines without incident. But warning received that Coy would probably move in a few days time. Special orders issued re transport, orders issued with a view to securing absolute uniformity of Dress and Equipment. New Company Sergt Major reported duty.	SS
	26-6-18		Considerable sickness in company owing to a bit of minor fatigue whilst semi general	SS
	27-6-18.			SS
	28-6-18		Work on Defence lines suffering considerably from shortage of plain wire were for anchoring the Hurdles. Considerable difficulty found in employing the many of the 4 Labour Coys.	SS
	29-6-18		OC went round all Defence Works and visited 2 Battle Hqrs, also new Reserve Communication Trenches.	SS
	30-6-18		Sunday - Company Drilling all morning, Rifle Exercises and infantry Drill.	U

[signature]
Major OC
89 Field Coy

A5834 Wt.W4973/M687 750,000 8/16 D. D. & L. Ltd. Forms/C.2118/13.

WAR DIARY
or
INTELLIGENCE SUMMARY.

(Erase heading not required.)

Army Form C. 2118.

89th Coy R.E.

Place	Date	Hour	Summary of Events and Information	Remarks and references to Appendices
LE CORNET BRISSART	1-7-18		C.R.E. visited Coy H.Qrs. and informed O.C. that Coy would probably support the 14 (Light) Division on either Wednesday or Thursday. The Division having been at rest getting reinforcements. Practically all labour now on Reserve Line.	L
	2-7-18		Major Stewart R.E. took over control of KILLERS-STEENBECQUE DEFENCE LINE.	L
	3-7-18		25% of the Company sick with a kind of fever "Spanish Spleusis" because of its supposed origin in Spain. Special precautions taken to prevent its spreading. Patients isolated and strong stimulant obtained for invalids. 2 Officers Lts. Holliwell and Oldfield with ill with fever. Weather extremely fine generally but very cold wind blowing.	L
	4-7-18		Coy. ration strength down to 146 instead of 220. Considerable trouble on works owing to shortage of material, it being gradually impossible to provide work to 1500 men employed there. Communication trench commenced between front line and Rear Line (Reserve) screening only within 30 yards of Reserve Line so that if enemy attacked and took the front line he would not be able to bomb down Communication trenches.	L
	5-7-18		Large quantities of revetting wire for netting backs all the hurdles which had been made to want of it, now able to be dealt with and many yards of headwork completed.	L

Army Form C. 2118.

WAR DIARY
or
INTELLIGENCE SUMMARY.
(Erase heading not required.)

Instructions regarding War Diaries and Intelligence Summaries are contained in F.S. Regs., Part II. and the Staff Manual respectively. Title pages will be prepared in manuscript.

Place	Date	Hour	Summary of Events and Information	Remarks and references to Appendices
LE CORNET BRASSART.	6-7-18		Major Stewart visited O.C. and discussed various questions priority of work, stores, supply O.C. estimated 10 days work on Reserve Lg. would see completion. Stores came up at the rate of 200 Hurdles a day with 25 Coils of plain wire. Large quantities of Barbed wire required to complete the lining. 35 Coils of wire being required per hundred yards.	A
	7-7-18		Sunday. Company had full marching order parade at 9AM with stores inspection and afternoon was 2½ hours drill. Usual pay parade at 11-30 AM. Afternoon left free to men for sports, resting, to. Warning Order received from CRE that the Coy. would in all probability move at very short notice.	A
	8-7-18		Preparing "handing over reports" for the 4 Labour Coy. to enable them to carry on with work pending the arrival of other Field Coy. Operation Order for the move received at 7.30 P.M. O= C.R.E. officer attached to C.O.b. would take over and the Labour Coys. would not take over this work. This rather upset arrangements, as just handing over having then to be arranged. These were completed however by midnight and all work detail, stores & Labour questions arranged in advance to completion of the work.	A
	9-7-18		Transport of Coy. moved off at 6 A.M. whilst the remainder of the Coy. were transported in Lorries to a point 4 miles N. of ST OMER, and one mile from LEDERZEELE. (Sheet 27 S.33 a 8.5). Dismounted Section arrived at destination at 1.30 P.M.	A

LEDERZEELE. (Sheet 27 S.33 a 8.5).

A5834. Wt.W4973/M687 750,000 8/16 D.D. & L. Ltd. Forms/C.2118/13.

Army Form C. 2118.

WAR DIARY
or
INTELLIGENCE SUMMARY.
(Erase heading not required.)

Place	Date	Hour	Summary of Events and Information	Remarks and references to Appendices
LEDEZEELE	9/7/18		Mounted Section arrived at 5.30PM. and by 6.0AM whole of company was settled down comfortably in a new camp with billets of huts & tents. Company camp arrangements made. C.R.E.S.G.H.Q Defences called and stated that the Coy would stand by for 3 days and would then move to a new place.	A.
"	10/7/18		Assistance given to G.H.Q Defences in the neighbourhood. One Officer and 8 NCOs etc to a few men in supervision and wiring of the Defences. Use of Baths for our officers and men granted. Message received from G.O.C. VIII Corps troops, to meet C.E VIII Corps on 11th inst. at Corps Hqrs.	S.J.
"	11/7/18		Lt. 89 Coy. and Chief Engineer VIII Corps and went round the Trench System of the WINNIZEELE DEFENCE LINE. Arrangements made for work to be commenced there at once. O.C. returned to Coy Hqrs and made out all orders for the move to St. SYLVESTRE CAPPEL on 12th July 1918.	A.
"	12/7/18		Company paraded at 10 AM. for the march in complete marching order. Weather very bad, extremely heavy showers commenced early in the morning and continued until 1 PM. Company went by way of CASSEL and reached their destination at 3.30 PM. MAP Ref. Sheet 27, P.23 central. Storms several and within 4 hours company had settled in under canvas.	A.
	13/7/18		The portion of the company not being central with their work, was moved the day 6 o'clock to the TERDEGHEM village. Sheet P.11, a.4.0.	A.

Army Form C. 2118.

WAR DIARY
or
INTELLIGENCE SUMMARY.
(Erase heading not required.)

Place	Date	Hour	Summary of Events and Information	Remarks and references to Appendices
TERDEGHEM	14/7/18		The day spent in reconnoitring the track line from RWELDE ST. SYLVESTRE CAPPEL.	A
	15/7/18		Preparations being made to commence work on the 16th inst. Company employed in putting bomb proof cover walls around the huts or tents.	A
	16/7/18		Work commenced. Preparing execution markers ready for working parties arrival on 17th inst. O.C. E9 Coy visited O.C. 20 Middlesex Regt. repairing work.	A
	17/7/18		Working parties from 20 Battn. Middlesex Regt. in Breastworks sections from ground level. 60 cubic feet per man. The working party was the first detachment of the 14th Division reformed at home after the Battle of ST. QUENTIN.	A
	18/7/18		2 Coys of another Battn. of the 14th Division, the 6th Battn. WILTSHIRES, arrived and proceeded to work. Sections of work upon which 89 & J10 by is engaged divided into 2 portions the work under 2Lt Hallowell with the left Half Coy. and 2Lt Moore P2. with the Right Half Coy. on the Southern Half.	A
	19/7/18		An Observation Post commenced at various points of the line.	A

Army Form C. 2118.

WAR DIARY
or
INTELLIGENCE SUMMARY.
(Erase heading not required.)

Instructions regarding War Diaries and Intelligence Summaries are contained in F. S. Regs., Part II. and the Staff Manual respectively. Title pages will be prepared in manuscript.

Place	Date	Hour	Summary of Events and Information	Remarks and references to Appendices
TERDEGHEM.	20/7/18		New works proposed, M.G. Pill Boxes, ruined Observation Post in the Windmill at P.7. (known as ZION MILL).	A.
	21/7/18		Sunday, Company training in the morning and resting in afternoon. Reinforcements, some 30 strong had arrived some days ago and proved to be men of declined physique in general. C.O. met O.C. Northern part of our line to set Observation Posts.	A.
	22/7/18		Weather at this time very bad very heavy heavy showers all day with occasional periods of sunshine, ground very heavy made work very slow. Work on Observation Posts at ZION MILL (Sht. 27) P17 a 3.8. with No 2 Section. Good start made.	B
	23/7/18		C.R.E. came round trench system with Chief Engineer VIII Corps. No 1 Section with 6th Wiltshire Regt. working near ST SYLVESTRE. no Breastworks giving 6 feet of cover. No 2 Section near the mill at P17 a 3.8. with 2 Companies of the 20 Middlesex Regt.	A.
	24/7/18		Warning received that 2nd Field Coy R.E. would shortly be moved into training area for a rest. The Company having been hard at work or rather fighting and working since January the 26th 1918.	A.
	25/7/18		Work being pushed on. No particular event to record	A.

A 5834 Wt.W4973/M687 750,000 8/16 D. D. & L. Ltd. Forms/C.2118/13.

WAR DIARY
or
INTELLIGENCE SUMMARY.

Army Form C. 2118.

Place	Date	Hour	Summary of Events and Information	Remarks and references to Appendices
TERDEGHEM	26-7-18		Chief Engineer in Corps visited the Coy Camp and expressed his satisfaction with it. Weather very bad consequently little excavating could be carried out	
"	27-7-18		Orders received that 89 Field Coy R.E. would not move, programme of Coy Work accordingly altered.	
"	28-7-18		Having received that 89 Field Coy R.E. would resume to Training area and the section No 4 under Lt-O'Keefe would came to WESTROVE near ST OMER in the 29R moved at 7AM by lorry. A quantity of Coy Bridging equipment was recovered. There this day being Sunday company trained returning Hats in afternoon, men free for their own amusement at 5 P.M.	
"	29-7-18		No 4 section and limbers left for WESTROVE at 7AM arriving subsequently at noon. Handing over reconnaissance with O.C. 62 CoyRE into returning over in the afternoon. Only 2 Coys of 6th W.R. Reg't being available to work Estry. Having done reports made out and sent to O.C. 62 Coy RE at 7 P.M.	
"	30-7-18.			
"	31-7-18		89 Field Coy RE moved to L-FORTEFIE for night of 30 July and 1st August, the intention being to move on August 1st 1918. to WESTROVE.	

Chuck
Major R.E.
O.C. 89 Field Coy R.E.

WAR DIARY or INTELLIGENCE SUMMARY

Army Form C. 2118.

89th Coy R.E.
W.D. 36

Place	Date	Hour	Summary of Events and Information	Remarks and references to Appendices
LEDER-ZEELE	21/8/18		Coy moved by march to a small village south west of F.P.FR.LECQUES.	L.3
F.P.FR.LECQUES	2/8/18		Coy settling down in comfortable billets. good messes for Officers Seniors & Junior NCOs. OC went to Committee meeting of the Divisional Horse Show at DU AYRE.	L.1
" "	3/8/18		The whole Company engaged in preparing a show-ground for 19 Divisional Horse Show to be held on August 5.19.18. (Bank Holiday)	L.1
	4/8/18		Training programme made out with a view to commencing on the 6th inst after Horse Show had been completed. 30 Sappers under 2 Lt Holland paraded before 2 Army Commander.	L.1
	5/8/18		Coy entries for 6 events in the Horse Show met succeeded in gaining seven medals for their Water Cart, but owing to qualify of animals being below the average no prize was awarded.	L.1
	6/8/18		75 Sappers of the Coy available for training. Three men under 2 Lt Hollowell carried out bridging practise with pontoon gear. Programme of Training attended. Excellent facilities for bridging with pontoons on the River HOULLE at HOULLE	L.1
	7/8/18		Training continued. Weather ideal.	L.3
	8/8/18		Coy training according to programme.	L.3
	9/8/18		do do do	L.3
	10/8/18		do do do	

Army Form C. 2118.

WAR DIARY
or
INTELLIGENCE SUMMARY.
(Erase heading not required.)

Instructions regarding War Diaries and Intelligence Summaries are contained in F.S. Regs., Part II. and the Staff Manual respectively. Title pages will be prepared in manuscript.

Place	Date	Hour	Summary of Events and Information	Remarks and references to Appendices
EPERLECQUES	12-8-18		A Hollowell and party of 20 Sappers repaired the parade on this day as for the previous Sunday, but before His Majesty the King at TERDEGHEM. Remainder of Company went to ST. OMER for Pleasure trip. Weekly pay at 10.30 A.M.	A
	13-8-18		Training continued	A
	14-8-18		Coy spent the day on 400 yds. Rifle Range and put in some good practice	A
	15-8-18		Coy preparing for inspection by G.O.C. (4 Division) on Saturday 18-8-18	A
	16-8-18		Training chiefly consisted of Infantry Drill, and lectures of a technical nature	
	17-8-18		Finishing touches being put to Coy transport equipment etc. 35% of the Coy during this training period were employed on making articles for other units, meatsafes, etc.	
	18-8-18		Inspection by G.O.C. 14 Division and Chief Engr. XVIII Corps at 10 A.M. G.O.C. congratulates Coy on appearance and general turnout	A
	19-8-18		Coy moved to WATTEN where they were billeted in the town. (at 10 A.M.)	A
	20-8-18		Coy entrained at 10 A.M. WATTEN STATION and arrived PROVEN STATION at 2.15 P.M. Marched to WILKINS CAMP at (SLC27) F.25.A. arriving at 4.15 P.M., billets in a very foul condition, all had to be cleaned out before being habitable.	A
	21-8-18		O.C. Coy went round the West POPERINGHE SWITCH DEFENCE LINE with C.R.E. XVIII and C.E. 2 Corps. Arrangements made to commence work on lines at once with an American Battalion for a working party.	A

Army Form C. 2118.

WAR DIARY
or
INTELLIGENCE SUMMARY.
(Erase heading not required.)

Instructions regarding War Diaries and Intelligence Summaries are contained in F.S. Regs., Part II. and the Staff Manual respectively. Title pages will be prepared in manuscript.

Place	Date	Hour	Summary of Events and Information	Remarks and references to Appendices
ST JANSTER BIEZEN.	22/8/18		Work on the Roeme line of the system commenced. Task given = 900 cubic feet. Battalion areas the 3rd of the 117 Regt 30th Division (American)	U.
	23/8/18		Work continued. Great shortage of stores, the reasons for defence lines being apparently died down somewhat.	U.
	24/8/18 25/8/18		Preparation made for work on Defence line with 3 Battalions, 1 Battalion a work.	U.
	26/8/18		Weather broke up, heavy storms all day. Sudden change of views caused a slight "new up" with working parties. One Battalion only doing a good day's work.	U.
	27/8/18		Orders received that the 14th Division would relieve the 30 Division in the line at YPRES. O.C. visits O.C. 207 Field Coy R.E. with a view to taking over the line from him.	
	28/8/18		Coy moved at 5 P.M. to billets of 207 Field Coy R.E. at "Dirty Bucket" Camp. near YPRES.	U.
	29/8/18		Work commenced as taken over from the 207 Coy R.E. New Buildings for Russian Disinfectors, Delousing Station and construction of Posts near VLAMERTINGHE on the "GREEN LINE". Coy on "Roeme" Divisional Works. C.R.E. visits Coy Hqrs.	U.
	30/8/18		O.C. visited all works and arranged for Horse Standings & Camp Fittings to be salved	U.
	31/8/18		O.C. visits BRAKE CAMP and arranged for alterations & recent schemes for Disinfecting Station	U.

TRAINING PROGRAMME.

89th. Field Coy. R.E.

	Morning.	Afternoon.
1st. Day. Aug. 2nd.1918	Physical Training. 7.15a.m.till 7.35 a.m. Infantry Drill & Rifle Exercises. 9.A.M. till 10.A.M. Interval. 10.A.M. till 10.30.A.M. Musketry,including Aiming & Trigger pressing.lecture on the rifle, rapid loading,different firing positions, 10.30 - 11.30.A.M. Lecture. 11.30.A.M.-12.30.P.M.	Military Engineering, Knotting & Lashing, care of ropes etc. Practical Demonstration to Nos.1.2.3.&.4.Sections from 2.P.M.- 4.30.P.M. Insert after,care of ropes etc.:- Splicing,strength of ropes etc.
2nd.Day. Aug.3rd.1918	Physical Training. 7.15 - 7.35.A.M. As for 1st.Day. { 9.A.M.-10.A.M. 10.A.M.-10.30.A.M. 10.30 - 11.30.A.M. Nos.1 & 2.Sections.Weldon Trestle erection.Nos.3 & 4.Secs.Bridging Scheme for 2 N.C.Os. & 30 men to erect Double Lock Bridge in 3 hours; 1 hour allowed for reconnaisance & obtaining Stores.11.30.A.M.-12.30.P.M.	To complete Double Lock Bridge not later than 4.30.P.M. 20 men training for Army Commanders Parade.
3rd. Day. Aug.4th.1918	Programme "Cut out"as all available men are required on works. 1 Officer & 20 men to Army Commanders Parade Sunday Aug.4th.1918.	Any available men on fatigues,completion of Sapper's Mess,disinfecting barns & limewashing barns Cookhouses completed.
4th.Day.	All men sent to Divisional Horse Show.	
5th.Day. Aug.6th.1918	Physical Training. 7.15.A.M.-7.45.A.M. Infantry Drill.9. -10.A.M. Musketry, Aiming, & Trigger pressing. also fire control.10.30-11.30.A.M. 11.40.A.M. Nos.2 & 3 Sections, arranging pontooning stores for following day's Bridging Course. Nos. 1 & 4 Sects. Extended Order Drill. 11.30 A.M.till 12.30 P.M.	2.- 4.30.P.M. No. 1 Sect. dismantling a Double Lock Bridge of 45'span. Nos. 2 & 3 Sects.(each section 34 strong, rein- forced by Sappers from Nos 1 & 4 Sections). Lecture on Floating Bridges with a view to preparing the following day's work,also all stores fashioned ready for work e.g. cables, & lashings whipped & cut to correct lengths: No. 4 Sec to build a Crows Nest O.P. at 45' height in tree.

20 men will report for inoculation,as per Coy. Orders.

6th.Day. Aug.7th.1918. 70 men on bridging over the River Houlle at HOULLE. Practical lecture and explanation of the parts of the pontoon,and its

TRAINING PROGRAMME.(CONTINUED).

6th. Day.
Aug. 7th. 1918.
(continued)
bridging capacity. Pontoon Rowing Drill, every man to have training as time will permit.
Trestle Bridging, erection of Weldon Trestles on the ground.
Building up trestles with rough round timbers for medium bridge.
Times,- leave Coy.Hd.Qrs. 7.30.A.M., one hour for mid-day meal and work until 4.P.M. then march back.
Strict discipline to be enforced on the march & on parades, so that the Standard of Infantry Drill will not be lowered. Insert:- See Remainder of Coy. will be inoculated After lowered.
Special instructions issued on 1st. Day's work.

7th. Day.
Aug. 8th. 1918
Bridging for same two sections, most of the work will be steady Drill in "forming up" the pontoon bridge, if time permits a raft may be built. Spare men will be interchanged but will continue construction of trestle bridge 2 trestles being at present ready for launching.

8th. Day.
Aug. 9th. 1918.
Construction of pontoon rafts, sappers will be trained in the handling of the raft, in rowing and steering to different points. Bridge of four half-pontoons for infantry in file will be built if time permits.
Improvised bridges will be constructed, to the extent material will allow.
Weldon trestles will be launched, and other trestle bridges in hand finished.

9th. Day.
10th. Aug. 1918.
Cask piers will be made if casks are available. Competition should be worked up between different squads, after steady training a squad of 14 men should make a cask pier in 1½ minutes.
Pontoon rafting will be continued also the Trestle Bridging
Lecture on "Gas Defence" by D.G.O. 11.30.A.M. till 12.30.P.M.

10th. Day.
Aug. 11th. 1918.
Sunday.
40 minutes steady drill for all sections from 9.AM till 9.40.A.M.
Box Respirators to be examined, and drill with same.
Church Parade at 11.A.M.
No parades for the remainder of the day.

11th. Day.
Aug. 12th. 1917.
Musketry Course on 400 yards range for all available.
5 rounds will be fired per man at following ranges and targets:-

No.	Target.	Practice.	Range.	Rounds.	Conditions.
1.	2nd.Class Bull.	Grouping.	100yds.	5.	Lying. Cover.
2.	" "	Fig.Applicat'n.	200 "	5.	" "
3.	" "	" "	300 "	5.	" "
4.	" "	" "	400 "	5.	Lying. Round. Cover.

89 Fd Coy R.E.

WM 37

Army Form C. 2118.

WAR DIARY
or
INTELLIGENCE SUMMARY.
(Erase heading not required.)

Instructions regarding War Diaries and Intelligence Summaries are contained in F. S. Regs., Part II. and the Staff Manual respectively. Title pages will be prepared in manuscript.

Place	Date	Hour	Summary of Events and Information	Remarks and references to Appendices
Dickey Bushes Camp	1/18		O.C. went out & over. Attended C.R.E.'s conference at 61st Fd Coy H.Q. No. 1 Section Readying Y/Bridges, No. 3 Section Johring 85., Bomb Store, Batt House No. 3 Section Rome Farm Switch & C.T. to Green Line, No. 4 Section Camp Work	Intl.
D	2-3d		Work same as 1st	Intl
D	6th		No. 1 Section withdrawing shapes from bridges. Orders received from C.R.E. Nos. 2, 3 & 4 Sections same as 1st.	Intl
D	7th		Most opp. from 62nd Fd Cy R.E.M.E. Taking out & put ignites at 7hos. Sections same as 1st	Intl
D	8th		Enlarging statha (62nd) for our use. Sections worked same as 1st. Church service in evening.	Intl
D	9th		2nd Lt Nairn rejoined Coy. went out under Lt Moore	Intl
D	10th		2nd Lt Deverall rejoined Coy.	Intl
D	11th		Went out new sites for refilling points with C.R.E. (work same as 1st)	Intl
D	12th		No. 1 Section withdrawing charges and erecting windows Readings, No. 2 Delousing Station, Batt Store and Gas Caison, No. 3 Rome Farm Switch, No. 4 Refilling Points (3). Moved into new standings.	Intl

A 3834 Wt. W4973/M687 750,000 8/16 D. D. & L. Ltd. Forms/C.2118/13.

Army Form C. 2118.

WAR DIARY
or
INTELLIGENCE SUMMARY.
(Erase heading not required.)

Instructions regarding War Diaries and Intelligence Summaries are contained in F. S. Regs., Part II. and the Staff Manual respectively. Title pages will be prepared in manuscript.

Place	Date	Hour	Summary of Events and Information	Remarks and references to Appendices
DIRTY BUCKET Camp.	13.		No.1 Section preparing new Horse Standings; No.2 Section Bus. Convoy, Boat Stove and Delivering Stations; No.3 Section Rome Farm Switch; No.4 Section Refilling Points (3).	Nil.
Do.	14-15		As on 13th.	Nil.
Ross Camp.	16		Left DIRTY BUCKET for ROSS CAMP.	Nil.
ORWELL Camp	17		Left Ross Camp for ORWELL CAMP. Erecting huts at ORWELL Camp for Div. HQ Ord.	Nil.
Do.	18		Erecting huts at ORWELL Camp. 2nd Lt. G.H.R. OLDFIELD proceeded on leave.	Nil.
do.	19		As on 18th.	Nil.
LEGER Fm.	20		Left ORWELL Camp for LEGER FARM. Handed over work at Div. HQ G.A. to 61st Fd. Coy. R.E.	Nil.
do.	21-27		No 1, 2, & 4 Sections Mule Track to Canal; No. 3 Section making and repairing Bridges on Canal.	Nil.
do.	28		No. 3 Section proceeded early this morning to repair Bridges over Canal to Lt. Infantry in attack. Repair work completed. No. 1, 2 & 4 Sections on ST ELOI – HOLLEBEKE Road	Nil.

A5834 Wt. W4973/M687 750,000 8/16 D. D. & L., Ltd. Forms/C.2118/13.

Army Form C. 2118.

WAR DIARY
or
INTELLIGENCE SUMMARY.

(Erase heading not required.)

Instructions regarding War Diaries and Intelligence Summaries are contained in F. S. Regs., Part II. and the Staff Manual respectively. Title pages will be prepared in manuscript.

Place	Date	Hour	Summary of Events and Information	Remarks and references to Appendices
LEGER Front	28-30		Nos 1, 2, 3, 4 Sections repairing Roads & take Field Guns to HOLLEBEKE.	Nil

Lieut. for Capt. E. R.E.
O.C. 89th Field Coy R.E.
1.10.18

Army Form C. 2118.

89 M Corps
Nov 38

WAR DIARY
or
INTELLIGENCE SUMMARY.
(Erase heading not required.)

Instructions regarding War Diaries and Intelligence Summaries are contained in F. S. Regs., Part II. and the Staff Manual respectively. Title pages will be prepared in manuscript.

Place	Date.	Hour	Summary of Events and Information	Remarks and references to Appendices
WULVERGHEM	1-10-18		Company moved from LEGER FARM (Sh.28 H30a 80:40) to WYTSCHAETE where the night of 1st & 2nd was spent, the company bivouaced at the Cross Roads of the village.	A
"	2-10-18		Company moved to vicinity of WULVERGHEM to dugouts in the old British trench system. Map location Sh.28/T6.c.6.5.	B
"	3-10-18		Company working on the section of Lezenes on the WOTNETON road from MESSINES and the erection of a new Divisional H.Qrs. near WULVERGHEM.	C
"	4-10-18		OC visited Brigade (the 41st) and arranged to reconnoitre the "LYS" River with a view to crossing same. 2Lt DEVERALL, 2Lt NAIRN RE carried out the reconnaissance. Lt. NAIRN after a 7 hour patrol reached his objective. brought back a good report. Lt DEVERALL had no success owing to heavy Machine Gun fire from the southern bank of the River by which the enemy held in great force, the infantry patrol accompanying him suffered heavy casualties.	D
"	5/10/18		Reports of reconnaissance handed to CRE and Brigade. The former expressed his great satisfaction with the work done in reconnoitring the River "LYS".	E

WAR DIARY
or
INTELLIGENCE SUMMARY.

Army Form C. 2118.

Place	Date	Hour	Summary of Events and Information	Remarks and references to Appendices
WULVERGHEM.	6-10-18		OC visited Brigade Hqrs. Work commenced on defence work from GOPPARD to MESSINES.	✓
	7-10-18		2 Officers engaged on reconnaissance of roads from DOSTAVERNE to WARNETON also examination of a pill box for a German "Booby" trap. Valuable work done in giving information re condition of ground area.	✓
	8-10-18		Work continued as follows :- Nos 1.3.4 Sections on screening the MESSINES-WARNETON RD. No 2 Section preparing track from MESSINES to GAPPARD.	✓
	9-10-18		Owing to probability of future bridging operations being carried out small detachments from each section were kept in camp. Barrel rafts being prepared.	
	10-10-18		Work as previously carried on. Officers busy reconnoitring the forward area near the River Lys. with a view to bridging same in face of enemy. On two outposts along the River Lys banks 1500 yards from the "our fact", Lieut R.J. NAIRN of No 1 Section made an excellent reconnaissance between WARNETON and BAS WARNETON. He brought back excellent information of great value.	✓

WAR DIARY
INTELLIGENCE SUMMARY

Army Form C. 2118.

Place	Date	Hour	Summary of Events and Information	Remarks and references to Appendices
	11-10-18		Works on road without incident. Stores being sent forward ready for bridging River "Lys".	1
	12-10-18		"Lys". Roads heavily shelled with gas shells and high explosive.	1
	13-10-18		Conference at CRE's office. 89 Coy ordered to co-operate with Infantry in forcing the passage of the River Lys between BAS WARNETON and a point midway between COMINES and WERVICQ. O.C. arranged for artillery barrages to cover the construction of bridges. Full details of operation as carried out on the 14th and 15th of October attached.	3
			Coy. busy on the screening of roads and preparing fascines.	
	14-10-18		Coy. engaged on operation in the first toe is the forcing of the passage of the River Lys.	4
	15-10-18		Coy. succeeded in throwing 4 bridges over the River Lys notwithstanding heavy enemy resistance. Operation described in appendix X	X, 5
	16-10-18		Coy. returned to billets that the day's rest. Coy. finished for Baths in afternoon.	
	17-10-18		Coy. moved to WERVICQ vil ex German billets. O.C. reconnoitred the destroyed bridges over the "Lys". Decided work on bridge at 28 Q 31 C.	3

Army Form C. 2118.

WAR DIARY
or
INTELLIGENCE SUMMARY.
(Erase heading not required.)

Place	Date	Hour	Summary of Events and Information	Remarks and references to Appendices
WERVICQ.	17-10-18		(Cont'd) near Chateau near BROUER. Coy arrived at 4 P.M. and at once settled into billets.	G
	18-10-18		Coy working on Heavy transport bridge with all 16 section Infantry Bridge being built at the site. Letters of congratulation from B.G.E. & 1 Infantry Bde. and O.C. 29 D.Li. received, these referred to operations in crossing the River Lys. The results of this battle were that the enemy decided to fall back a considerable distance leaving in our hands many Large towns and villages.	G
	19-10-18		Coy constructed pontoon bridge for horse traffic near WERVICQ. at night coy received orders to move to TOURCOING.	G
	20-10-18		Coy moved at 09.00 hrs to TOURCOING via BOUSEBECQ and RONCQ. Very excellent billets being obtained in what was formerly a German HOSPITAL, every man having a bed and mattress.	G
	21-10-18		Coy proceeded to work on bridges between WATTRELOS and TOURCOING. Party of 1 Officer & 50 O.Rs of "Australian Army" arrived for pioneer work with the Coy.	G

WAR DIARY
or
INTELLIGENCE SUMMARY.
(Erase heading not required.)

Army Form C. 2118.

Place	Date	Hour	Summary of Events and Information	Remarks and references to Appendices
TOURCOING	22.10.18		Considerable trouble on bridge works owing to scarcity of heavy timbers or girders.	J.
	23.10.18		Old bridge completely dismantled, both at WATTRELOS and on the TOURCOING - WATTRELOS ROAD. 26 charges of Perdite (thre early removed from forts in TOURCOING STATION). Work on bridge progressing satisfactorily. A series of large German mines found in the 6' way between the 2 sets of rails in goods station of the MOUSCRON.	J.
	24.10.18		2 Heavy Bridges for all traffic (except tanks) erected at WATTRELOS for 3rd (A'Webs:4.9) Sketches of the 2 Bridges attached.	M. ① and ②
MOUSCRON	25.10.18		Coy. move to billets in a large factory near MOUSCRON.	J.
	26.10.18		Coy. working with the exception of N°2 Section who were busy repairing mines from the MOUSCRON-TOURNAI RAILWAY. They removed two various strong points the 22nd October. 26 large 200 lb German Trench Mortar shells which had been laid either on the crown of the railway arches, or has been put in the abutments of bridges with delay action fuzes etc. This is in addition to those demined on the 22nd inst. During this present the	J.
	27.10.18		Coy. examined many factories for unexposed mines. German Coy. at rest (Sunday) refitting. Photos in the afternoon.	J.

WAR DIARY
or
INTELLIGENCE SUMMARY.
(Erase heading not required.)

Army Form C. 2118.

Place	Date	Hour	Summary of Events and Information	Remarks and references to Appendices
MOUSCRON	28/10/18		Coy. resting. All equipment being prepared, checked and cleaned up ready for operations. Report on Coy crossing sent to CRE Coy stocked.	
	29/10/18		Coy. at Baths and packing up ready for the move.	
	30/10/18		OC Visited CRE at DES HEPS regarding work during forward operations. Arrangements made to move the Coy. to a point North East of DOTTIGNIES.	
	31/10/18		Coy moved at approx. to LE HAIRERIE FARM (Sheet 29 T.30.a.3.6) following orders of moves made to the Coy. as a result of the "flu" epidemic:- 2/L R.J. NAIRN R.E. - The Military Cross - 2 Lieut (a/capt) F.W. COOPER R.E. L/Cpl (a/cpl mjr) G.A. HARVEY, 2nd Corp W. VICKERS, and SAPPER C. WILDERSPIN - all awarded the Military Medal. The Corps and Divisional Commanders also the C.R.E sent their congratulations. Coy settled into Billets by 12 hrs	

[signatures]
Myrick
O.C. 89 Field Coy R.E.

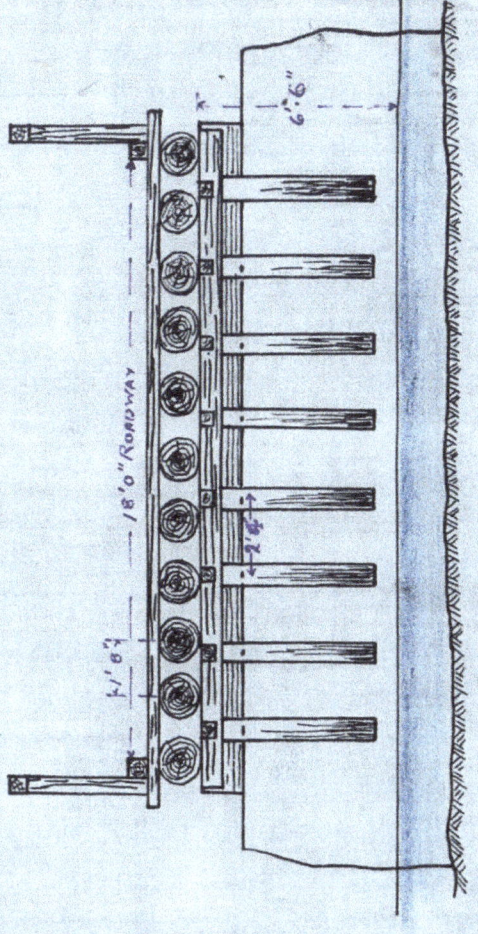

SECTION A.B

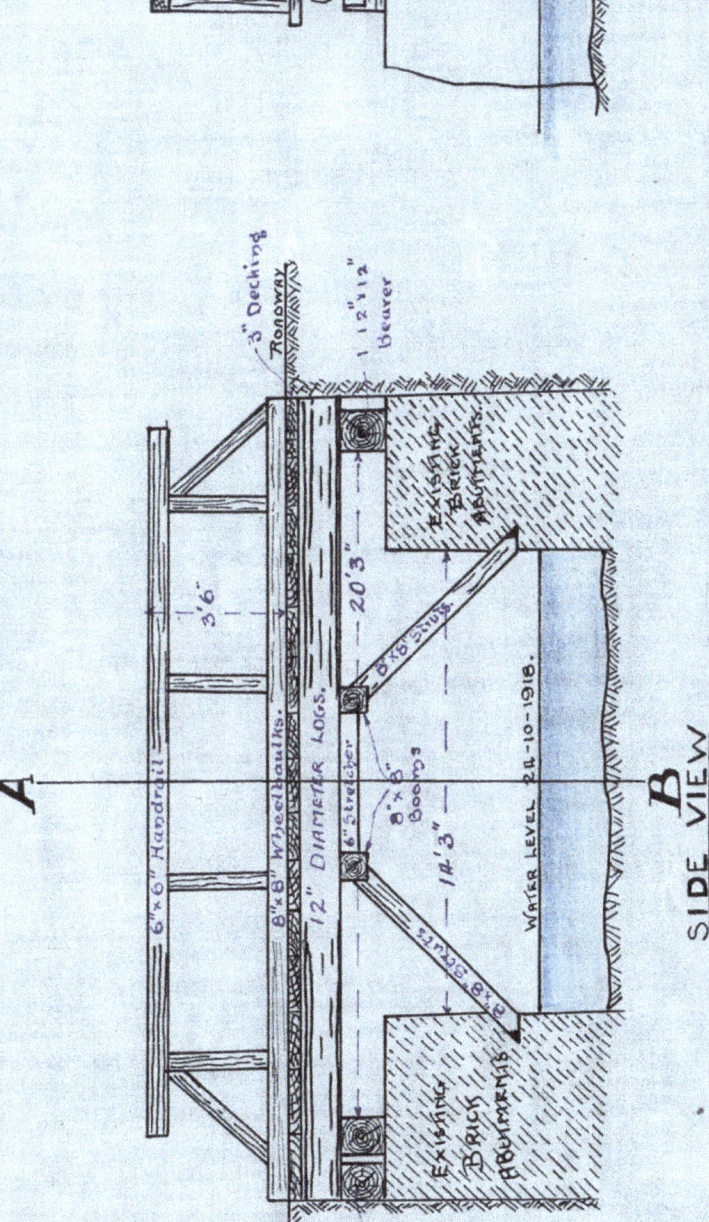

SIDE VIEW

TO CARRY 17 ENGLISH TONS.

HEAVY BRIDGE
RECONSTRUCTED OCTᵇᴿ 1918
BY 89ᵀᴴ FIELD Cᵒʸ R.E.
IN WATTRELOS (37.A.22.a.15:40.)

89ᵀᴴ FIELD Cᵒʸ R.E.
B.E.F.
27-10-1918

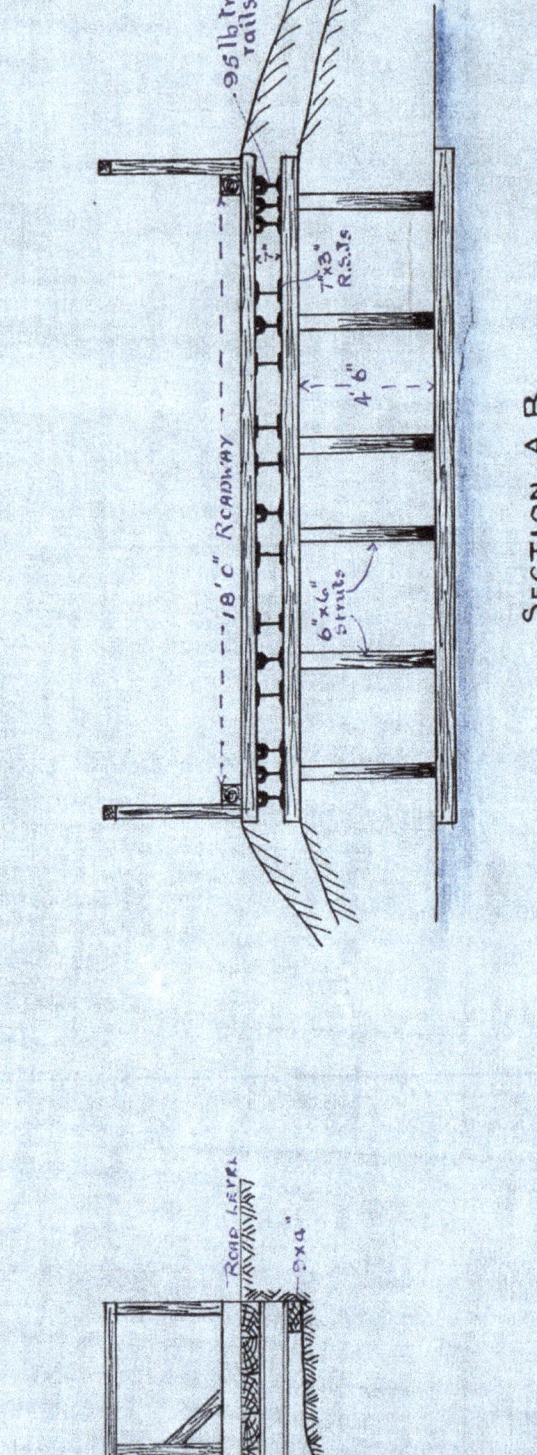

89th FIELD COY R.E.
B.E.F
28-10-1918

SECTION A B

SIDE ELEVATION.

HEAVY ROAD BRIDGE, WATTRELOS–TOURCOING ROAD.
RECONSTRUCTED BY 89TH FIELD COY R.E.
OCT 1918. MAP REF (37A14b 15:40)
To Carry 17 Tons.

WAR DIARY
or
INTELLIGENCE SUMMARY.
(Erase heading not required.)

Army Form C. 2118.

89 7 A Coy / Sep / 39

Place	Date	Hour	Summary of Events and Information	Remarks and references to Appendices
COYEGHEM.	1-11-18.		Company settling down into billets	G.
	2-11-18		Company "cleaning up", refitting and resting	G.
	3-11-18		Company making platform & testing pontoons for crossing the River ESCAUT.	G.
			at HELCHIN, as there would be every likelihood of the Division attacking across the river in a few days time.	G.
	4-11-18		Work continued as above, all pontoons and trestle gear being overhauled and repaired. This proved very necessary as it had been subjected to very rough usage. Coy. went to HEULE STATION (Nr. COURTRAI) to practice with INGLIS BRIDGE.	G.
	5-11-18		O.C. reconnoitred the River ESCAUT approaches near HELCHIN with a view to bridging the same at an early date.	G.
	6-11-18		Preparations in full progress for the future operations	G.
	7-11-18		3 Platoons on bridge seating prepared for INGLIS BRIDGE.	G.
	8-11-18		Half Company assisting 61 Field Coy R.E. to put bridge over the River ESCAUT north of HELCHIN. Several casualties suffered by O9 Coy. & O.C. one sapper killed.	G.
	9-11-18		Enemy retired from the line of the Schelde or River ESCAUT. Company	G.

WAR DIARY
or
INTELLIGENCE SUMMARY.
(Erase heading not required.)

Army Form C. 2118.

Place	Date	Hour	Summary of Events and Information	Remarks and references to Appendices
			Proceeded to HELCHIN ready to erect the INGLIS BRIDGE. Abutments built up and span decided upon was 96 feet. The first lorries bringing the bridge from AFDLE arrived at 16.15 hrs. No work could be done therefore on this day. It was decided to make a very early start the following day.	
	10-11-18		Full daylight on the INGLIS BRIDGE, work commenced at 06.30 hrs and ended at 18.30 hrs. The bridge being almost complete with the exception of 2 bays. All materials for this bridge instead of being brought up in order of construction were mixed and this caused considerable delay.	D
	11.11.18		Bridge erected on shore but considerable trouble experienced in launching and owing to heavy rain in the afternoon & early darkness work had to be suspended, 2 bays being bodied out over the river when the launching finally held off its roadway. News received that an ARMISTICE between belligerents had been signed.	A
	12.11.18		After much trouble the bridge was landed on the opposite shore, work was then carried out dismantling the Causte Balance trap.	D

WAR DIARY
or
INTELLIGENCE SUMMARY.

Army Form C. 2118.

Place	Date	Hour	Summary of Events and Information	Remarks and references to Appendices
	12.11.18		(Cont'd) At 19.30 hrs. work ceased, the Bridge being complete with exception of decking Seventeen but there still remained a little work in connecting up to existing March Track. Plans showing scheme carried out & details also Sezie elevation of Bridge.	
	13.11.18		Bridge opened for traffic at 14 hrs. From beginning to end the Bridge took 35 hrs to complete.	
	14.11.18		Company resting after 14 days very heavy work. Truth gear taken from the River.	SEPT
	15.11.18		Orders received that the Company was to move the following day to TOURCOING.	
	16.11.18		Company moved via DOTTIGNIES – WATTRELOS – to TOURCOING. Personnel taken in lorries transmits section by March route as above to same destination arriving at noon. Billets very unsatisfactory, too much furniture & no bedding.	
	17.11.18		Company inspected, afterwards relieved from duty that day. A detachment of 12 men sent to Church Parade on Thanksgiving Service at ROUBAIX. After the service the party marching with other detachments from the "Second Army" marched past the Army Commander.	
	18.11.18		Company lectured on the new Educational Scheme & Demobilization Scheme.	

WAR DIARY or INTELLIGENCE SUMMARY

Army Form C. 2118.

Place	Date	Hour	Summary of Events and Information	Remarks and references to Appendices
TOURCOING	19.11.18		Orders received that the Company would move back to HELCHIN on the 20th inst. The Pontoon Bridge at HELCHIN dismantled by a detachment of 1 NCO and 16 Sappers, in addition to similar party proceeded from another Field Coy of the Division.	M.
HELCHIN	20.11.18		Company moved from TOURCOING to HELCHIN - arriving at Billets 15.30 P.M. Trestle gear dumped at R.E. Park TOURCOING before leaving. Sappers left on guard.	L.?M.
"	21.11.18		Two Sections employed clearing the RIVER ESCAUT of debris. Arrangements made for re-milling of village. 3 lorry loads of material delivered. 62nd Field Coy sent 3 Pontoon Wagons. Sappers employed loading up same with Pontoons & Trestle gear.	L.?M.
"	22.11.18		Company employed on re-constructional work in Village. Football match in afternoon.	L.?M.
"	23.11.18		Completed clearing river of debris. Rebuilding village food store etc.	L.?M.
"	24.11.18		The Sappers went Northwards for Route march in the morning. Erected temporary Bath.	L.?M.
TOURCOING	25.11.18		The Pontoons were loaded up and Transport left HELCHIN at 10 a.m. in accordance with orders for TOURCOING. The Sappers following in the afternoon by Lorries. LT. MOORE met C.R.E. (MAJOR TEMPERLEY) in TOURCOING and was shown 4 Demolished Bridges and instructed to prepare a scheme for bridging one of the gaps and consider the removal of steelwork in the other cases.	L.?M.

Army Form C. 2118.

WAR DIARY
or
INTELLIGENCE SUMMARY.
(Erase heading not required.)

Place	Date	Hour	Summary of Events and Information	Remarks and references to Appendices
TOURCOING	26.11.18		Company settling into billets. Clearing wagons etc. Scheme for bridging gap over Canal. Boulevard GAMBETTA. TOURCOING prepared.	L.?.M.
"	27.11.18		Sappers. Drill parade and various fatigues. CAPT LYON rejoined.	L.?.M.
"	28.11.18		Company employed in erecting Delousing Chambers at Divisional Baths at BONDUES.	L.?.M.
"	29.11.18 30.11.18		Sappers making preparations for TORCHLIGHT TATTOO at ROUBAIX.	L.?.M.
"			Major Snell rejoined.	L.?.M.

I P Moore L? RE
89th Field Coy RE.

INGLIS BRIDGE.

ERECTED AT 37/C/Sb 30:50 ON 13-11-18.

BY

89TH FIELD COY. R.E.

SCALE 8'0" TO 1"

96'-0"

12'-0"

PLANK ROAD

Shaded portion of banks not to be dug away.

SLOPE

SECTION SHOWING ROAD JUNCTION.

3" ROAD DECKING.
3" ROAD BEARERS
6"×6"
8"×4" R.S.J.
6"×2" CHEEKS
STANDARD ROAD BEARER
MUD SEAT SIZE 6'×13' AREA 78 □FT. BUILT OF 9"×3"

89TH FIELD COY. R.E.
B.E.F. 14-11-18.

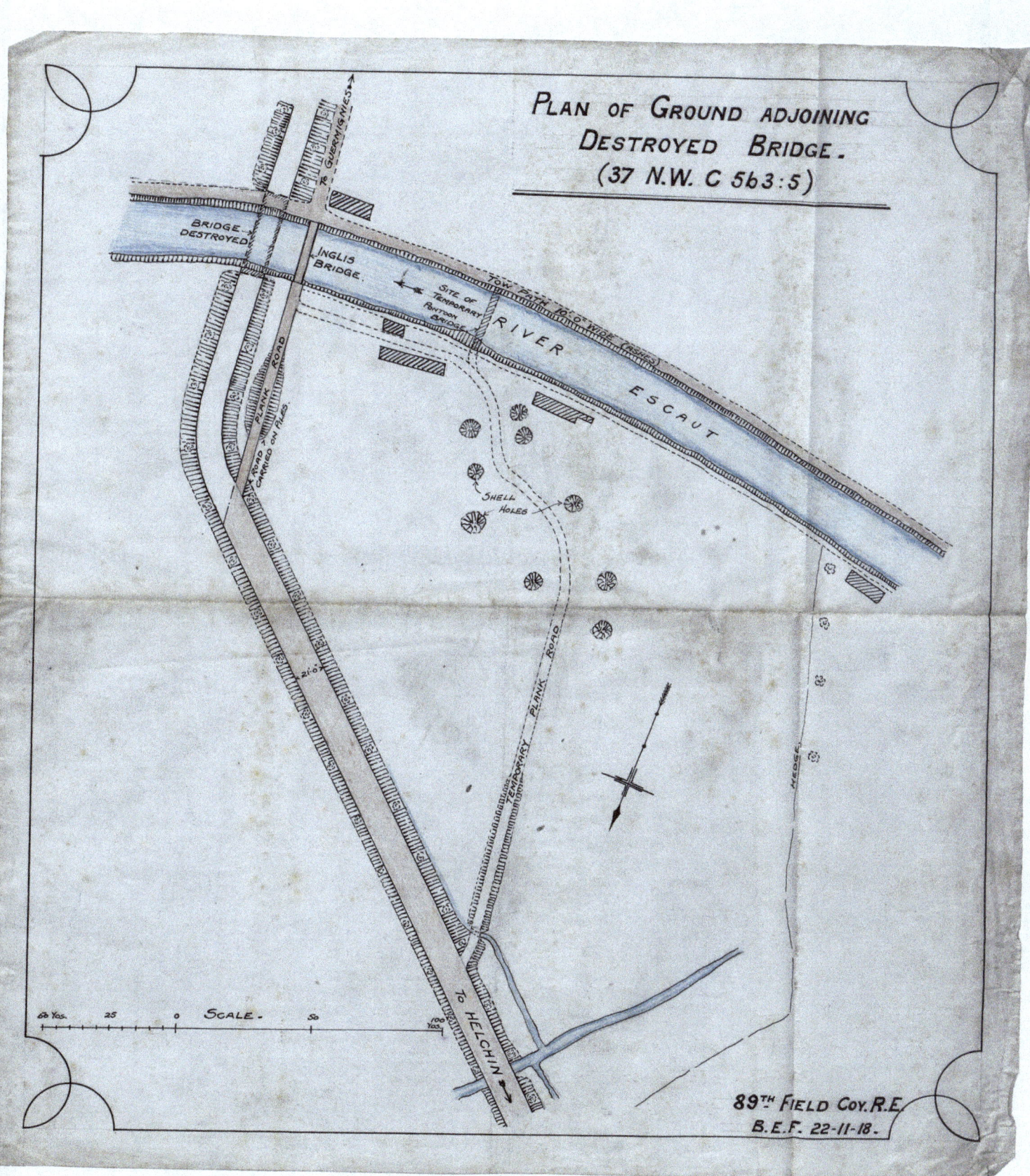

Army Form C. 2118.

WAR DIARY
or
INTELLIGENCE SUMMARY.
(Erase heading not required.)

897th Coy R.E.
Vol 40

Instructions regarding War Diaries and Intelligence Summaries are contained in F.S. Regs., Part II. and the Staff Manual respectively. Title pages will be prepared in manuscript.

Place	Date	Hour	Summary of Events and Information	Remarks and references to Appendices
TOURCOING	1-12-18		Coy employed on minor repair work, eg. fixing up baths for Infantry Brigade.	A.
	2-12-18		Reports being made of damaged bridges over the CANAL DE TOURCOING and schemes presented to the CRE for demolishing same	A.
	3-12-18		Apart from minor repair jobs Coy engaged in improvements to billets, fixing up boxing ring at local theatre, and generally cleaning up.	A.
	4-12-18		Educational scheme for the Company under the direction of Lt MOORE M.C. R.E. began in earnest. A French class of 19 members was formed and a Sapper with good knowledge of French was employed as instructor.	A.
	5-12-18		Coy preparing for the rehearsal of a Divisional Inspection by the Army Commander. Workshops for carpenters started in the men's billets	A.
	6-12-18		Coy. took part in a rehearsal with the Division. Coy marched past saluting point & marched into the Division in review order. Everything satisfactory.	A.
	7-12-18		CRE visited the Coy and inspected billets, workshops. He expressed satisfaction at everything shown to him.	A.

Army Form C. 2118.

WAR DIARY
or
INTELLIGENCE SUMMARY.
(Erase heading not required.)

Instructions regarding War Diaries and Intelligence Summaries are contained in F. S. Regs., Part II. and the Staff Manual respectively. Title pages will be prepared in manuscript.

Place	Date	Hour	Summary of Events and Information	Remarks and references to Appendices
TOURCOING	8-12-18		Sunday – Coy preparing the large "Square" in TOURCOING for reception of TORCHLIGHT TATTOO visit. Torchlight procession to be held at 18 hrs Monday the 9th inst.	H
	9-12-18		Coy preparing for final inspection of the Division by the Army Commander.	H
	10/12/18		Inspection of the Division by the 5th Army Commander. Weather bad, heavy rain all day. After the march past Coy marched off to their respective back billets.	
	11-12-18		Coy went in the morning to a lecture in the "Cirque" TOURCOING on "OLIVER TWIST". In the afternoon employed on repair work to various huts, billets etc. Lecture stage being erected in the "CIRQUE".	H
	12-12-18		OC went to local Industrial School with a view to arranging the hire of a carpenter's shop with machinery and all accessories complete.	H
	13-12-18		Designs made out for bridging the Canal DE ROUBAIX where it passes under the BOULEVARD GAMBETTA.	H
	14-12-18		Various minor works engaged nearly all men of the Company. Arrangements made to open Carpenters school of instruction in the "Ecole INDUSTRIELLE" TOURCOING on MONDAY the 16th inst. and 6 class doors there carried on in the Coy billets.	H

Army Form C. 2118.

WAR DIARY
or
INTELLIGENCE SUMMARY.
(Erase heading not required.)

Place	Date	Hour	Summary of Events and Information	Remarks and references to Appendices
TOURCOING	15/12/18		Sunday. The Coy rested and had Church Service in the morning.	A.
	16/12/18 to 21/12/18		Work continued on the Bridge over CANAL DE ROUBAIX. Width of gap to be spanned 110 feet. It was decided to use 5 bays and trouble trestles, the centre span to be 31 feet in order to allow tow path on the ROUBAIX side. Lock walls completely blown away and entirely of old brick work completely demolished and covered with many cubic yards of debris. Good progress made with this work.	B.
	22/12/18		Arrangements put in hand for a full days entertainment on XMAS DAY for the men in the Coy. Chairs, crockery etc hired. Concert room prepared and a great variety of Christmas fare purchased.	C.
	23/12/18		Work on bridge occupied most of the time of the Coy. Party of sappers sent to NIEUWERSHED to erect crosses over the graves of NCO's and men killed in the "HS" crossing.	D.
	24/12/18		Work on bridge as usual.	E.
	25/12/18		XMAS DAY. Coy works this day. Church Parade in morning. Whist Drive in afternoon and Dinner in evening afterwards a concert was held. The day ended very successfully.	F.
	26/12/18			

Army Form C. 2118.

WAR DIARY
or
INTELLIGENCE SUMMARY.
(Erase heading not required.)

Instructions regarding War Diaries and Intelligence Summaries are contained in F. S. Regs., Part II, and the Staff Manual respectively. Title pages will be prepared in manuscript.

Place	Date	Hour	Summary of Events and Information	Remarks and references to Appendices
TOURCOING	26/12/18		BOXING DAY. A football match was played in the afternoon and in the evening a dance was given, the civilians of Tourcoing joined the Coy and spent a very merry evening	A. 1
	27/12/18		Work was again resumed and the carpenters school also opened again.	A. 1
	28/12/18		Considerable trouble experienced in getting 40-foot girders from ROUBAIX to TOURCOING owing to lack of a strong wagon, trouble was experienced with the bad roads which shook the improvised vehicle to pieces.	A.
	29/12/18 to 31/12/18		Work on the bridge as usual, no incident of importance to report upon, foundations of the old Irish culvert over the CANAL DE ROUBAIX were cleared and 2 trestles for the store dump prepared. Eleven men have left the Company during the month for demobilisation in England, mostly coalminers, they belonged chiefly to the chosen Section so no experienced men forthcoming the company accordingly placed.	A.

Major R.E.
O.C. 89 Field Coy R.E.

Army Form C. 2118.

89th Field Coy R.E.

Vol 41 /14

WAR DIARY or INTELLIGENCE SUMMARY.

(Erase heading not required.)

Instructions regarding War Diaries and Intelligence Summaries are contained in F. S. Regs., Part II. and the Staff Manual respectively. Title pages will be prepared in manuscript.

Place	Date	Hour	Summary of Events and Information	Remarks and references to Appendices
			Three sections of the Coy employed throughout this period on the tramway Bridge over the CANAL DE ROUBAIX in TOURCOING. (BOULEVARDE GAMBETTA)	
	Jan 1.19		Bridge consists of 5 bays over a span of 100 feet, the centre span over the canal being 38 feet in length. 4 Heavy turn timber trestles providing necessary piers. A great deal of excavating required also light traffic bridge for pedestrians built at side of works.	A
			No 2 Section maintaining bridges in Corps area and constructing Refuse Destructor for Corps Sanitary scheme in Town of TOURCOING. This work for the 4 Sections fully occupied the Company. Demobilisation proceeding rapidly nearly 40 sappers and N.C.Os having left the Coy to return to civil life in England.	A
	Jan 24. 19		Weekly dances and whist drives arranged for the Coy were a great success, both with soldiers & civilians. All animals belonging to the Company marked off in Categories for dispersal in Australia.	A

89th Field Co. R.E.

Army Form C. 2118.

WAR DIARY
or
INTELLIGENCE SUMMARY.
(Erase heading not required.)

Place	Date	Hour	Summary of Events and Information	Remarks and references to Appendices
TOURCOING	Jan 1/19 to Jan 24/19		No Section with the help of 25 German Prisoners of War improving accommodation for sections in TOURCOING Football Ground. Heavy girders 2'-9" X (1'-2" X 1'-6") X 40' being launched over centre span of the Bridge over CANAL DE ROUBAIX. R.E. went on leave to U.K. Girders are one span of Bridge placed in position and a start made with the Jacking. Demobilization proceeding rapidly about 80 Sappers & N.C.O.s have left the Coy. Lt. OLDFIELD proceeded on leave to the U.K. on the 29th. Weekly dance held on the 29th was a great success.	A.
TOURCOING	25/19 to 31/19			

L.M. Lyon, Capt. R.E.
89th Field Coy. R.E.

Army Form C. 2118.

WAR DIARY
or
INTELLIGENCE SUMMARY.
(Erase heading not required.)

Vol 42

Place	Date	Hour	Summary of Events and Information	Remarks and references to Appendices
TOURCOING.	1st Feb.		Coy. strength reduced to 140 due to demobilisation. All available sappers working on Bridge over Canal between TOURCOING & ROUBAIX. Sappers weekly leaves going strong and providing great convenience, not only for themselves but also for the rest of the people.	Nil.
	10th Feb.		O.C. returned from leave. All sappers working on Bridge. Coy. strength reduced to 95. Sappers held a Bal Masqué which was a great success. Over 150 couples being present.	Nil.
	11th Feb.		Coy. ration strength now reduced to 85. The few sappers left available for work were employed on Bridge over CANAL DE ROUBAIX in the BOULEVARDE GAMBETTA.	↓
	"			↓
	21st Feb.		Bridge over CANAL DE ROUBAIX completed. Local workmen commenced work in relaying of tramway lines and coupling it to the line laid across the Bridge.	↓
	26th Feb.		No particular incident to report, routine works carried out daily. Strength of Coy about 80 o.r. and 30 aspirants.	↓

Lionel Glyn OE
O.C. 8 9 Field Coy RE

WAR DIARY
or
INTELLIGENCE SUMMARY.
(Erase heading not required.)

Army Form C. 2118.

88th (FIELD) COMPANY · ROYAL ENGINEERS · 8 MAR 1919

Place	Date	Hour	Summary of Events and Information	Remarks and references to Appendices
TOURCOING	1-3-19 to		Bridge over CANAL DE ROUBAIX completed. Local tramway authority asked to complete works on rail connections.	A
	8-3-19		Orders received for Coy transport to be moved on or by the 10th inst to PETIT AUDENARDE (near the BELGIAN FRONTIER near ROUBAIX).	A
	9-3-19		Coy complete with transport vacate billets at TOURCOING and vacate to PETIT AUDENARDE. Hqrs. at No 57 Billets in the village.	A
	10-3-19 to		Coy. engaged in clearing up the new billets, fixing mess, latrines ablution huts, cookhouse etc.	A
	20-3-19		12 animals sent to TOURCOING CONCENTRATION CAMP for despatch to England. Company suppt left with 4 animals. Coy employed about maintenance of Bridges.	S
	21-3-19		35 O.R. left the Coy. for 231 Field Coy RE for service in the Army of Occupation. this included 10 volunteers.	A
	23-3-19		2Lt. NORRIS B3 left the Coy. on the 21st inst to join Army of Occupation as a Volunteer. 2Lt R.J. NAIRN left the Coy. on the 22nd inst for demobilisation in Group 45a. 2Lt G.H.R. OLDFIELD left the Coy for demobilisation as fitted men 28th inst.	A
	to 31-3-19		No R.E. work carried out since 21-3-19 owing to shortage of men. All animals withdrawn from the Coy.	A

O.C. 88TH FIELD COY RE

J.B. McAlpine? Major RE
OC Coy.

WAR DIARY or INTELLIGENCE SUMMARY.

Army Form C. 2118.

Instructions regarding War Diaries and Intelligence Summaries are contained in F. S. Regs., Part II. and the Staff Manual respectively. Title pages will be prepared in manuscript.

(Erase heading not required.)

Place	Date	Hour	Summary of Events and Information	Remarks and references to Appendices
PETIT AUDEN-ARDE (BELGIUM)	1-4-19		No works in progress. Company strength varying throughout the month for	
		30 to 40.		
	"		Considerable dissatisfaction among all ranks of the Coy about the delay in demobilization, practically all the men of the Coy having enlisted in 1914 and having served in France continuously since May 1915, also all or nearly all men	
	15-4-19		making the complaints had employment awaiting them at home.	
			On representation being made to C.R.E. by 3 F.d. Coys. the Coy Commander	
	16-4-19		Brig. Gen. Sir R. Leveson-Gower CMG DSO visited the Coy and explained the situation to the Coys concerned. Names of men demanding demobilisation on compassionate grounds were taken and full particulars sent to Division.	
	"		No events of importance to record.	
	27-4-19		In view of an inspection of Ordnance Stores by DD DOS of the 14 Division	
	"		full and complete inspection of the Coys equipment being made, all deficiencies & damaged stores being listed for inspection.	
	30-4-19		The weather throughout the month was very unsettled.	
			Only 1 OS officer remained with the Division since the 23rd inst. Cavalry were engaged by local contractors employment engineers	

[signature] RE
OC 89TH FIELD COY. RE

WAR DIARY
or
INTELLIGENCE SUMMARY
(Erase heading not required.)

Army Form C. 2118.

89th Coy R.E.

Place	Date	Hour	Summary of Events and Information	Remarks and references to Appendices
PETIT AUDENARDE (BELGIUM)	1-5-19		Coy. strength one officer and 36 O.R.s. Work consisted entirely of guarding equipment. All men on strength of the Co. are without leave for over six months. Sent on leave for 14 days to England. Information received that cadres would begin to move—about the 1st inst — to England.	
	6		Party of 7 O.Rs went to BRUSSELS on a "joy ride" returning on the 17th inst. having spent 48 hours in the city. Nothing further of incident to set down. New information received on 31st that the Division would begin to move on the 4th of June, also that Cadres would be reduced by 75% of the original cadre establishment—thus making the Cadre of a Field Coy. Re. 1 Officer and 13 O.R.s.	
	31-5-19			

Sd/ Haynes
O.C 89 Field Coy R.E.

WM 46
ceased

WAR DIARY
89th FIELD Co. R.E.
FINAL.

WAR DIARY
or
INTELLIGENCE SUMMARY

Army Form C. 2118.

Place	Date	Hour	Summary of Events and Information	Remarks and references to Appendices
PETIT AUDENARDE	1-6/19		Information received that the CADRES i.e. 1 Officer and 13 ORs for the "EQUIPMENT GUARD" would be despatched to ST ANDRE CONCENTRATION CAMP on June 14th, and that Brigades would be grouped after that to form "Equipment Guard" Groups. Four men Equipment Guard will in no case leave Workshops arrangements made for the demobilization of	A
	13/6/19		the Cadre for the disposal of surplus equipment thoroughly inspected. Men on leave will on and after return by the 13th July (20 Telegraphing)	A
	10/6/19	10hrs	the Cadre of the Coy (less Equipment Group) consisting of 9 & 22 ORs under CSM LOSEMORE proceeded by lorry from PETIT AUDENARDE to ST. P. ANDRE via LILLE to entrain for demobilization. Equipment Guard under Major S. SMITH busy packing up. Entraining Station HERSEAUX, GERMAN PRISONERS at war would load up at STATION	A
	15/6/19		under 8 & to Supervision. Orders received that by transport & Guard would leave 17th next	A
	16/6/19		Coy transport moved to Station by animals, sent for to Corps HORSE BILLETING CAMP.	A
	17/6/19		The last part of the 89 Fd Coy RE left HERSEAUX for ENGLAND to H.M. First	A

WAR DIARY
or
INTELLIGENCE SUMMARY.

Army Form C. 2118.

(Erase heading not required.)

Place	Date	Hour	Summary of Events and Information	Remarks and references to Appendices
PETIT AUDENARDE	17/6/19		at Ascension Sty 22 group. The route would be via ANTWERP, the journey from AERSEAU occupying 2½ hours approx. Final destination to be "AINTREE" Station. Responsibility for equipment to party disembarkation to rest with O.C. store to hand over these to the Brixton R.E. Coy. respinsible for transporting the equipment to final destination. Personnel forming the Equipment Guard to be demobilised thro' the nearest Dispersal Port Disembarkation. The 89 Field Coy R.E. thus completed 4.9 months Service with British Army in FRANCE and FLANDERS. The identity of the Coy to be retained for the "INTERIM ARMY".	T. S. H. M. T.

[Signature]
Major R.E.
89TH FIELD COY. R.E.

[Stamp: 89 (FIELD) COMPANY ROYAL ENGINEERS 17 JUN 1919]

www.ingramcontent.com/pod-product-compliance
Lightning Source LLC
Chambersburg PA
CBHW080920230426
43668CB00014B/2167